The Global Debt Bomb

The Global Debt Bomb

JAMES L. CLAYTON

M.E.Sharpe
Armonk, New York
London, England

Library of Congress Cataloging-in-Publication Data

Clayton, James L.
The global debt bomb / James L. Clayton.
p.   c.m.
Includes bibliographical references and index.
ISBN 0–7656–0475–2 (hardcover : alk. paper)
1. Debt. 2. Debts, Public. I. Title.
HG3701.C575 2000
336.3′4—dc21   99–22986
CIP

Printed in the United States of America

The paper used in this publication meets the minimum requirements of
American National Standard for Information Sciences—
Permanence of Paper for Printed Library Materials,
ANSI Z 39.48-1984.

BM (c)   10   9   8   7   6   5   4   3   2   1

For Gerrie, with love

Table of Contents

List of Tables and Figures

Tables

Figures

Preface

It is commonly assumed that the United States has entered "a new era of budget surpluses," that over the next several years—through fiscal 2007—the administration expects to have a total budget surplus well in excess of a trillion dollars. If true, this would be the first time since the 1920s that the U.S. government has had a steady run of surpluses. The message conveyed by the administration and Congress is that Americans no longer need to worry about rising public indebtedness—that a growing economy and a continually rising stock market will solve the debt problem that has plagued the nation for several generations.

This euphoric outlook is even more evident regarding rising private-sector debt. Private-sector debt in the United States in 1999 was about 130 percent of the gross domestic product (GDP), the highest level on record. In 1928, the peak of the last private-sector debt binge, that figure was about 100 percent of GDP. Equity prices, which have risen faster in the United States than in any other major nation since 1990, are often used to justify this level of private indebtedness and unprecedented optimism. A rapidly rising stock market is thought to have increased the net worth of corporations and households, thus justifying historically high levels of debt. This stock-inflated net worth is also used to justify a zero household savings rate.

In truth, when one cuts through all the budgetary hoopla, the audacious assumptions, and fiscal gimmicks used to make the numbers add up, the U.S. government will have a very difficult time maintaining its budget surplus. Current public spending levels are clearly not sustainable long-term—especially when unfunded pensions are included. International economic and financial conditions have been deteriorating (except in the United States), imprudent lending and borrowing patterns in a variety of countries are becoming more evident with each passing month, commodity prices are falling, and uncertainty looms about the future of the world economy. In the United States, the current economic expansion has gone on a very long time by historical standards, as has the rising stock market. Since capitalism has always been prone to fiscal crises, this prolonged bout of excessive optimism suggests that, rather than entering "a new era of prosperity," the United States is more likely in the later stages of a debt-fueled expansion that will be inevitably followed by contraction. In short, these *feel* like good times—people have jobs, inflation has been tamed, and the stock market has been on a roll—but the underpinnings of this late-stage expansion are especially precarious because of the historically high levels of private indebtedness.

Most of the other industrial countries of the world have also increased their public indebtedness since 1990. In some (Italy and Belgium), their debt is now larger than their GDP. Only Korea, Norway, and Finland have had sustained budget surpluses in recent years. These recent increases in public debt have come on top of very substantial debt growth in the 1970s and 1980s, and they do not include unfunded promises to pay state pensions, which for some nations are over 100 percent of their GDP. Clearly, rising public indebtedness is a worldwide problem.

Growing private debt is also becoming a problem in the industrial world. Private-sector debt has been growing as a percentage of GDP in most nations since the 1960s. In Germany and Japan, private-sector debt is now larger than GDP. In 1998, corporate debt as a ratio of GDP in the United States was the highest it has been for decades, and debt/equity ratios in manufacturing are the highest they have been since the mid-1980s. In late 1998, while profits were weakening, business debt was growing faster than at any time since the beginning of the expansion in the early 1990s. As most people know, U.S. household debt as a percentage of income has reached historical highs—just like personal bankruptcy rates—while household savings rates have reached historical lows. For the G–7 nations, household liabilities as a percentage of disposable income have risen from an average of 53 percent in 1985 to 74 percent in 1996. Rising stock markets in all these countries (except Japan) make this level of debt seem unalarming; but in all these countries, market bubbles are evident and sooner or later will burst—as they have always done. When that happens, net worth will fall—perhaps rapidly—but the debts will remain. When this global debt bomb explodes, the dangers of excessive debt will be abundantly clear to all. The purpose of this book is to persuade the public and policymakers that a global debt bomb exists and that its timing mechanism is already ticking; I will also suggest ways to defuse this crisis before it happens, or at least mitigate its effects.

In the chapters that follow, I analyze the causes and consequences—both positive and negative—of rapidly rising public and private debt over the past three decades in the G–7 nations. A wide variety of works by historians, economists, and public policy experts provide context for a deeper understanding of these events and their consequences. I have taken an international and interdisciplinary approach in the belief that only by looking at the experience of several nations over a long period of time and from the perspective of several disciplines can we grasp the full meaning of this debt threat. My main conclusions are that public and private debt levels in all the G–7 nations and in most of the rest of the industrial world have reached levels that are not sustainable, and that these nations are particularly vulnerable to a serious and prolonged market correction.

Several organizations have allowed me access to their facilities and have helped me to conceptualize, research, and write this book. The Organization for Economic Cooperation and Development (OECD), headquartered in Paris, allowed me the use of its library for an extended period. Cambridge University was equally generous with its resources, as was the London School of Economics and Politics. The International Monetary Fund (IMF) and the World Bank in Washington, D.C., also allowed me to use their open sources for a brief period, for which I am grateful. A highly informative conference on the federal budget at the Brookings Institution in Washington, D.C., was especially useful in conceptualizing this project. I am also deeply indebted to the Ministry of Foreign Affairs of the Japanese government—and particularly to Shunji Yansi, Consul General in San Francisco—for inviting me to spend two weeks at several locations in Japan at the government's expense, talking with national and academic officials about a variety of subjects. This time spent in Japan gave me a valuable new perspective on public and private debt. On this same point, I have also lived for nearly five years in Berlin, Vienna, Hannover, and other German and Austrian cities, which afforded me yet another perspective through which to process this material. Last, but not least, I express appreciation to the central administration of the University of Utah—and most especially to former President Chase Peterson—for several generous grants and professional leaves to do this research.

Several academic and corporate colleagues have also been very helpful to me at various stages of this project. I owe a special debt to J.C. Mutchler, who read the entire manuscript and offered numerous suggestions to make sure this book would be clear to the nonspecialist. James Rock and Clayne Pope, both economists, were also helpful early on in conceptualizing the public debt section of this work. A long friendship with Ian Cumming, Chief Executive Officer (CEO) of Leucadia Financial Corporation, and Phil Horsley, CEO of Horsley-Bridge, gave me a real-world perspective on global financial matters not easily available to academics. Several colleagues at the University of Utah also offered encouragement and suggestions of various kinds along the way. They include Peter Stang, David Pershing, Dean May, Robert Goldberg, Ronald Smelser, James Gardner, and John Flynn. I have also learned a lot over the years about budgets from Robert Huefner and Tony Morgan. Holly Campbell and the Tanner Humanities Center provided a forum for discussing some of the ideas that went into this book.

Lavina Fielding Anderson edited the entire manuscript and generated the bibliography prior to its submission to the publisher. One could not ask for a better editor. I also want to thank Sean Culhane, Economics Editor at M.E. Sharpe Inc., who initiated this project and followed it to completion, as well as his administrative assistant, Esther L. Clark, and the copyeditor for this book, Georgia Kornbluth.

Finally, I thank my wife, Gerrie Clayton, for her constant encouragement and numerous sacrifices over four decades in support of my administrative and academic interests, and my ninety-seven-year-old mother, Olita Clayton, who never let me forget to include the moral aspects of this topic.

The Global Debt Bomb

Chapter 1

An Introduction to
the Debt Culture

The era of the deficit is over . . . . Ignore the Cassandras.

—Mortimer B. Zuckerman[1]

This expansion will run forever.

—Rudi Dornbusch[2]

Rarely is a hardened consensus right at an economic or financial turning point.

—James Grant[3]

When conventional wisdom says the time for worrying is over—well, that may be just the time to start worrying again.

—Bernard Wysocki Jr.[4]

The Emergence of the Culture of Debt

The amount and, more importantly, the burden of debt, both public and private, has been rising rapidly in recent decades throughout the industrial world. This increase is clearly evident from a variety of sources whether measured as a ratio of public debt to gross domestic product (GDP), debt to asset ratios for corporations, or the ratio of household debt to after-tax income. To illustrate, the gross public debt of industrial countries has risen to more than 70 percent of GDP, up dramatically from 41 percent in 1970.[5] Private-sector debt as a percentage of GDP in recent years has climbed to more than 100 percent of all goods and services produced in a given year in most large industrial countries and to more than 200 percent in Japan.[6] Private nonfinancial debt as a percentage of GDP is now nearly 150 percent of GDP in the United States, having climbed up from 55 percent in 1952 and 100 percent in 1975.[7] A similar picture is evident with household debt in the United States. Prior to World War II, the ratio of household debt to after-tax income was less than 10 percent; by the 1950s, it had risen above 30 percent; and in 1998 it was over 100 percent. Corporate debt/equity ratios have also risen in recent decades in the G–7 nations (United States, Canada, Japan, Germany, France, Italy, and the United Kingdom), albeit much more modestly.[8] The G–7 country classification is used here because it has evolved over time as a way of facilitating analysis. Rather than being based on strict criteria, economic or otherwise, the G–7 simply signifies the seven largest countries in the world in terms of GDP. They are also referred to as "the major industrial countries."

At the same time debt has been rising, savings have been falling. According to the International Monetary Fund (IMF), long-run historical data indicate that before countries industrialize they have very low savings rates.[9] Once they industrialize, those savings rates move up to the 20 percent of GDP range. Since the 1970s, however, world savings rates have begun to decline, primarily because of a decline in public-sector saving which in turn was caused by massive increases in social welfare spending and substantial increases in defense spending. This decline in world saving is part of a longer decline in the ethic of thrift and the rise of the consumption ethic.[10] Over the long term, the most important funding obligation of governments is public pension liabilities. With aging populations, a financial crunch seems unavoidable, according to the IMF, and both public and private saving rates will have to increase. But world saving rates are not increasing, and private saving rates in advanced countries are actually declining.[11] This is especially true in the United States, where private savings rates have fallen below zero.

The expansion of public- and private-sector indebtedness during recent decades exceeded the expansion of economic activity and the capacity to fund this debt by a wide margin. Virtually all industrial countries expanded their public sectors well beyond their revenue streams. Many countries also experienced a boom in asset markets closely associated with this unprecedented buildup in debt. These temporary increases in wealth led to a reduction in both household and business saving rates and probably encouraged speculation in the stock markets on the expectation of further asset appreciation, according to the IMF.[12]

The expansion of public and private indebtedness, especially since the 1980s, has left many countries unusually vulnerable to the inevitable cyclical developments, especially asset price declines. This phenomenon, along with a rise in real interest rates and a general decline in saving rates, has severely diminished the private sector's ability to service its debts and has increased the financial fragility of the financial systems of many countries, especially in Southeast Asia and Japan.

More recently, most stock markets have also risen to record heights based on this same optimistic debt-financed outlook, with many markets in Europe and North America showing historically high price/earnings and price/equity ratios. The rapidly rising bull market is rooted in the belief that sound money is here to stay, the years of inflation are over, interest rates will be stable or fall, and high-tech industries will create earnings that will justify ever-higher price/equity ratios. This new-era economy is further enhanced by cost cutting and downsizing, made possible by substituting goods for labor. Growth will be faster and recessions shorter, it is asserted. The bear-market case rests largely on the belief that soaring stock markets have begun to create equity and asset "bubbles," which suggest that at some future date they will burst or at least deflate rapidly. Some of these equity bubbles have already burst—Japan's for example—and some Southeast Asia nations have suffered major debt-related fiscal crises. By October 1998, several of the world's stock markets had gone into a tailspin, falling more than 20 percent from their 1998 peak. These nations included Russia (with a percentage decline of 84 percent in U.S. dollar terms), Colombia (35 percent), Argentina (35 percent), Indonesia (39 percent), Mexico (41 percent), and Turkey (58 percent).[13] Except for Japan, the G–7 stock markets have not collapsed, but by early 1999, all were in the advanced stages of a market bubble that began to move sharply upward in 1995.[14]

What is clear at this point is that the capacity to service these very high levels of public and private debt, whose interest payments depend on a growing economy and a healthy and reasonably predictable market, are now jeopardized by the growing possibility of widespread market crashes like those that have already occurred in Asia, Russia, South America, and some European countries. It is this *combination* of high debt, which is manageable in good times, and emerging asset bubbles that has the potential to create a serious global fiscal crisis.

This book will describe the growth of public and private debt in the G–7 nations in recent decades, why these debt levels are unsustainable in the long run, and why a global debt crisis looms in the event of a sustained stock market downturn. The methods used to gain an understanding of this problem will be primarily historical, because I believe experience is the best guide to understanding the present and projecting the future; I have also employed economic theories and statistical analysis where they can be useful. I shall argue that both public and private debt crises reflect basic human drives and, as such, are part of the present as well as the past. Booms and busts have occurred regularly for the past 400 years. The same is true of debt crises—they occur unpredictably but periodically, and another major one appears to be on the horizon for the United States and other G–7 nations.[15] I will also discuss policies and practices that have proved useful in reducing risk and avoiding fiscal disasters.

The primary focus of this book is the United States, because the best data are available for that country and because of its global importance. The next level of emphasis is on the English-speaking nations, which have higher lending ratios and lower saving ratios than any other group of countries, thus making them more vulnerable to debt excess. America's equity bubble is also among those most likely to burst because its current bull market originated in 1982, with an eightfold increase since then. Equity prices in the United States have risen faster and farther since 1990 than in the other major European economies, followed by the United Kingdom, Germany, and France. America's economy is also especially vulnerable to a sharp reduction in investment by firms, according to the *Economist*, because American companies also have a "negative savings ratio."[16] What this means is that American firms have been borrowing to invest, whereas most European firms have not financed their capital spending by going deeper into debt. Ominously, as most of the major stock markets have been rising rapidly, corporate profits have been in a long-term downward trend since the mid-1980s. By the early 1990s, the world economy could be likened to two boats, according to Alan Murray of the *Wall Street Journal*. "One carries most of the nations of the world and is sputtering under the burden of a global financial crisis. The other holds only the United States and speeds through the choppy waters as if nothing much has happened."[17] Both Federal Reserve Chairman Alan Greenspan and Secretary of the Treasury Robert Rubin have warned that the United States cannot remain an "oasis of prosperity" while the rest of the world languishes.[18]

There are also two boats that ply the world debt seas: a public one and a private one. Public debt has been the major concern of world leaders for at least a decade, while private debt has hardly registered on the intellectual radar screen. Public spending has now been brought into balance in the United States and Canada, and is currently receding as a major political issue. But as concern for the federal deficit has declined, dangerous signs of excess in the private debt sector have emerged. This is why any thorough analysis of indebtedness has to consider both public and private debt together. For several decades they have tended to move in reverse coupling in the United States; as public debt has risen, private debt has fallen and vice versa. Recently, however, both have been rising because both public and private debt trends are rooted in the same problem: insatiable wants that must be satisfied by a growth machine that, except in America, appears to be stalling.

Table 1.1 shows the increase in the burden of public and private debt for

Table 1.1

Credit Market Debt Outstanding in the United States, 1960–1997
(as a percentage of GDP)

Category	1960	1970	1980	1990	1997
Government					
Federal	46	29	27	47	47
State	12	14	11	12	13
Corporate	26	35	32	39	41
Households	11	12	51	65	69
Total	166	179	170	239	261

Source: U.S. Bureau of the Census, *Statistical Abstract of the United States: 1998*, p. 512; and U.S. Bureau of the Census, *Historical Statistics of the United States: Colonial Times to 1970*, p. 989.

the United States since 1960. After rapidly falling from 114 percent of GDP following World War II, federal debt held by the public reached a low of 25 percent of GDP in 1974. This downward trend then reversed itself and has been climbing ever since, reaching 47 percent of GDP by 1997. State debt has remained a constant share of GDP since 1960, largely because the vast majority of states are prohibited by their constitutions or by law from accumulating deficits. Corporate debt has risen dramatically since 1960, from 26 to 41 percent of GDP. Business liabilities now exceed business assets by a wide margin.[19]

U.S. household debt has risen sixfold as a percentage of GDP and is now more than 100 percent of disposable income, having risen from about 30 percent in the early 1950s. U.S. consumers have been on a spending spree for five decades as their outlays have grown much faster than their personal disposable, or after tax, income. Americans resorted to borrowing to achieve the "American Dream" they felt entitled to, but could no longer afford to finance out of earned income because real earnings (that is adjusted for inflation) for most people have remained virtually flat since the early 1970s. As a result, the median net worth of the average American family has been declining since the late 1980s when measured in dollars of constant purchasing power. Personal bankruptcy rates have also risen dramatically in recent years. The ratio of debt *payments* to family income has not increased much in recent years because the length of debt payments have been expanded substantially. For example, we used to pay for our cars in two years; now the average is five. We also used to have a goal of paying off the mortgage prior to retirement. Now almost a third of American households have home mortgages or home equity loans after age sixty-five.[20] This change in attitude toward debt has had a major impact on total debt levels. Total credit market debt in the United States hovered around

150 percent of GDP from World War I to the 1970s. When public debt rose, private debt fell. Since the 1970s, both public and private debt have been rising, and total debt today is *massively* higher than it has ever been.

In other major industrial countries, gross public debt, a somewhat more inclusive measurement than credit market debt, has risen to an average of 72 percent of GDP in 1994, up from 41 percent in 1970.[21] Despite increasing concern about public debt levels throughout the world, public debt is still rising. Nor should current fiscal surpluses and projections of continued surpluses be taken too seriously. Long experience has shown that forecasts of either deficits or surpluses can be extremely unreliable, and both U.S. political parties ignored the spending caps on public debt the very first year after the surplus occurred.

Corporate debt/GDP ratios of the G–7 nations have also increased since the 1960s, especially in Japan.[22] In the United States and the United Kingdom, a protracted period of corporate debt accumulation occurred during the 1980s, mostly in commercial real estate and in corporate mergers and leveraged buyouts financed by substituting debt for equity. In both countries, business net worth declined from the early 1970s to the early 1990s.[23] In the United States, debt/equity ratios in the manufacturing sector have also been rising since the mid-1980s, from 121 percent in 1985 to 159 percent in 1995. Corporate debt/equity ratios in Japan for the same period were much higher and are one of the reasons Japan is in economic trouble.[24]

Household debt data for the major industrial nations is quite limited, but what data exist indicate considerable increases in this period in the ratio of personal debt to income as well as to assets, particularly for Japan and the United Kingdom.[25] Mortgage liabilities, a good proxy for household debt, rose from 20 percent of disposable income in the United Kingdom in 1963, to nearly 80 percent of disposable income by 1991. Most of these countries also experienced easier access to credit, declining rates of personal savings, and rising levels of loan default. Germany was the exception to these trends, and household borrowing during the 1980s actually declined as a percentage of income in that country.

The fundamental reasons for this increase in debt vary greatly by nation, sector, and time period. But as Adam Smith pointed out two centuries ago, common to all of these reasons is a general discontent by large numbers of people with their present condition, not knowing when they were well off, and a willingness to sacrifice future income to enhance present consumption.[26] Specific reasons for increasing public and private indebtedness may be to establish a new governmental program, to smooth private consumption over time, or to maximize long-term profits, as well as a host of other reasons. When all this works out as planned, debt is considered beneficial and justified. Both borrowers and lenders are happy. But when debt grows faster than assets over long periods of time, or when assets are largely based on stock market bubbles, then debt levels can become burdensome and even dangerous.

The Consequences of Rising Indebtedness

Until a few years ago, the worldwide increase in *public* indebtedness was generally understood to present no really serious or immediate problems—that is to say, current benefits derived from increasing public indebtedness were clearly evident, but the eventual costs, if any, were not generally perceived to be alarming. What alarm that did exist was largely concentrated in the United States, not in Europe or Japan. More recently, many Americans have come to believe that the public debt problem has been solved, or at least is no longer a salient issue, because the United States is, for the first time since 1969, running a budget surplus *according to current budget policy.* Conveniently overlooked are the $14 trillion of unfunded public obligations for the retirement and health-care benefits of the baby-boomer generation. When these obligations are included, as they should be, the real deficit for fiscal year 1998 is $106 billion, and the United States will not have a surplus until the year 2007.[27] Canada and the United Kingdom are also expected to have near-term surpluses if pension liabilities are ignored.

Unfortunately, these current "surpluses" are not the result of long-term commitments by the public to cut budgets or raise taxes, but the consequences of reduced defense spending[28] and unexpected increases in government revenues owing to a strong economy and tax receipts from surging capital gains resulting from rising asset prices.[29] At best, these revenue surpluses are temporary and will evaporate when the market turns down again. At worst, these budget surpluses will touch off a new round of tax cuts and spending increases which, in the long run, will drive up the deficit once again. Moreover, the long-term outlook for continued surpluses is not very good because projected increases in health-care outlays are anything but encouraging.[30]

Rising household debt is still widely perceived to present little risk in the private sector, in part because assets have tended to accumulate at about the same rate as debt has. During the 1960s, corporate debt generally grew faster than corporate assets; but later on, the reverse was true. Today, privately held debt, whether corporate or household, is generally considered to be manageable, largely because the value of assets to fund that debt has risen so rapidly. It is, moreover, very difficult to determine conclusively whether any given level of debt is based on profligacy or a wise use of assets.

But an increasing number of government officials, economists, and major financial institutions have come to believe that there may well be a problem of debt "sustainability" in the public sector, that further indebtedness may bring more disadvantages than advantages to the debtor nation, and that public debt ought to be paid down.[31] Public budgets around the world began to deteriorate after the oil-price shock in the early 1970s, improved somewhat during the 1980s, but then began to deteriorate once again in the 1990s. Although controversial, many experts have come to the conclusion that high public debt levels lead to higher real interest rates, decreasing investment, reduced policy flexibility, and falling expectations for the future.[32] Rapidly growing long-term unfunded public entitlement commitments and the recent debt crises in Asia have given new urgency to the problems created by excessive public indebtedness. In addition, recent attempts to reduce public deficits by fiscal policy have actually made matters worse by ratcheting up existing deficits because of the political difficulty of raising taxes or cutting spending.[33] The immediate good news is that G–7 budget deficits are currently generally declining owing to revenues generated by the equity and asset bubbles that are emerging. The bad news is that, when these bubbles pop, the situation will likely become worse than before.

Even larger and potentially more serious problems loom in the private sector in the form of emerging asset and market bubbles. We have already seen what can happen when Japanese banks ran up huge private-sector debts in a "binge of reckless lending" during the Japanese bubble economy of the late 1980s. That burst bubble cost Japan more wealth, both in absolute and relative terms, than it lost during World War II.[34] America is now experiencing a very serious, if not alarming, asset-price bubble, along with the massive corporate mergers and excessive monetary growth usually associated with the final stages of a bull market.[35] Several European economies are also in the advanced stages of overheating. This disturbing situation has grown out of a long expansion propelled by private consumption that is based on a combination of financial liberalization and rapidly expanding credit and asset prices.

The current stock market bubble in the United States is even larger in real terms than was the disastrous bubble of the late 1920s.[36] As the *Economist* has pointed out, "America's economy is more vulnerable to falling share prices than Europe's": American households' equity holdings were worth 143 percent of disposable income in 1997. The equivalent figure for Germany was 19 percent. French families held even less.[37] This "share fever" has created an "equity cult" in which about 45 percent of all adult Americans now hold stock, through either mutual funds or pension plans, compared to about 10 percent in Europe. Only a quarter of American citizens held stock prior to the crash of 1987. About a third of Britons hold shares, and that ratio is also growing. Wider share ownership also means that a drop in share prices may now have a much bigger effect on the market than in earlier times. Moreover, as George

Soros points out, the capacity of the state to regulate the market has also declined; consequently, when the bubble does burst, its consequences will be more difficult to ameliorate.[38] It may, in fact, be not a bubble but a bomb.

Rapidly rising prices of shares traded in the G–7 nations since 1985 illustrate how bubbles occur. From 1985 to 1996, the value of shares traded in France increased seventeen times, in Germany nine times, in the United Kingdom more than seven times, and in the United States more than six times. Since 1996, all these markets have risen further. Japan saw its market rise four times in value before its bubble burst. By most traditional measures, European and American stock market values are grossly overvalued today. At the same time, savings rates have fallen throughout the world, and household saving in the United States is at the lowest level in several decades. Despite these unprecedented levels of exposure, and a long list of major figures who have warned of the dangers of such exposure, the public generally, both here and abroad, shows little concern about the possibility of a stock market crash and great optimism about the future. This optimism is perhaps best captured in the common expression "cash is trash." Such contemptuously carefree comments were also common in the late 1920s.

It is true that inflation and unemployment rates are very low in the United States; but average real hourly earnings have also fallen to their mid-1960s level, more than half of all manufacturing jobs have been lost in the past twenty-five years, and nearly half of all workers fear that they will lose their jobs. As Paul Krugman, professor of economics at Massachusetts Institute of Technology (MIT), has pointed out, nothing fundamental has changed— our growth rate has not accelerated, productivity has not risen—yet we have become "startlingly triumphalist" in the past couple of years.[39] The Federal Reserve Board, although generally upbeat in its assessments, reported to Congress in March 1998 that there was a greater-than-usual degree of uncertainty at this time.[40] Since that time the IMF has continued to warn of growing downside risks in the world economy.[41]

The Global Debt Bubble

Traditionally, persistent increases in public debt levels have often been compared to termites in the house. You can ignore these pests for quite a while, but eventually you will have a very big problem. Add to the emerging fiscal problem a long-term decline in savings rates, an aging population, an unresponsive public, and growing frustration with the political process itself, and this half of the debt problem—the public debt side—seems very volatile. The other half of the debt problem—the private debt side—is usually ignored. But household debt in the United States, for example, is much larger than federal debt—$5.4 trillion versus $3.8 trillion—and the ratio of house-hold debt to disposable income is much larger than the ratio of federal debt to GDP. As economists Wynne Godley and George McCarthy have pointed out, borrowing by U.S. households "has been proceeding at such a pace that the burden of indebtedness now represents a serious threat to stability."[42] Place both halves of the debt problem in the context of rapidly rising equity and asset prices in most of the industrial world, and the potential for a debt explosion is obvious. Put the Japanese stock market crash into this mixture as a precedent of what can happen to a major nation when it goes on a debt binge, and it seems only a matter of time before other nations have similar experiences.

It is widely agreed that public debt in excess of about 60 percent of GDP may be unsustainable and that public debt over 100 percent of GDP (in Italy for example) is clearly excessive.[43] The current situation in America is like an expanding balloon. Long-term public indebtedness trends are sharply upward; sporadic attempts to reduce this debt have been largely unsuccessful (even in good times); and therefore the equity and asset bubbles now on the horizon are likely to cause severe recessions and even greater indebtedness when they burst.

International corporate debt/GDP ratios have also generally increased since 1970, as have corporate debt/profit and debt/asset ratios, but at a much slower rate, according to E.P. Davis in his excellent study on this topic, entitled *Debt, Financial Fragility, and Systemic Risk*.[44] For the United States, the debt/equity ratios in the manufacturing sector have climbed steadily from 121 percent in 1985 to 149 percent in 1990 and 159 percent in 1995.[45] By 1997 this ratio had reached levels comparable to those in Japan in some sectors of the economy, including machinery, electrical equipment, petroleum and coal products, and motor vehicles and equipment.[46]

It is the use or quality of this corporate debt, rather than its quantity, that is most important, however. There is no consensus on the threshold of peril for the corporate sector, unlike the public sector. In the United States, the default rate on corporate bonds is currently extremely low, and the delinquency rate of corporate borrowing is also low, suggesting that there is no impending crisis here so long as profits remain high. But the current expansion is one of the longest on record, and profit margins are beginning to be squeezed. Current corporate debt levels could easily *become* a serious burden if the stock market crashed; if the economy moved into a recession; or if deflation replaced inflation, as has already happened in Japan. What is important to keep in mind, as Felix Rohatyn, U.S. ambassador to France and a key player in resolving New York City's default some years ago, has pointed out, is that, as the quantity of debt increases, there is a tendency for the quality of that debt to decline.[47]

Figure 1.1. **U.S. Household Debt as a Ratio of After-Tax Income, 1952–1998**

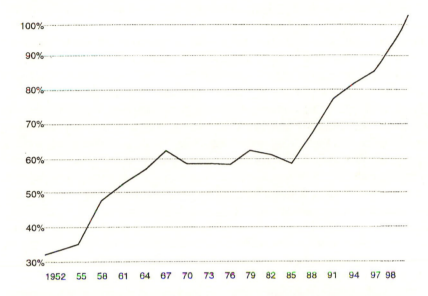

Source: Federal Reserve Board, Bureau of Economic Analysis, as compiled by Hoisington Investment Management Co.; *World Economic Outlook*, May 1989, p. 61.

Household indebtedness as a percentage of GDP has increased dramatically in the United States, especially since the 1980s. It has risen as a percentage of disposable income from 35 percent in 1952 to 65 percent in the early 1880s to 100 percent in 1998 (see Figure 1.1). About half of this debt is in home mortgages. Household net worth has grown even faster, reaching its highest ratio to disposable personal income in 1997. But, according to the Federal Reserve Board, most of this increase in net worth is based on inflated values of household assets and dramatic price increases of corporate equities held by households.[48] A bursting stock market bubble and a continuing decline in real wages would place a severe burden on many American households, especially since home equity loans have also been rising sharply. Rapidly rising personal bankruptcy rates in recent years, when unemployment rates have been at near historic lows, further suggest that the current level of personal indebtedness is already a problem for a growing number of people. It would not take much to turn currently comfortable levels of household debt into a serious national problem.

An Explanatory Theory

I believe that the best underlying economic-historical model, which can explain more aspects of the global debt crisis than any other, is the Hyman Minsky–Charles Kindleberger financial crisis model, which itself is based on the ideas of a host of distinguished earlier economists.[49] Minsky, who recently died, was a professor of economics at Berkeley and believed that, during the 1970s, world capitalism entered a new phase: "money-manager" capitalism. From the cautious use of debt and the prosperity that ensued following World War II, the world—in both its public and its private sectors—began to rely more and more on increasing debt and shorter-term financing. The inevitable result was an increasing fragility in the world's economic system. At the same time, major corporations began to manage their ever-growing stock portfolios solely for the benefit of the investors, including a growing number of mutual fund holders. This desire to maximize profits for shareholders encouraged mergers, acquisitions, leveraged buyouts, stock buybacks, and corporate downsizing. Money-manager capitalism favors the "fortunate fifth," who hold a majority of traded stocks and bonds, but results in a declining share of the nation's wealth for the rest of the population.[50]

What Charles Kindleberger, former professor of economics at MIT, contributes to this model is an insightful analysis of its crisis phase. A long period of depression-free growth inevitably leads to "euphoria," excessive debt ratios (often called "gearing" in the economic literature), and eventually a "bubble." The closer one gets to the peak of the cycle, the more evidence there is of chicanery and swindles, Kindleberger believes. This is not new. Jefferson believed, for instance, that public debt was the most corrupting thing there is.[51] He died bankrupt, as did many of the Virginia gentry. Alexander Hamilton, although usually thought of as the person who authored the idea that public debts are "a public blessing," actually was only referring to public debts that were "properly funded."[52] Like Jefferson, Hamilton believed that public debts invite prodigality and are liable to dangerous abuse. Kindleberger takes the firm view that warnings of impending crisis almost always go unheeded. Eventually the best-informed insiders decide to bail out, and/or a crisis occurs—sometimes outside the system—and there is a rush to liquidity. A very good candidate for signaling the onset of a bear market is a sudden credit tightening when share prices are extremely high.[53] Prices suddenly decline, bankruptcies increase, and the bubble bursts—not necessarily all at once, but more often at about the same rate that the bubble inflated.[54]

The IMF recently added a further dimension to this theoretical base by analyzing currency and banking crises from 1975 to 1997 for fifty industrial and developing countries.[55] Many of these crises were the

Table 1.2

Stock Market Capitalization in G–7 Nations, 1985–1995
(as a percentage of GDP)

Nation	1985	1995
Canada	46	68
France	8	34
Germany	15	26
Italy	9	19
Japan	35	71
United Kingdom	50	127
United States	56	95

Source: U.S. Bureau of the Census, *Statistical Abstract of the United States: 1997*, pp. 838, 854.

result of overly expansionary monetary and fiscal policies that "spurred lending booms, excessive debt accumulation, and overinvestment in real assets, which have driven up equity and real estate prices to unsustainable levels." The "inevitable correction of asset prices, has then led to a slowdown in economic activity, debt-servicing difficulties, declining collateral values and net worth, and rising levels of nonperforming loans that threaten banks' solvency."[56] High levels of short-term debt, as well as overborrowing for unproductive uses, make things even worse. Stock market crashes are often followed by sharp corrections in other asset markets, notably real estate. Such crises cannot be reliably predicted; but according to this excellent study, "In the lead-up to a currency or banking crisis, the economy is overheated: inflation is relatively high, the real exchange rate is appreciated, the current account deficit has widened, domestic credit has been growing at a rapid pace, and asset prices have often been inflated."[57]

Both Minsky and Kindleberger came to believe that Wall Street increasingly dominated the overall economy. Table 1.2 shows the increase from 1985 to 1995 of stock market capitalization as a percentage of GNP in the G–7 nations. By 1997, U.S. stock market capitalization had risen to 140 percent of GDP, which would tend to support Minsky's thesis. In fact, the mutual fund industry now has greater assets than the U.S. banking industry. All the G–7 nations have seen a substantial increase in the size of their stock markets in recent years, when measured as a share of GNP; several ratios have more than doubled. Moreover, most of these markets are near or above their historical peaks in share prices.

The basic reasons for this rapid increase in share prices include declining inflation, the shift of savings into equities, low bond yields, good corporate earnings, and momentum buying. During 1998, the broad-based money supply in almost all these countries also increased much faster than GDP, productivity, or inflation. The fastest growth in the money supply was in the United States, with an increase of 11 percent. Increases of this magnitude in both stock prices and the money supply indicate emerging bubbles.[58]

In recent years, Kindleberger has focused his attention on what he called "a mutual funds mania bubble" in the U.S. market.[59] Other analysts believe Wall Street's influence on the U.S. economy amounts to an "equity cult." Most observers, no matter what their political persuasion, would now agree that stock markets play a much larger role than they used to and that, when the next serious downturn arrives, it could have a much greater negative impact on the economy than in the past because far more people own stock. A sharp worldwide market downturn would hurt English-speaking nations far more than other nations because Americans, Canadians, and the English have far *more* equity holdings as a percentage of disposable income than anyone else and far *lower* household savings rates than most other nations do.[60] Stock market margin debt, moveover, is especially high in the United States.

Those who are most likely to disagree with this theoretical approach are those who believe that historical cycles are now a thing of the past and that the world has entered an entirely "new" era.[61] But evidence that anything really new has happened is almost totally lacking, while evidence of the continuing validity of conventional valuation ratios is overwhelming.[62] If, or perhaps more appropriately, when these bubbles burst, one expects to hear considerably less about "new paradigms."

That the U.S. stock market was at a historical high by the end of 1998 can best be seen in Figure 1.2, which charts the Dow Jones Industrial Average (DJIA) in constant prices back to 1900. The most striking item about this pattern is how far out of line the current Dow is by historical standards. The other striking aspect of this graph is the evenness of the cycles: *what goes up also comes down—and at approximately the same rate.* If DJIA history repeats itself, as it always has done during the past century, then the U.S. market should fall to somewhere near the level it was in real terms in 1982, and take about fifteen years to do so. So far as I know, no one is predicting a crash of this magnitude, but this is what the historical record says could happen. Whatever one believes about market cycles, a hundred years of data that show several clearly defined and extraordinarily uniform market cycles cannot simply be dismissed out of hand.[63] As markets begin to fall—and especially if they persist in falling—historical interpretations should gain more credibility.

Both Minsky and Kindleberger believe that this debt-crisis cycle can be

Figure 1.2. **Inflation-Adjusted Dow Jones Industrial Average, 1900–1998**

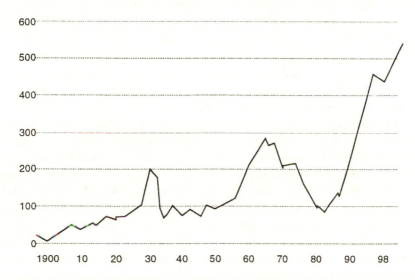

Source: John R. Dorfman, *Wall Street Journal*, May 28, 1996, and subsequent DJIA data.

ameliorated, if not reversed, by government action, especially by a "lender of last resort"—such as the IMF. This view appears to have wide support, even in Japan where several governmental stimulation packages have been tried in recent years to reverse the effects of their crashed bubble—all to little effect. But a "lender-of-last-resort" policy can do only so much. It was designed to assist relatively poor countries over a hard spot; it is not powerful or rich enough to do much for a G–7 nation that gets into trouble.[64] There is also evidence that the IMF, by attempting to bail out certain countries with fiscal problems, has also encouraged other countries to go further into debt than they would have done in the IMF's absence—the "moral hazard" problem.[65] The Mexico bail-out clearly helped the lenders but has nearly impoverished the Mexican people, and too many markets are falling too rapidly for the IMF to be able to do much about it in a well-ordered way. Indeed, to a significant degree the solution has now become the problem.[66]

Even with the best of efforts by the IMF, Kindleberger believes that a "day of reckoning" is likely anyway—probably before the turn of the century, he hypothesized in 1995.[67] Many other economists also believe that we have reached a time of "financial fragility"—that excessive borrowing, especially by households, now represents a threat to economic stability.[68] Still others believe that a crash would be a good thing in the long run, eradicating the excesses of recent years and teaching prudent lessons of lasting worth.[69]

I shall apply this basic economic model to the emerging global debt crisis outlined above. Since one major debt bubble has already burst in Japan, we also have an excellent case study for the larger G–7 nations. I believe, along with many others, that shares in the G–7 nations are overvalued, particularly in the United States. It is this combination of overvalued shares and unprecedented public and private debt levels that have started a global debt bomb ticking. Since household savings rates have fallen during the 1990s in most of the major nations of the industrial world, and most especially in the English-speaking nations, households are especially vulnerable now to a market crash. Because several equity bubbles now appear to be on the verge of bursting in several other G–7 countries, we have an excellent database for early debt cycle comparisons here, too. Bursting stock market bubbles are increasingly evident in other regions of the world and will be considered where appropriate.

Historians as well as economists can contribute to our understanding of why these debt bubbles occur and what can be done about them. Economists apply technical skills and theoretical models of considerable sophistication to the problem, but historians bring a much longer perspective and deal with noneconomic, but still relevant, topics that cannot always be quantified. Economists bring insights to quantifiable or measurable factors; historians bring understanding to the human side of life, often unpredictable and always imperfect. The past is a good, if not the best, guide to the present; and since all knowledge is subjective, different disciplines are needed to explain different factors and discover different relationships. Each discipline brings a different perspective to bear; each tries to answer different questions. Both perspectives are necessary to a full understanding of the problem of debt in the modern world. We cannot expect to predict human behavior; but we can, with careful analysis and a wide range of tools, observe useful patterns over time, which, when used judiciously, can help us as a society and as individuals to achieve greater happiness.

Preview

If Chapter 1 introduces the reader to the debt culture and the global debt problem, Chapter 2 establishes its context, introduces the reader to the international culture of debt, both public and private, and analyzes its origins, the course of its development, and its distinguishing features. The economic challenges that gave rise to increasing indebtedness are discussed, particularly sluggish productivity, falling savings, rising economic inequality, persistent unemployment in Europe, rising global competition, and unfunded pensions. The changing roles of credit and debt and how they relate to these trends are also described. The composition of debt in various countries is introduced, as are the requirements for medium-term stability and eventual debt reduction. Discussions of which nations appear to be most at risk and which are most successful in meeting these debt-related challenges round out this chapter.

Chapter 3, "The Nature of Debt," is the most technical chapter. It introduces the moral aspects of debt and the reasons for their decline as debt-limiting agents. This chapter includes a critique of the more sensational studies of public debt and deficits and an analysis of various economic theories of debt. The problem of "sustainability" is introduced, along with the question of whether there are leading indicators of excessive debt. "Debt traps," the "invisible" debt problem, and debt cycles are also presented for discussion. I also address the question of why rising household debt may be a greater problem than public debt, when growth rates are declining. Finally, viewing debt as a series of relationships, rather than as simple numbers, introduces the reader to the concept of "the ghost in the debt machine."

Chapter 4, "Private Debt," begins a discussion of the components of debt in the private sector. Corporate debt, noncorporate private debt, mortgage debt, consumer debt, farm debt, and other forms of indebtedness are examined. Each has its own history, and each its own pitfalls. Overall, American corporations have had the best record of debt management in recent years; young people, mostly Americans, with excessive credit card debt have had the worst. Nationally, the United States is better off in the public debt area than many other nations; but in the private debt area, the United States is not nearly so well off as Germany.

"Public Debt," Chapter 5, is by far the best-understood component of debt. I have little new to offer here except to put the work of others into a larger historical context and to add the dimension of asset and equity bubbles—which of course dramatically changes many traditional conclusions about the sustainability of public debt. I also discuss why constitutional amendments and legislative limitations on public indebtedness are largely ineffective, and I spend some time introducing the reader to the "smoke-and-mirrors" approaches to public budgeting. Why current efforts in the United States to balance the federal budget over the long term very likely will *not* succeed and why quite different efforts to do the same thing in New Zealand and possibly Canada likely *will* succeed complete the discussion in this chapter.

Chapter 6, "Disarming the Debt Bomb," focuses on the major human and economic barriers that prevent, or seriously hamper, solutions to several emerging debt trends. Barriers vary by country, income, level of development, religion, and a host of other factors. Inclinations toward saving or consuming are deeply embedded in a nation's past, but culture is not always the controlling factor.

Halting and temporary progress toward solving debt problems has been the rule in recent years, and debt crises are therefore becoming increasingly common. Following a long period of prosperity, disaster myopia is now far advanced in the United States; and years after a major market and asset crash in Japan, denial is still a major problem there. Excessive public spending commitments and unfunded pensions are problems that Europe has yet to face. A major change therefore will probably take some kind of sharp and prolonged crisis in more than just Japan to get the industrial world to change course, since debt problems are now largely structural, embedded within the cultures of most modern nations.

Chapter 6 concludes by examining specific policies and practices that have been successful in reducing debt in the public sector over long periods of time. How to create the will to change, not just what needs to be done, is the focus here. Lessons from the corporate debt sector—arguably the best-managed sector—will be analyzed with an eye to their applicability in other debt relationships. The long-term value of market crashes and corporate and household debt defaults will be presented; and once that counterintuitive analysis is fully digested, the study ends with some reasons for long-term optimism. "Manias, panics, and crashes" are always followed by better days, but only if these bursting bubbles are allowed to work their inimitable magic.

The most ominous challenge in solving the global debt crisis is raised by Japan. Private and public debt levels have grown so large there that the usually effective neo-Keynesian solutions do not appear to be working. Because public debt levels are already very high, and even higher pension obligations loom in the near future, further deficit spending is difficult to justify. Even when the government tries to expand the economy, the Japanese people prefer to hold cash, thus creating a classic "liquidity trap."[70] Once a "miracle" economy is shown to have feet of clay, a deep pessimism can affect the national psyche and last for years. This is Japan's problem. Could the Japanese disease spread to other G–7 countries? It is not inconceivable. America has been the "miracle" economy of the 1990s, a debt-financed oasis in a sea of troubles. Should the American bubble burst, like the Japanese bubble did, would Americans hunker down as the Japanese have? Would their world-renowned optimism turn to a depression-like pessimism? Would the world's biggest spenders become the world's biggest savers once again? Would Americans begin to heed the lessons of history because they have been forced to relive them? If so, this could be by far the most significant consequence of the global debt crisis.

Chapter 2

The Global Debt Picture

Understanding the nature of debt in the aggregate is more important than understanding any single debt component. As the old saying goes, "If you look only at the trees, you don't see the forest." This chapter focuses on the forest, the global debt picture as it appears in the major industrial nations of the world at the end of the twentieth century. The level and trends of public and private debt—to nations, corporations, households, and future generations—and whether current levels of indebtedness are sustainable will be our concern here.

The Urban Institute, a nonprofit policy research and educational organization located in Washington, D.C., recently published an excellent volume entitled *The New World Fiscal Order.*[1] Its essays concentrate entirely on public debt, the rapidly rising public debt levels of recent years, and industrial democracies' declining ability to control federal budgets. My concern in this book is with debt in general, *both public and private*. To see the system whole, at least at first, let us see how each of the parts is interconnected and how best to measure their cumulative impact. Dauntingly complex, global debt is one of the cogs in the much larger process of global capitalism and can be understood fully only by combining its private and its public components.

Not all players on the global debt field are of equal importance. The United States will, and should be, given most attention because the United States is the largest public debtor in the world[2] and the most economically powerful player in the world market. Not least as a reason for concentrating on the United States here is that by far the best data on all aspects of debt are available for this country. Japan and Germany come next in importance—Japan because it is the world's principal exporter of capital,[3] America's most serious competitor, and the leading economic power in the Pacific; and Germany because it is the leading power in Europe. Thereafter, I shall look at the other G–7 countries: Italy, France, Canada, the United Kingdom, and, where relevant to this study, certain less significant industrial nations.[4] As the discussion of debt progresses, the subject will be further broken down by type of debt: public, private, federal, state, corporate, and household.

Importance of This Subject

During the past two decades, the United States and the rest of the industrial world have gone through economic challenges of major proportions. Productivity growth has been sluggish; the rates of public and private saving have fallen; the rate of investment has declined; economic inequality has risen; equity and asset bubbles have appeared and, in some cases, burst; and recovery from the recession of the early 1990s has been exceptionally slow. In the United States, persons with only a high school education have lost one-fifth of their real income since the early 1970s, and middle-class wages have stagnated. Saving rates for all age groups have fallen in the United States and most other countries, and real interest rates have been exceptionally high by historical standards. As we approach the millennium, the U.S. trade deficit continues to grow, manufacturing employment continues to shift from the economically advanced nations to the newly emerging nations, and an oversupply of unaffordable goods threatens the world economy.[5]

Since the early 1980s, the United States has faced four major shocks to its financial sector: the developing country debt crisis of the early 1980s when all the Latin American nations announced they would no longer pay the interest and principal on their debts; the dramatic worldwide 1987 stock market crash; the savings and loan debacle a few years later; and a large number of commercial bank failures following the sharp increase in oil prices and decrease in real estate prices in the Northeast.[6] During the 1990s, the gap between the well-off and the rest of America grew wider, a bigger share of Americans were living in poverty than was the case a generation earlier, and the stock market became more volatile. The risks of economic crisis appeared to be greater than a couple of decades previously.

Closely related to all these challenges is the basic fuel that drives the modern economy: credit. Credit—both how much is available and how it is used—is directly relevant to economic growth, productivity, savings and interest rates, trade and budget deficits, the value of the dollar, and a host of other economic issues. Indeed, few important matters today are not deeply affected by the flow of credit, both in the United States and abroad. Understanding how credit works, and how credit interacts with inflation, investment, and interest rates, is crucial to understanding a modern economy.

Debt is an inherent part of credit, the obverse side of the coin, if you will. Debt is something owed, the unpaid residue of credit already advanced. All financial debts are contractual claims usually expressed in monetary units.

The terms of these contracts vary widely. Some have to be paid on a specific date; some need never be paid off as long as the interest is kept current. Some debts are negotiable; some are not. Some debts are secured by assets; others are secured only with a promise to pay back the principal later. Credit is what is loaned; debt is what must be paid back. This study is primarily concerned with the latter.

The amount of debt in a modern economy like America's is surprisingly large. Total credit market debt in the United States in 1998 amounted to more than $21 *trillion*, or two and a half times the nation's gross domestic product (GDP).[7] For other countries the level of debt as a percentage of GDP is generally comparable, with the United States falling somewhere in the middle of the G–7 nations with regard to public and private debt.

From the data in Table 2.1, it is evident that substantial debt characterizes the economies of all of the G–7, sometimes called the major industrial countries of the world. Switzerland, Sweden, and Holland would also be high on the list of heavily indebted countries, since they all have high public and private debt/GDP ratios. It is also evident that overall indebtedness varies by country—with very high debt levels in Japan because of high public and private debt, and rather modest debt levels in France and the United Kingdom. Japan has a special problem so far as debt is concerned. David Asher, a research fellow at the Massachusetts Institute of Technology Japan Program, recently wrote an op-ed piece for the *Wall Street Journal* in which he pointed out that "Japan's biggest economic problem is an overabundance of debt—not just bad debt, but debt, period."[8] He added that Japanese nonfinancial firms have a debt/equity ratio of 4:1, and that general government debt will likely reach 130 percent in 1999 because of huge stimulus packages and declining government revenues. If off-budget liabilities are included, Japan's public indebtedness would probably be closer to 200 percent of GDP.

Credit is widely considered to be the most efficient instrument of commercial exchange. Without it, little would get done, or it would take much longer to do. Given this fact, most governments have established tax systems that artificially stimulate their economies by giving tax credits to individuals and firms that accumulate debt. But it is also important to know that the amount of credit available over time must mirror the amount of savings available. When savings fall, credit must eventually get more expensive. And when a given economy is saturated with credit, further cuts in interest rates may lead only to more speculation, rather than to growth.

We also know that countries, corporations, financial institutions, and households tend to underestimate the risks of debt finance, especially during stock market bubbles.[9] Furthermore, debt bubbles more often end with a bang than a whimper. The tendency to idolize central bankers in good times,

Table 2.1

Public and Private Debt in the G–7 Nations, 1993
(as a percentage of GDP)

Nation	Debt
Japan	277
Canada	204
Germany	188
United States	186
Italy	183
United Kingdom	160
France	145

Source: IMF, *World Economic Outlook,* May 1996, pp. 18–19; *The Economist,* October 5, 1995, p. 123.
Note: Public debt is gross debt, excluding foreign and nonfinancial debt.

giving them too much credit for the good things that happen, flips to blaming them too severely when things go wrong. This phenomenon seems to be occurring in America today, just as it did in the late 1920s. The size of a nation's level of debt does not necessarily in itself indicate that a nation's debt level is too high—except in the case of Japan—or that a crisis is impending—again excepting Japan—but it does suggest the need for continued vigilance in all cases. In all events, it is good to think about debt as a cyclical phenomenon, with inevitable ups and downs, just like the economy.

Turning now to the major components of debt, the best-understood and most studied portion of the world debt picture is public or governmental debt. Public debt is best measured as a percentage of GDP. Table 2.2 describes both the size of and recent trends in public indebtedness in the G–7 nations, listed alphabetically.

As indicated in Table 2.2, the United States ranked fifth among the G–7 nations in gross public indebtedness in 1998 and fourth in 1970. The largest increase was in Japan, which experienced an increase of staggering proportions—from 12 to 114 percent of GDP. All the G–7 nations, except for France and the United Kingdom, have gross debt levels that are above 60 percent of GDP, the level above which debts are not sustainable, according to the European Union's Maastricht Treaty.

These large public debts play both a positive and a negative role in a nation's economy. So long as they are not excessive, over, say, 60 percent of GDP, deficit spending can smooth out the economic bumps, target funds for defense or other important purposes, and compensate for deficiencies in

Table 2.2

Gross Public Debt of the G–7 Nations, 1970–1998
(as a percentage of GDP)

Nation	1970	1975	1980	1985	1990	1995	1998
Canada	52	43	45	65	73	98	92
France	53	41	31	39	40	53	59
Germany	18	25	33	43	44	58	61
Italy	42	60	59	84	101	123	119
Japan	12	22	52	68	70	87	117
United Kingdom	82	64	54	53	35	51	52
United States	45	43	38	48	55	68	62

Source: C. Eugene Steuerle and Masahiro Kawai, eds., *The New World Fiscal Order*, pp. 238–39; and IMF, *World Economic Outlook*, May 1999, p. 18.

the private economy. By channeling savings into productive investments, debt bridges the gap between the present and the future. It encourages rapid transactions in a market that otherwise might be moribund. Without large amounts of debt, our modern economy simply could not function, let alone grow. But large and persistent public debts may bias interest rates upward, reduce investment by "crowding out" private borrowers, and telescope too many future resources into the present generation, thus reducing the standard of living for our children. The fundamental issue therefore is the *sustainability* of current levels of debt, and whether the debt is being well managed, not the amount of debt per se.

Many insights can be gained by combining public and private debt and looking at the total debt picture. Private debt levels, both business and individual, tend to rise in times of prosperity, whereas public debt levels tend to rise in times of adversity—especially during depressions and wars. From the 1920s until the 1980s, these trends tended to cancel each other out in the United States. Consequently, total debt tended to fluctuate narrowly between about 140 and 150 percent of GDP.[10] Beginning in the late 1970s, total debt as a percentage of GDP began to climb rapidly. By 1998, it stood at nearly 250 percent of GDP, more than a hundred points higher than it had been for the previous decades since World War I. This high debt/GDP ratio is unprecedented in American history and is largely due to increases in public and personal debt, rather than corporate debt.

To summarize, a very large amount of debt is necessary to the smooth functioning of any major modern economy. Like gasoline, debt fuels the system. But also, like gasoline, debt can be very dangerous if not handled properly. What makes this topic important at this time is that virtually all experts believe, some strongly, that current public debt levels cannot be sustained in the long run, and that serious efforts therefore need to be made to reduce the level of public debt worldwide. There is also a growing consensus that rapidly rising household debt levels, especially in the United States and the United Kingdom, are not sustainable.[11] Whether this is so and what can be done about it will be the topic of later chapters.

Composition of Global Debt

We do not have extensive and reliable data on *overall* debt trends for any nation except the United States, but we do have reasonably good data for public debt levels for all the major nations, and some data on private debt for several of the larger countries. Based on these data, it is evident that strikingly similar things are happening around the world, and have been happening for some time. First, the clearest message from the data available is that debt, both public and private, has been rapidly increasing for most countries, especially during the 1980s. The best data on this topic exists for the United States and is published in the "flow of funds" accounts compiled by the U.S. Treasury.[12] For other countries, the World Bank and the International Monetary Fund (IMF) publications, especially their semiannual economic outlook series, are perhaps the best generally available sources.

The overall composition of indebtedness can perhaps best be studied initially by looking at the United States. The total debt owed to all sources and sectors of the United States is technically called "total credit market debt" and can be found in the *Statistical Abstract of the United States*, published annually, or in the monthly *Federal Reserve Bulletin* (see Table 2.3). In early 1998, America's total debt amounted to $21.7 trillion, or 258 percent of all of the goods and services produced during that year. Most of this debt was held by commercial banks, life insurance companies, federally managed mortgage pools, and other financial sectors of the economy. Financial sectors owe about $4 trillion of that sum to each other; it should be deducted from the total to avoid double counting, leaving the actual "nonfinancial domestic and foreign debt" owed at just over $16 trillion, or about 190 percent of GDP.

As noted, except during the Great Depression and World War II, total nonfinancial debt hovered around 140 percent of GDP, until the early 1980s, when it climbed rapidly to its present height of 190 percent of GDP. Significantly, since the 1980s both of the major sectors—public and private—have participated in this increasing indebtedness. Within these larger categories, however, are exceptions: The levels of state debt, corporate debt, and farm debt have remained essentially unchanged as a constant ratio of GDP over the past twenty-five years. Whether other major industrial countries have experienced a similar debt explosion is

Table 2.3

Credit Market Debt in the United States, 1970–1998
(as a percentage of GDP)

Category	1970	1980	1990	1998
Government				
Federal	29	27	47	45
State and local	14	11	12	14
Private				
Corporate	35	32	39	41
Nonfarm, noncorporate	26	17	22	15
Household	12	52	70	66
Farm	6	6	3	2
Total nonfinancial	150	149	194	191
Total credit market debt	179	174	245	260

Source: Federal Reserve Bulletin, "Flow of Funds Accounts." Data for 1998 are for the first quarter.

not entirely clear. We do know that gross *public* debt has been increasing in most of the G–7 nations in recent years. As Table 2.2 indicates, all but one of the G–7 nations have increased their public debt since 1970, some dramatically so. Only the United Kingdom has decreased its public debt after 1970; but since 1990, it also has been rising rapidly. Public debt levels have climbed rapidly in Australia, Belgium, Finland, the Netherlands, Spain, and Sweden, according to the Organization for Economic Cooperation and Development (OECD).[13] Japan and the United Kingdom have comparable data for private nonfinancial debt. That debt rose from 130 percent of GDP in 1970 to 220 percent in 1990 in Japan and from 70 percent to 160 percent in the United Kingdom.[14] Clearly, the United States, Japan, and the United Kingdom have had dramatic overall *public and private debt* increases in recent years.

We also have comparable "domestic credit" data for the G–7 nations gathered by the IMF and published in its *International Financial Statistics Yearbook.* Table 2.4 presents domestic credit data for the G–7 nations in ten-year increments since 1965. These data include debt claims on the central, state, and local governments as well as the private sector. These data show that Japan, Germany, the United Kingdom, and France have had very substantial increases in domestic credit obligations, while the United States and Italy have not. This pattern, too, indicates growing indebtedness by most, if not all, industrial countries.

A further breakout of these data sets indicates that Germany and Japan have a much higher ratio of private-sector debt to total debt than the United

Table 2.4

Domestic Credit, 1965–1997
(as a percentage of GDP)

Nation	1965	1975	1985	1997
United Kingdom	56	51	47	121
Japan	88	100	118	112
Germany	68	86	112	105
France	36	50	85	79
Canada	31	40	51	69
United States	73	82	82	65
Italy	67	100	76	51

Source: IMF, *International Financial Statistics Yearbook*, for the years cited.

States. For Germany, private-sector debt in 1992 represented 80 percent of total credit outstanding; in the case of Japan, the private-sector ratio was 85 percent. In the United States, private debt was only 61 percent of the total. The point is that Germany and Japan are much more private-sector–oriented in their debt structure than the United States, which has a dramatically larger defense establishment and therefore a stronger orientation to the public sector. Both Germany and Japan also have much closer links between lenders and borrowers and, hence, may be able to sustain a higher level of indebtedness and a lower rate of default than is the case in the United States. All three countries have a "borrow-and-spend" philosophy, although taxes are higher in Germany than they are in Japan and the United States.

Still another way of measuring the composition of world debt is to look at private-sector debt as a percentage of GDP. The Bank for International Settlements made such computations for 1993, as indicated in Table 2.5. Again, one sees large differences in the private-sector debt, just as in the public sector, reflecting different cultural values, historical experience, and current policies.

Personal debt as a ratio to personal income has also been increasing in all of the G–7 nations for which we have data (Italy is the exception), especially since 1980. As Table 2.6 indicates, France has had the largest increase in personal debt since 1970, according to work done by E.P. Davis, a British economist.

A major paradox is evident in the global debt picture, at least in the United States. Concern about rising deficits and growing federal indebtedness has been unprecedented in recent years; consequently, the federal budget has been balanced for the first time since 1960 as a result of efforts by both political parties and a growing economy. On the other hand, there has been very little concern expressed about rising consumer indebtedness in the

Table 2.5

Private-Sector Debt, 1993
(as a percentage of GDP)

Nation	Debt
Japan	202
Germany	140
United Kingdom	120
United States	120
Canada	110
France	100
Italy	64

Source: The Economist, October 28, 1995, p. 123.

United States or elsewhere. Indeed, most official pronouncements on private debt in recent years have been low-key, even soothing. They deny that a serious problem really exists, asserting that the consumer debt cycle is always self-correcting.[15] Even the growing use of credit cards in supermarkets and doctors' offices gives little cause for concern. Whereas the debate over balancing the federal budget grew increasingly shrill and discordant, even shutting down the government for several days in early 1996, concern over rising consumer indebtedness has been placid and has never generated serious public debate.

However, household debt trends in the United States should cause considerable alarm. Household debt as a ratio of after-tax income in the United States has risen from 35 percent in the early 1950s to more than 100 percent in 1998. That is, it would take more than a year's entire income to pay off the debts of the average American household. Consumer debt and bankruptcy filings are at all-time highs, and many are not preparing for retirement. Those not overly concerned with these rising household debt levels respond that household assets have risen even faster than household debt, but most of this increase in assets is based on a rapidly expanding stock market and very high home ownership values, both of which could be temporary. Moreover, the increase in bankruptcy filings has been concentrated among middle-income consumers, suggesting that the increase is systemic, not just concentrated at the low or high end of the income spectrum. Additionally, credit card debt has also risen fivefold since 1980.[16] Nearly half of all Americans now have credit card debt. The average duration of household loans has also increased, especially on automobiles, thus diminishing the immediate debt burden but extending that burden over a longer period of time. Given that personal savings rates have been trending downward since the early 1980s and that they fell below zero in the fall of 1998, it can be argued that the

Table 2.6

Personal Debt/Income Ratios, 1970–1990

Nation	1970	1980	1990
United Kingdom	58	58	118
Japan	60	75	115
United States	65	78	100
Germany	60	75	87
Canada	80	85	86
France	22	40	60

Source: E.P. Davis, *Debt, Financial Fragility, and Systemic Risk,* p. 76. Figures should be seen as approximations; it is the trends that are important. Davis does not provide data for Italy.

average American household is not adequately preparing for retirement, for the possibility of a market crash or a major recession, for the loss of a job, or for a major medical emergency.

Concern about the level of the federal debt ranks consistently high on the list of public concerns measured by pollsters; consumer debt, on the other hand, has never risen even to the level of statistical visibility. Consumer debt in the United States is more than a *trillion* dollars higher than federal debt and must be paid off, whereas the federal government, being sovereign, does not have to pay its debts—ever. And should it want to, the federal government could print money to pay down its debt, as several European governments have done in the past. One suspects that only a country that has not experienced a serious depression in more than sixty years could have so much faith in the market's ability to solve all the foreseeable credit problems.

Although this study is about debt in the larger nations of the industrialized world, it is useful at the outset to note a few facts about debt in the developing nations. Third World debt has also been increasing steadily—from about 24 percent of GDP in the late 1970s to about 37 percent in the early 1990s.[17] In 1998 the external debt of developing countries reached $1.8 trillion, up from $1.0 trillion in 1985 and $639 billion in 1980. There has been a marked improvement in the fiscal positions of a large number of developing countries since the 1980s, according to the World Bank. This is particularly true of countries in Asia and in the western hemisphere, or at least this was the case prior to the Asian debt crisis. Private foreign investment is beginning to flow once again to the middle-income countries, and will never be paid off or even paid down significantly.[18]

To sum up the main points of this section, in recent decades the whole world has been going deeper and deeper into debt. This is true whether one is speaking of public debt or private debt; personal or household debt; or First, Second, or Third World debt. There are only a few exceptions to this generalization, such as New Zealand and Ireland, and it remains to be seen whether these countries' downward trends in public indebtedness can be maintained.[19] It is true that public *deficits* in some G–7 countries have been declining in recent years and that a few countries have actually balanced their public accounts, but few serious scholars think that any of the major countries will actually sustain a balanced budget over a very long period, and no one I know of is predicting a significant decline in public debt generally.[20]

Sustainability of Global Indebtedness

Since there has been a dramatic increase in public debt in all the G–7 nations and much of the rest of the world, and since there has been a similar and even more rapid increase in private debt, especially in Japan and the United Kingdom, the question of long-term sustainability of these debt trends arises. The fragility of the financial system and the increased degree of fiscal vigilance necessary to keep the system healthy are also salient issues. "Disaster myopia"—or the tendency of memories to fade regarding earlier debt catastrophes—is also a perennial issue. Above all, it should be remembered that debt and credit are troublesome and obstreperous by nature; hence, fiscal excess and occasional but severe debt "shocks" are a deeply ingrained part of the human condition.

The GDP provides the best overall *economic* indicator of a nation's ability to sustain its debt levels, along with its counterpart, the national income. An important *political* indicator of sustainability is economic fairness to different constituents. Laurence J. Kotlikoff, in his original and provocative work *Generational Accounting: Knowing Who Pays, and When, for What We Spend*, addresses this issue, as does Daniel Shaviro in *Do Deficits Matter?* At the private level, net debt as a ratio of disposable personal income and corporate income after taxes are good indicators of debt sustainability. For Third World debt, the best indicators of sustainability are the debt service ratio to GDP and to exports. At the outset, however, we should be forewarned that virtually all experts believe that there is a debt sustainability problem, even in the near term.[21]

The long-term fiscal outlook is extremely difficult to project for any nation or even for a particular debt sector within that nation. There are too many variables, none of which can be held constant, and too many unforeseeable events to contend with. However, the medium-term outlook, say within the next ten years, is a subject that can be carefully analyzed, and the IMF and the World Bank have done so, at least for the public sector.

As I have already emphasized, in the United States the overall nonfinancial debt level from 1920 until about 1980 fluctuated around a fairly narrow mean of about 140 percent of GDP. This was true for every decade except during the Great Depression, when nonfinancial debt climbed to over 200 percent of GDP, and during World War II, when nonfinancial debt rose to about 170 percent of GDP. As private debt declined, public debt grew, thus keeping the overall debt burden fairly constant. Since 1980, however, the nonfinancial debt ratio to GDP has risen from its historical level of about 140 percent of GDP to 191 percent in 1998. This ratio shift represents an increase in our overall debt burden by about one-third. Although this rate of increase is probably sustainable in the short run, it may not be sustainable in the long run.

Several classes of U.S. nonfinancial borrowers participated in this increased indebtedness during the past three decades. Households increased their debt the most, by 450 percent! The federal government increased its debt next most, by 55 percent, followed by corporations, which saw a 17 percent increase in indebtedness. Households began to increase their debt burden in the late 1970s by taking on more mortgage debt; and beginning in the early 1980s, both mortgage and consumer debt increased markedly.

The dramatic change in America's credit market in recent years can be seen in yet another way. In 1970, total net borrowing in the U.S. credit market was $88 billion. Of that total, the federal government borrowed 18 percent to pay its interest costs. By 1992, at the bottom of the recession, net borrowing in the U.S. credit market was $541 billion, of which 89 percent represented federal borrowing.[22] Following the recession, the federal government was still preempting one-half of the total credit market, even in the best of years. As Francis Cavanaugh, the senior career executive responsible for debt management policy advice in the Treasury Department has pointed out, from 1991 to 1995, the federal share of the total U.S. credit market—including government-sponsored enterprises—averaged 71 percent.[23] Not all this government funding crowds out private credit. Some government spending assists people in securing more credit by guaranteeing loans. But the S&L disaster—the massive insolvencies of hundreds of savings and loan associations during the 1980s—showed how aggressive financiers with government guarantees could create a fiscal crisis of the first order.[24] Competition between private borrowers and the federal government for a limited pool of funds for loans is clearly a new and disturbing element in our credit markets. Cavanaugh believes that, as the federal government and federally assisted agencies require more and more funding, serious problems of equitable allocation arise, and the quality of our credit markets, and therefore of their sustainability, becomes more problematic.[25]

Requirements for Debt Sustainability

The IMF believes public debt levels will increase in relation to GDP in most countries. Growing private debt trends in most countries lead to the same conclusion. Again, there are exceptions. Both Italy and Canada are expected to reduce their public debt slightly in the near term, but these are the two G–7 countries with the highest debt/GDP ratios. In the long term, Britain is expected to reduce its public debt, largely because its population is already relatively old and retirement benefits are less generous than elsewhere. In the private sector, markets provide a much more predictable and disciplined process of debt allocation, but that discipline can be erratic and slow to punish profligacy. Furthermore, the globalization of the debt market can also enable governments to be more profligate than was true in the past. For instance, global markets helped encourage the United States to finance both its fiscal deficits and its trade deficits in recent years by providing more capital than would have been available from the domestic market alone, thus transforming America into the world's largest creditor nation. As the *Economist* has pointed out, "the market imposes less discipline on giants than on dwarfs."[26]

Falling world savings rates and very high unemployment levels in the industrial world make addressing the problem of growing indebtedness more difficult. World saving as a percentage of GDP, although up a bit since the early 1990s, is still in 1998 below the levels of the 1970s and early 1980s.[27] The rate of saving has fallen even further in the more advanced countries. The very rapid buildup of private and public debt in recent years also indicates that simply stabilizing current debt levels is not enough: What is needed to achieve sustainability is a gradual reduction in the debt levels of all the G–7 countries and most of the middle- and low-income countries. The fact that unfunded pensions and other future entitlements are generally not included in conventional measures of public and private debt makes the need to reach a more sustainable posture even more important. The IMF estimates these unfunded pension liabilities to be at least as large as the public debt levels.[28]

According to the IMF and the leaders of the European Union, among others, when gross public debt levels rise above 60 percent of GDP, a nation should be concerned about sustainability.[29] Gross debt includes the assets held by the social security system. This was the public debt level set by the Maastricht Treaty of 1995 as a prerequisite for nations wishing to join the

European Monetary Union. The average country in the European Union had a gross public debt of 72 percent of GDP in 1998. This 60 percent goal is an arbitrary but not unreasonable figure. Of the G–7, only Japan, Italy, and Canada have gross public debts much above that figure, and Canada is expected to bring its net public debt below 60 percent by 2003. Whatever the threshold, running deficits over long periods of time do tend to make the recipients of these as-yet-unearned benefits feel wealthier than they really are and, hence, to consume more than they otherwise would.[30]

Whether a nation is consuming too much or too little is not easy to gauge.[31] But there is no doubt that public- and private-sector debt/asset ratios have risen sharply since the 1980s. And whether or not the rate of personal consumption in the United States is too high, it is higher than in the other G–7 nations and has been climbing as public and private debt have risen. Moreover, spending on items that require credit rose more rapidly than spending on other goods.[32] A sharp deceleration in asset values, such as a stock market crash, would make these already high debt/GDP ratios much more difficult to sustain. More importantly, the high historical levels of corporate and personal debt in many countries make the entire financial system particularly vulnerable.

With regard to private debt, the market is the best mechanism for determining debt-level sustainability. Bankruptcy is the ultimate stabilizer. Nevertheless, because total nonfinancial private-sector debt rose much more rapidly than GDP during the 1980s in the United States, Japan, and the United Kingdom, the sustainability of current private debt levels is also questionable. Private debt/GDP ratios over 200 percent of GDP, as in the case of Japan, seem excessive, particularly when the Japanese are saving less than they used to. Furthermore, Japanese debt levels appear to be especially excessive given the fact that net pension liabilities are also in excess of 200 percent of GDP, whereas America's private pension liabilities are only 43 percent of GDP.[33] More than doubling the rate of private indebtedness in a little over a decade, as Great Britain did, also appears to be unsustainable in the long run.

The sustainability of home mortgage indebtedness and household liabilities is harder to evaluate than overall debt. But it is clear that household liabilities as a percentage of disposable income have risen in the G–7 nations.[34] Home mortgage costs in the United States as a percentage of disposable income rose from under 40 percent in 1960 to nearly 70 percent in 1996. In the United Kingdom, mortgage costs in that same period rose from less than 20 percent to 76 percent. The increase in Canada was even higher. In the United States, home mortgage costs as a percentage of disposable income for first-time buyers have risen from 23 percent in 1976 to 35 percent in 1996. Mortgage rates at that level appear to be sustainable, but it is hard to imagine that they could go much higher. Household liabilities as a percentage of disposable income are five times higher in the United States, Japan, the United Kingdom, and Canada than they are in Germany and Italy. There may be a flash point out there, say beyond 100 percent of disposable income, where household debt levels would turn critical, but that is by no means certain. Still, high-level mortgage debt, when funded by floating-rate mortgages, as in the United Kingdom, is clearly more dangerous than moderate debt funded by a fixed rate. On the positive side of the ledger, Germany and Italy could probably increase their household debt dramatically, should they care to do so.[35]

The World Bank has established guidelines for excessive and unsustainable Third World debt. If the total debt service for a given nation rises above 80 percent of GDP, or 220 percent of that country's exports, the World Bank finds that country in fiscal trouble. Gross product is used as an index of that nation's income-generating power, and exports provide foreign exchange to service the debt. The penalty is that nations that cross these lines are denied credit in the world market, the situation for most sub-Saharan African nations. Meanwhile, nations with very low debt ratios attract further credit, the situation of the Czech Republic, South Korea, Portugal, and Thailand. Still, foreign direct investment cannot be relied upon. Domestic savings in one's own country is the only certain source of capital in the long run.

Attempts to Address the Global Debt Problem

Given the already heavy public debt burden in most industrial countries and the rapidly rising public debt levels of recent years, attempts have been made to reverse these trends and even to reduce the level of public debt in several countries. There have been some notable successes: Denmark (1983–1987), Ireland (1987–1989), and New Zealand (1984–present). In the Danish and Irish cases, public debt levels were very high and clearly unsustainable, and risk premiums on interest rates were therefore also extremely high. Both countries undertook front-loaded government expenditure reduction programs that brought their deficits back into structural balance for a brief period. An exchange market crisis in 1984 and growing frustration with their economic performance convinced New Zealanders to embark on a major deficit and debt reduction project. They cut public expenditures, denationalized government agencies and ran them like market-driven businesses, ended compulsory union membership, virtually abolished agricultural subsidies, and instituted a value-added tax (VAT).[36] A radical break with the past, this across-the-board approach was very successful, and New Zealand had a budget surplus from 1993 to 1996. But the "kiwis turned sour" in late 1996, according to the *Economist*.[37] The public tired of continued sacrifice and withdrew its support for the reform party; New Zealand slipped back into deficit financing once again. Irish fiscal reforms have led to two economies: "a still backward, unproductive and labor-intensive one owned by the Irish, and a modern, exceptionally productive and capital-intensive one owned by foreigners."[38]

Several other countries have had brief periods of general government fiscal balance, including social security surpluses. These include Australia (1987–1990), Japan (1987–1992), the United Kingdom (1988–1989), Sweden (1987–1990), and Finland (1988–1990).[39] According to Paul Posner and Barbara Bovbjerg, the director and assistant director of budget issues for the U.S. Government Accounting Office, political will was the key to these budget reductions.[40] But this level of political will was virtually impossible to sustain over a prolonged period of time, and none of these countries had a balanced budget in 1997. Norway, because of its North Sea oil, had prolonged budget surpluses during the 1970s and 1980s but has experienced a general government deficit during the early 1990s. Only Singapore, Hong Kong, and Taiwan have consistently had surpluses in recent years.

Although the long-term outlook for reduced public debt is not very encouraging for most countries, we have learned some lessons along the route toward balancing public budgets. First, spending cuts, rather than revenue increases, appear to be the best approach, since expenditure growth has been the driving force behind budget deficits in past years. Second, whatever is done has to be credible from the start. It is far better to actually reduce next year's budget a little than to promise large reductions in five years. Third, entitlements and unfunded pension plans must be included in the mix for the plan to work. Fourth, a nation does not have to wait for economically prosperous times to begin to reduce its deficit. Experience has shown that expenditure cuts do not necessarily lead to recession. Fifth, financial markets need to perceive that the budget-cutting attempt is substantive. Otherwise, interest rates will remain high and bond sales could be problematical. Finally, democracies generally do not take on big challenges unless they have to. A fiscal crisis, and more commonly a *sustained* fiscal crisis, appears to be the *sine qua non* for reversing long-term debt trends.

In the private sector, the picture is much different. Whereas virtually everyone agrees that current G–7 public debt levels are worrisome, virtually no one expresses concern about corporate debt in the G–7. In other words, it is widely believed that there is no corporate debt crisis.[41] Nor is there a strong link between corporate debt and public debt; each has its own fiscal path. There is, however, an ongoing banking crisis, especially in Japan, Italy, and France; but that crisis has not spilled over into the corporate sector, at least not yet. Both bankruptcy rates and debt/equity ratios are rising, and real interest rates remain high. These developments do not, as yet, constitute a "crisis" that requires major changes in the way corporations do business. Where there are problems, they seem to be related to the business cycle or are confined to certain corporate sectors. The global expansion is expected to continue over the medium term, and growing reliance on market forces is expected to solve any major corporate debt crises that may arise.

Despite marked increases in personal indebtedness and personal bankruptcy rates in the United States, the United Kingdom, and Canada, and a general rise in the ratio of debt to personal income in all G–7 countries, all these countries are relying on the usual market forces to address any household debt crises that might occur. In other words, the current wisdom holds that there is no personal debt crisis anywhere. This belief is held despite steadily rising personal indebtedness as a ratio of personal income, rapidly rising bankruptcies, and rising credit card balances in the United States and elsewhere. Consumer confidence remains high in all G–7 countries except Japan, and household wealth has been rising because of higher stock prices, again, except in Japan. A constant refrain, at least until mid-1998, was: "There is nothing to worry about."[42] A few people, most of them not economists, were even beginning to predict an end to the cycle of business expansions and contractions that is evident back to before the Civil War. Others, again not the experts, have begun to predict a new worldwide period of prosperity.[43] But some of the most respected experts on financial crises—people like Hyman Minsky, Charles Kindleberger, Henry Kaufman, and Benjamin Friedman—have for years warned that financial crises are an essential part of the upper turning point of the business cycle, a necessary consequence of the "excesses" of the previous boom.[44]

Other Debt Issues

There are a number of larger, less tangible issues that relate to the global debt picture, some of which I shall discuss later in this book. Each comes at the subject from a different angle, and when thoroughly understood, informs our understanding. Among these issues are the following four questions:

1. *Do Americans and others need to lower their expectations about what it is possible to achieve economically, given the worldwide decline in the rates of growth and productivity since the early 1970s?*

Several writers have addressed this question recently, among them Robert J. Samuelson in *The Good Life and Its Discontents*, Peter G. Peterson in *Facing Up*, Benjamin M. Friedman in *Day of Reckoning*, and Jeffrey Madrick in *The End of Affluence*. If this view is correct, then historically high borrowing levels—at least in the private sphere—may have to be adjusted downward, especially for the bottom 80 percent of the population. The current ideology of minimal government and maximum self-reliance may also have to be modified, putting greater pressure on governments to provide stronger safety nets for the less deserving, thus pushing up public debt levels.

Assuming that this need for diminished economic expectations is valid, most experts may well have underestimated the time frame in which debt sustainability will become a pressing issue. Household debt levels—particularly in the United States, Britain, and Japan—may become especially troublesome, since they grew rapidly on the expectation of a high rate of growth of the economy. Tax increases, benefit reductions, and rising interest rates also become more likely in this scenario of slower growth rates. Should economic growth and productivity continue to be sluggish in the G–7, more analysis will need to be given to the *transition* from unrealistic to realistic expectations, as Daniel Shaviro has argued,[45] rather than simply focusing on the current level of indebtedness, be it public or private, or its near-term sustainability.

2. Is the process of globalization changing stratification systems and social mobility in ways likely to have profound effects on the use of credit and debt?

What will be the impact of another 2 billion workers, mostly from developing economies, entering the world economy in the next decade or so? Will their increasing credit needs and capacity to incur debt clash with the decline in manufacturing jobs in the industrial world? Is the quintessential problem now facing the industrial world the oversupply of goods and an insufficient number of consumers to purchase them at current wages, as William Greider argues in his provocative and insightful book, *One World, Ready or Not*. Is "our wondrous machine" heading "toward some sort of abyss," as he contends?[46] If so, then current debt levels may be much more onerous than we think and will be much more difficult to pay down.

In a society that has traditionally stressed universalistic success norms, if these norms start to be questioned or rejected as unrealistic, what will be the impact on indebtedness? Will those being hurt call for higher taxes, more spending, and even more income transfers from the rich to the poor? James Medoff, Harvard professor of labor and industry, and his Harvard-trained colleague in economics, Andrew Harless, advocate precisely this course in their book, *The Indebted Society: Anatomy of an Ongoing Disaster*. Or will those for whom the dream has been shattered turn within themselves, reduce their expectations, and cut their indebtedness? The last time Americans were faced with a major crisis of expectations, during the Great Depression, they turned inward and cut spending dramatically. Might they do so again?

3. Has the very concept of debt become anachronistic?

From the beginning of our nation's history until the 1920s, "thrift" was considered to be a greater virtue than "debt." Saving, rather than spending, was the more respectable norm in the private sector. Beginning in the 1920s, consuming rather than saving began to be advocated, particularly by the business community. Thrift began to decline, becoming an almost obsolescent virtue by the 1980s.[47] Abhorrence of debt has shifted subtly to respect for credit and its first cousin, "leverage." A similar shift in public sentiment occurred in the public sector in most nations following the Great Depression. Compensatory spending to make up for a depressed economy, an idea usually associated with John Maynard Keynes, began to take center stage among the world's finance ministers. Since then, the American public has not felt nearly as strongly about balancing the federal budget. "Conservative flags which are more often saluted than followed" is how economist Herbert Stein describes the goal of a balanced budget.[48]

Our attitudes toward debt are, of course, closely related to our attitudes toward broader social norms. In the larger society over recent decades, traditional normative ideals like thrift, respect for authority, hard work, and the central importance of character have lost much of their potency. People no longer fear economic depressions and expect to be protected from financial catastrophe by the federal government. In such a world, debt is stripped of its fearfulness, and going excessively into debt is no longer considered sinful. The amount of one's indebtedness becomes an issue of personal choice rather than a moral issue. Audacious action is often rewarded, and a swashbuckling style frequently admired.[49] Formerly outrageous behavior, if it leads to great wealth, is often excused or overlooked. Gambling institutions can become more profitable than thrift institutions, as was the case in the United States beginning in the early 1990s.[50] Some argue that all these changes mean we have entered a new "Casino Age."[51] If so, then perhaps we should begin to look at debt in some respects as a form of gambling.

To fully understand the global debt picture we must see it as a reflection of a larger order of things. Today, banks have largely lost their historic role as guardians of the nation's credit, custodians of rectitude, and paragons of fiscal virtue. They are now regular players at the commercial table—the cause of fiscal excess as often as they are examples of fiscal probity. Most economists no longer agree with Adam Smith that thrift has its roots in human nature, as David M. Tucker points out in his book *The Decline of Thrift in America: Our Cultural Shift from Saving to Spending.*[52] The very existence of human nature itself is now in question. There is no longer a close or necessary connection between thrift and virtue, or thrift and respectable behavior. In fact, according to a new rational life-cycle theory advocated by

Franco Modigliani, one of the economic profession's greats, people should plan to spend everything they have before they die.[53] Descendants should fend for themselves. Generations are unconnected. History has no unifying role to play and therefore neither does the future.

This is not just a fanciful idea of some dead economist. It has persuasive empirical support. As Andrew Hacker has recently pointed out in *Money: Who Has How Much and Why*, the middle 20 percent of American households over age sixty-five have a net worth of only $68,000 above the value of the family home.[54] How long will that last? After a lifetime of working, the average head of a U.S. household has saved enough to support himself or herself and dependents for about two years, although most people live for at least another ten years following retirement. Fewer than half of all retirees have private pensions. They will have gone Modigliani one better: They will have spent all their personally earned assets *long before death arrives*.

Nor is the picture much better on the public side. As Peter Peterson has shown, "Most retired Americans today receive two to five times more in social security benefits—and at least ten times more in tax-free Medicare benefits—than what they and their employers contributed, including the interest on their contributions."[55] In short, most Americans over sixty-five soon exhaust their own resources and soon use up what the government has taken from them over the years in the form of taxes. Shortly after they retire, most Americans are in fact living "on the dole" as we use to call it before the Great Depression.

There has been a massive disintegration of all fiscal rules, not just those related to public finance. As Herbert Stein has pointed out, Americans now only give "ritual obeisance" to a balanced budget.[56] In reality, most leaders of industrial nations really want public debt to increase, just as they themselves have taken on greater personal debt in the private sphere. Nor are they much different from their constituents. "At no point did anything near a majority of Americans indicate a willingness to solve the deficit problem either by cutting programs or by raising taxes," American Enterprise Institute authors John Makin and Norman Ornstein concluded after an extensive examination of American public opinion polls taken in recent years.[57] Those politicians who do not recognize this fundamental fact are often punished at the ballot box. To expect otherwise would be to ignore this new, powerful, and ubiquitous debt ethos that has emerged in recent decades.

4. If the environmental movement continues to grow and a new environmental ethic takes deeper root, what will be its likely impact on current attitudes toward debt?

A new emphasis on sustainable growth, the earth's carrying capacity, and ecology could make the public more critical of consumerism and more favorable toward reducing their wants. Environmentalists have not been concerned much about debt per se but have rather been concerned with the long-term costs to the environment of rising consumption. Some see the tendency to ignore long-term environmental costs as a form of deficit financing.[58] Were environmental costs factored into public spending more adequately, surely there would be some pressure to decrease those costs. Many environmentalists also want to shift the tax burden away from income taxes and toward consumption taxes to reduce consumption. Higher consumption taxes, such as the VAT, could—but not necessarily would—reduce debt finance. In general, there is no evidence that the VAT has reduced debt in Europe: People simply pay the tax and go on consuming.

Some environmentalists and most religious leaders advocate an increase in spirituality; this ethos too could perhaps help to establish some limits to upwardly spiraling consumer indebtedness. But there is currently no evidence that household debt is correlated with religious belief, that environmentally oriented states have less state debt than more conservative ones, or that states with high religious affiliation are less indebted than those with lower church membership.

Conclusions

The world has become much more heavily indebted in recent decades. When *both* public and private debt are included, none of the industrialized nations now have debt/GDP ratios comparable to what they used to be and most have experienced dramatic increases in their private as well as their public debt in recent years. Third World debt continues to grow and is now back up to its early 1980s level—the level at which the international debt crisis occurred. The developing nations are likewise following the industrialized nations toward greater indebtedness. Although various nations have made sporadic and temporary attempts to scale back their public debts, and although corporations and households have held debt levels constant for short periods, the long-term global trends in both public and private debt have been ever upward.

These rapidly rising public debt ratios as a percentage of GDP, moderately rising corporate debt/GDP and debt/profit ratios, and very rapidly rising personal debt levels as a percentage of disposable income for households are not sustainable in the long run. On this point, there is widespread agreement among scholars, governments, and financial institutions. But clearly identifiable and widely agreed upon benchmarks that indicate precisely *at what point* debt becomes excessive are not determinable. Nevertheless, the movement toward a European monetary union and, more specifically, the

Maastricht Treaty, has laid down specific criteria for those nations wishing to join with it. One of those criteria is that gross public debt should not exceed 60 percent of GDP. All but two—France and the United Kingdom—of the G–7 nations exceeded that guideline in 1998. Japan, Italy, and Canada did so by a substantial amount. Whatever that illusive crossover point may be, there is widespread concern by international agencies and the governments of major nations that public debt levels are too high and that concern about corporate, household, and personal debt is too low.

What is clear is that a profound change in public attitudes toward debt has occurred in recent decades in every part of the world. This change is evident to anyone who has spent even a modest amount of time studying this issue. The nature of this change in attitude is captured well by two different aphorisms: In the late Victorian era, a common expression, held by virtually all classes of society, was: "Out of debt, out of danger." That sentiment has disappeared almost everywhere. Today, the axiom that best captures the motivating ideology of the average person is: "Take the waiting out of wanting. Buy it now." The next couple of decades will likely give us convincing evidence about which maxim is the better guide to human happiness.

Chapter 3

The Nature of Debt

To enlarge our understanding of debt—what it is, how it works, and how to understand it better—we need to think about debt in new ways, to ask different questions, and to reach beyond common wisdom. The student should undertake the study of debt as he or she would a study of the Catholic Church—as a distinct topic with its own special characteristics, assumptions, doctrines, values, heresies, and mind-set. Debt is not just a branch of the finance department or something consumers acquire along the way. It has its own ethos, its own separate set of defining characteristics, and its own operating metaphors.

The Moral Aspects of Debt

"Credit is a financial term with a moral lineage," the well-known stock market analyst James Grant has written.[1] Until fairly recently, what we today commonly call "credit" was called "debt." Debt was based on "trust"—trust that what was loaned would be repaid, and trust itself was rooted in other powerful principles such as trust in God and doing unto others as you would be done by. In short, "debt" was traditionally understood to incorporate certain fundamental moral values. It was part of the natural order of things. So was scarcity. Hence, waste was a sin and luxury should be avoided. In early Christian times, avarice—insatiable greed for riches—was elevated to the status of one of the seven deadly sins, and seeking wealth to the exclusion of higher values was condemned. Biblical precepts were part of the broader culture—a wise man saved for the future, while a sinful and foolish man spent everything he earned, and the love of money was the root of all evil.[2]

In Puritan times, abstinence from debt was given high value and sumptuary laws prohibited luxurious living. In the Puritan view, human beings were placed on earth to glorify God, not themselves. This task required faith, industry, and frugality. To Cotton Mather, spending more than one earned was sinful. Debt placed one's soul at risk. In Benjamin Franklin's more secular times, debt endangered one's liberty. When in debt, you were always somebody else's man. " 'Tis hard for an empty Bag to stand upright," was Franklin's pithy maxim. In Thomas Jefferson's day, both public and private debts were viewed in the same way, and both were considered dangerous. Debt could too easily rise to excessive levels. Once those levels were reached, debt inclined individuals and nations to corruption, and threatened republicanism.[3] "Natural law" forbade one generation from making its successors pay the debts it had incurred, Jefferson believed. The sorry fact that our third president died bankrupt belies his lifelong concern for the horrors of unpaid obligations. Many among the entire Virginia gentry suffered a similar fate, suggesting that Jefferson was not alone in his views about the burden of excessive debt.[4]

It is widely believed that Alexander Hamilton thought a large public debt was a "blessing." This view is incorrect. It rests entirely on Hamilton's only known statement on the subject, a letter written in 1781 to Robert Morris: "A national debt, if it is not excessive, will be to us a national blessing." Almost never quoted is the subsequent sentence, stating that he was "far from acceding to the position . . . that "public debts are public benefits." Such a view, he declared, leads to "prodigality," and renders a nation's public credit liable "to dangerous abuse."[5]

In Victorian times, rigorous saving and paying cash for all purchases were marks of a "sound" family economy and a requirement for self-respect. Hardship was the lot of humankind; personal discipline was its necessary handmaiden. For Andrew Carnegie, drinking liquor was the greatest danger to a successful career, but the second greatest deterrent to a man's success was "speculation." By "speculation" Carnegie meant getting financial gain you had not earned—relying on a random turn of fortune's wheel—and living beyond your means. Carnegie believed: "There is one sure mark of the coming partner, the future millionaire; his revenues always exceed his expenditures. He begins to save early, almost as soon as he begins to earn."[6] Avoiding debt because it was sinful had now been transformed into avoiding debt to be successful. But being successful still meant avoiding extravagance, a trait that would trigger public disapproval. For example, Bradley Martin held a ball at the Waldorf Hotel in New York in 1897 that attempted to duplicate the splendors of Versailles for 800 guests at a cost of about $400,000; the Martins were so universally condemned that they felt compelled to move to London.[7]

The twentieth century ushered in an even more radical change in the concept of debt. Rising incomes after 1900, increased leisure time, and the secularization of moral values created a new kind of individual: the consumer who purchased on credit. Merchants devised new ways to sell more goods by arousing unsatisfied longings. A new way to finance consumer purchases was also created: the installment plan. Buy now, pay later. Eventually, this new way of financing purchases evolved into a secular gospel, one based on increasing personal debt by telescoping future income into the present.[8]

By the late 1920s, the older, morally laden concept of "debt" had evolved into the newer, morally neutral concept of "credit." Robert S. Lynd, a prominent sociologist of that period, captured this shift in sentiment when he wrote that the "lingering Puritan tradition of abstinence" and "paying cash" had by then become a "duty" to spend by "utilizing installment credit."[9] Values were now things to be bought in stores. Thereafter, debt—or now more commonly, credit—could be viewed neutrally, as either good or bad, depending on whether it was used for investment or consumption. However, even frank consumerism no longer had the same opprobrium; consumer goods increasingly became consolations for needs previously satisfied by religion, thereby achieving a secularized and psychologized justification. When production outpaced desire, new desires were created by advertising. If actual economic needs were already satisfied, dreams replaced needs. The evils of prodigality were relegated to the past; self-indulgence was the new norm.

The joys of credit gradually replaced the evils of debt as a new moral ethic. From being among the world's best savers, Americans, especially the secular elite, now began holding the older Victorian values in contempt. By the late 1920s, spending had become the norm. Moral limitations on the pursuit of self-interest rapidly diminished thereafter. R.H. Tawney in his classic *The Acquisitive Society* (1920) described and decried the new credit ethic, the resulting primary focus on wealth, and the decline of moral limitations on consumption and debt. This secular order would inevitably lead to fiscal excess, he believed. The decline of frugality resulted in the decline of morality.[10] Some authors date the decline of moral considerations and the rise of private indebtedness in the United States from the post–World War II period.[11] But the separation of morals and debt actually happened much earlier. According to Census Bureau data, private debt increased from 119 percent of GDP in 1920, to 157 percent in 1930, and 219 percent in 1933.[12] This indebtedness increase was true of both corporate and individual debt. The decline of moral considerations where debt was concerned followed the decline of moral concerns in economic thought, history, and political science in both the United States and Europe. As a trend, it is a part of the larger process of the secularization of modern society.

The consequences of separating debt from moral considerations are striking, especially when coupled with the consequences of separating the market from the consequences of unbridled laissez-faire economics. This point is well illustrated by the example of J. Pierpont Morgan, virtually the voice of the American financial world before the Federal Reserve System was founded in 1914. Morgan's conservative fiscal views were strongly influenced by his fundamentalist religious beliefs and by the severe panics of 1857 and 1873, which had been cataclysmic for him and his influential father. Morgan's mistrust of debt was rooted in Episcopal values of honesty, straight dealing, personal charity, order, beauty, and veneration of the past. His banking experiences taught him to be "slow and sure," or "sound," in the language of that era. Together, the unregulated market and an omnipotent God held the financial system constant—imposing limits on excess. The free market punished those who strayed from fiscal responsibility; eternal judgment awaited the profligate.[13] Like Jefferson, Morgan did not always live up to his avowed standards, but his beliefs were clear: The universe itself required frugality, and debt, especially for ostentatious consumption, was to be avoided at all costs.[14]

The final decoupling of morality from debt occurred in the 1930s. Victorian fiscal morality dictated adherence to strict federal and state budget balance.[15] Even in times of depression, government budgets had to be balanced. Governments, like families, were expected to live within their means. Emergencies did not change the rules. One simply waited for the depression to end. Based on long-standing rules going back at least to Adam Smith and his classic *Wealth of Nations* (1776), Victorian principles of public finance assumed that governments must keep their financial affairs in order just as individuals and families must. Consequently, government deficits should be avoided except in time of war. Parsimony in peacetime made possible the expansion of debt in time of war. History taught, Adam Smith believed, that deficit funding "gradually enfeebled every state which has adopted [this practice] . . . enriching in most cases the idle and profuse debtor at the expense of the industrious and frugal creditor."[16]

The Great Depression and John Maynard Keynes permanently swept away the last vestiges of this fiscal morality. As Stein documents in *The Fiscal Revolution in America*, moral concerns about public debt eroded during the Great Depression and were virtually gone by the late 1930s. The Great Depression convinced most Americans that the economic system was flawed. Keynes argued that the economy could be fixed only by compensatory government spending. Keynes and those who accepted his views eventually persuaded Franklin D. Roosevelt that the government would bring the economy out of the depression by increasing public spending, a move that required going into debt. Similarly, what worked for governments could also work for families. Debt, or compensatory spending, was the way out of depression and want. This idea caught on slowly, but the massive deficit spending of World War II provided Keynes's proof: Prosperity returned. Deficit spending became the norm. By the 1960s, references to the immorality of public indebtedness were largely considered ritualistic and old-fashioned—as previously quoted, Stein's "conservative flags which are more often saluted than followed."[17] Although the public, the media, and political leaders continued to worry that government (or household) deficits might become excessive, the moral dimension—the sense that debt was morally wrong—was absent.

By the 1990s, credit had ceased to be related to moral behavior, and had become an essential *function* of the marketplace. Debt could be either a blessing or a curse, depending on its use. Its new purpose was to leverage income to maximize, or at least smooth, the process of investment and consumption. Beginning in the late 1970s, public debt as a ratio of GDP began to climb, and household debt began to soar. Deficit phobia was clearly evident in the heated rhetoric of public discussions,[18] but public and private debt climbed in tandem.

There were no longer any moral rules about the proper level of public or private indebtedness. Nor did there seem to be any clearly observable moral consequences following what used to be considered excessive debt levels, either public or private. It is not uncommon now for corporations to pay 50 percent or more of their earnings in a given year to interest on accrued debt;[19] and household debt exceeded 100 percent of annual after-tax income in the United States by the late 1990s.[20] Federal participation in U.S. credit markets—because of the massive borrowing required to roll over the growing federal debt—preempted up to 89 percent of total net borrowing in some years but was never, after 1990, less than 45 percent of the funds available in the U.S. credit market.[21] In recent years, consumer spending has risen twice as fast as income in the United States, and personal savings rates turned negative (individuals withdrew more money than they put into their savings accounts) in the fall of 1998 for the first time since the 1930s. Debt now drives the financial system formerly governed by moral rectitude.

With the separation of moral concerns from the market system, a process largely completed by the end of World War II, a new financial architecture was needed. Since punishment for wrongdoing was now passé, a new mechanism for avoiding punishment needed to be put in place. A regulator of last resort would take the place earlier served by morality and the workings of the unregulated marketplace. In the United States, that regulator was the Federal Reserve Board (FRB). Internationally, it was the International Monetary Fund (IMF). The objective of both agencies was to provide more credit in recessions or periods of financial crisis, thus continuing and enhancing the driving force of the new financial system. In theory, the FRB and the

IMF were methods of helping a temporarily illiquid bank or group of bankers to prevent a localized banking failure from becoming a systemic breakdown. A wave of bank failures like those in the Great Depression would destroy the creation of credit, the very lifeblood of a debtor society. Banks, therefore, must not be allowed to fail, because debt must be perpetuated. An international lender of last resort would do the same thing for countries that went bankrupt: The countries would be given more money by the IMF to extend their debts, thus forestalling default. Excessive debt, in short, would be addressed by creating even more debt. When countries attempted to default, as Mexico did in 1995 or Russia did in 1998, the IMF extended more credit to them and rolled over their debts. Since debt has lost all moral attributes and become merely a means to greater prosperity, it seems only natural to use more of it than ever before. The IMF rescue packages are not trivial. From mid-1997 through 1998, the IMF "loaned" $180 billion to Asia, Russia, and Brazil, of which $61 billion came from U.S. taxpayers.[22]

The IMF and some economists still talk as if there were a "moral hazard" that banks and governments may take otherwise unacceptable risks because this lender of last resort will bail them out. But there is neither a "moral" problem nor much of a "hazard" of going bust anymore. In times past, a lender of last resort lent freely to banks that were distressed but solvent, against collateral, and at a penal rate of interest.[23] Insolvent banks and countries were allowed to fail because they had acted immorally. Now, governments and banks default all the time and are routinely bailed out with public funds. The Asian crisis of the late 1990s perfectly illustrates this new debt ethic: (1) excessive borrowing was the root cause of the Asia financial crisis,[24] and (2) even more borrowing from the IMF proved to be the preferred solution to the crisis.

However, the IMF's prediction was accurate. With the elimination of any moral stigma in debt accumulation, risk taking increased. The spectacular performance of equity markets around the world in recent years has increased this appetite for risk among mutual fund investors, bankers, and governments. Allowing a big bank or a developing country to fail would not only require the lenders of capital to write off those loans but could also curtail other lending. Limitation on lending is unacceptable. Debt itself is the "contagion" which has engulfed the global financial system. New loans only add to the exposure of countries already excessively in debt. The possibility of default is only an afterthought. "Moral hazard" is no longer closely related to religion, nor even to morality generally. The moral part has been decoupled from the hazard part. Moral hazard is now more of an economic construct than it is a moral principle and, as such, is measured statistically rather than religiously or philosophically. We know that the era has passed when balancing the budget—once considered absolutely essential to human happiness—can now be referred to as "deficit hysteria."[25]

The Technical Aspects of Debt

Understanding the disappearance of the moral foundations of debt is relatively easy compared to grasping the technical aspects of debt in modern society. Anyone seriously interested in penetrating this technical thicket faces a "minefield of ambiguities." Definitional problems, inadequate theory, limited data sources, inconsistent findings, and overheated rhetoric plague this subject.[26]

Editors and news pundits regularly warn of the perils of public debt, yet many well-trained economists react to these announcements with increasing skepticism, from both a theoretical and a statistical analysis of these issues.[27] Private debt is treated less frequently and with considerably less ongoing concern, yet the amount of private debt in many, if not most, major countries is much larger than public debt, and its rate of increase in recent years has been much faster.[28]

Even how we go about measuring debt, especially public debt, is a complicated issue.[29] Several approaches are possible; and different measurements are used for different purposes. Comparing public or private debt levels among different countries can be even more difficult. Cross-country comparisons can be extremely deceptive, reliance on certain concepts of accounting can be misleading, and a nation's assets have to be included in these comparisons, because assets reflect ability to repay debt. What determines public or private solvency is not always clear. Is Russia solvent? Is Brazil? Who can say for sure? The debt process is always fluid, constantly changing, and full of surprises.

There is, moreover, a huge body of alarmist literature on this subject, particularly in the public sector, although I suspect this literature is abating somewhat among experts in the United States and Britain.[30] Still, alarmist books are more likely than scholarly analyses of the growing debt crisis to reach the best-seller list. A recent example is Harry E. Figgie's and Gerald J. Swanson's 1992 *Bankruptcy 1995: The Coming Collapse of America and How to Stop It.* They write that in 1995, "the United States as we know it will most likely be dead."[31] The authors' public debt projections for the United States were way off the mark within less than a year after publication, because they used faulty assumptions and straight-line projections of increasing public debt. Even Nobel Laureate James Buchanan, an expert on public debt, has had considerable trouble convincing his colleagues to take his concerns about debt seriously.[32] This is largely because Buchanan evaluates public and private debt as classical scholars have traditionally done, while most modern economists view public and private debt as very different things. Buchanan's theories are also difficult either to prove or to reject.[33]

Nor have those who criticize this alarmist view fared much better. Robert Eisner, a well-known economist who is skeptical about even modest public debt levels, has also failed to persuade his more complacent colleagues of his restrained approach to understanding public debt. He has, however, made considerable progress in getting people to measure public debt more intelligently by including all government debt as one statistical entity, not federal debt alone, by separating investment from consumption, and by measuring debt in real rather than nominal terms.[34]

Adding to this methodological "minefield" is the larger context in which this subject has to be placed for any in-depth understanding. "Debt" is a part of the obverse of "saving." Declining savings among virtually all industrial countries is one of the root causes of growing indebtedness.[35] According to the IMF, inadequate savings has led to relatively high global real interest rates, diminished investment, and lower real income growth rates. Diminished saving itself is part of the even larger process of "modernization." Modernization, or the movement of religion from the center to the periphery of society, has been largely responsible for the decline in the concept of debt as a "sin," which, as discussed above, used to be a major barrier to increasing indebtedness. As countries modernized, they changed their attitude toward debt profoundly—from a generalized fear of the consequences of rising indebtedness to an increasing acceptance of rising debt levels, although they have done so at markedly different rates.[36]

Along with one of the lowest savings rate in the industrial world, the United States has the highest consumption rate.[37] To illustrate, in 1965 the rate of personal consumption as a percentage of net national product was 68 percent; by 1991 that figure had risen to 77 percent.[38] This substantial increase comes at the expense of *everything* else. Furthermore, a 77 percent rate of consumption in the United States is considerably higher than the rate of consumption in Japan (67 percent) or Germany (62 percent) or the other G–7 nations for that year. As Peter Peterson, who was secretary of commerce during the 1970s, has long argued, this strong desire to consume is part of our policy of growth maximization and entitlement mentality.[39] Over time, consumption has come to hold a position of exclusive predominance among competing interests. It drives all before it. Our rapidly expanding entitlements are derivative of this larger desire to consume. Debt is the vehicle by which greater consumption is made possible, in both the private and the public sector, particularly when real incomes are falling. Therefore, if we really want to understand the fundamentals of debt, we must consider public and private debt together, and must consider *both* of them as part of the larger drive toward ever increasing consumption.

Like the proverbial stone thrown into a lake, understanding debt leads to ever-widening concentric circles of context. In the United States, scholarly concern has focused on rising federal debt and declining savings; in Japan—which had little federal debt until recently—even greater concern is centered on unfunded public pension liabilities; and in Germany, fear of debt is so strong that the use of credit cards has yet to find widespread acceptance.[40]

Deep and abiding concern about public debt has not really been strong in the United States since the 1960s; but as Herbert Stein has pointed out in his monumental *Fiscal Revolution in America*, "ritual obeisance" to the *concept* of a balanced budget is still considered important.[41] Italy, with the highest level of public debt among the G–7 nations, as well as the highest level of unfunded public pensions,[42] seems almost unconcerned about its fiscal situation. It has certainly made very little progress in reducing its extremely high level of public debt; simultaneously, Italians, per household, are saving only half what they saved in the early 1980s.

Each debt sector varies by country and by time period. American households have increased their liabilities as a percentage of disposable income from 74 percent in 1984 to 100 percent in 1996.[43] In Germany and France, the ratio of household liabilities to personal income has been constant for several years. In Italy, Canada, and the United Kingdom, that ratio has been rising rapidly. Each of the major industrial countries has a different basic attitude toward saving, and manages its debt in different ways. In the United States, net saving as a percentage of GDP has been falling since the latter part of the nineteenth century; today it is less than half the Japanese rate and well below the savings rates of most G–7 nations. All age groups and persons in all income levels save less than they used to in United States.[44] Italians, despite the sharp drop in household savings, still save much more than Americans do. Thus, even though their public debt is much larger than in America, so, too, is their ability to finance it. Comparisons must therefore be made very carefully. However, with some certainty we can say that there is considerable evidence of inadequate world savings, which leads to relatively high global real interest rates, which in turn reduces investment, productivity, and income growth.[45]

Add to these systemic problems of debt analysis the artificial ones of fiscal gimmickry, now highly developed in all advanced countries, and we can begin to appreciate the technical complexity of debt analysis. For example, recent public debt reduction laws have little to do with debt reduction; they are designed only to reduce the rate of debt *increases*. Balanced budget projections are almost always meaningless beyond two years, yet they are constantly announced. Public opinion polls are notoriously unreliable indicators of what the public will tolerate fiscally, yet public polls are taken almost every day. More and more budget items are being taken "off budget" so that they can be hidden and ignored. Hundreds of budget items are no longer included in official budgets, from social security to trust funds for minute activities. Although most states have constitutional provisions or laws prohibiting deficit spending, virtually all have deficits, and far more state debt is now off budget than on—that is to say, nonguaranteed state bonds now far exceed full faith and credit funding, or funding which is tied legally to tax revenues.[46] States have paid little more than lip service to these constitutional restrictions for several decades.[47]

Other anomalies come to mind. Money market mutual funds are widely thought to be a form of savings, but they are not insured in the United States and are not even legal in Germany. Most Americans no longer think that investing in the stock market is speculation, and apparently they no longer think putting money in a savings account is a good idea. Derivatives are supposed to be a method of reducing risk, but to date they seem to have increased it. Debt exposure is much harder to measure today because of these new instruments, and mismanagement of debt using derivatives can result in debt exposure of several multiples more than that of recorded debt. The collapse of Long Term Capital Management, a high-flying hedge fund which had a balance sheet of about $100 billion on an equity base of $5 billion, is only the most public example of the dangers of leveraged debt. Social Security is thought of as an insurance program; but in reality, most U.S. retirees get back three to five times more than they put into the system.[48] Deficit doves tell us not to worry, yet fifteen countries in Europe had deficits in 1994, and only two, Italy and Holland, have seen their deficits shrink in the previous four years.[49] By 1998, five of the G–7 nations still had government deficits, as did most of Europe outside Scandinavia. Gross government debt/GDP ratios within the European Union are not expected to change much in the foreseeable future, according to the IMF, despite all the euphoric rhetoric by politicians in various nations stating that the deficit problem has been solved.[50]

Debt has, since earliest times, been an intractable problem. For hundreds of years nations have gone through cycles of excessive debt creation followed by some kind of financial crisis. It is simply part of the capitalist system, if not a part of human nature itself. Lord Overstone, a notable banker in England during the early nineteenth century, vividly described this debt cycle as follows: "First we find it in a state of quiescence, next improvement, growing confidence, prosperity, excitement, overtrading, convulsion, pressure, stagnation, distress, ending again in quiescence."[51] Most major economists since Overstone's day have accepted this view, at least in general. My point here is that credit is by nature unruly, and financial mismanagement can lead to disastrous economic events. All attempts to eliminate this debt cycle have been unsuccessful, as evidenced by the most recent financial crisis in Asia.

Equal in importance to viewing debt as cyclical is the importance of understanding debt as a series of direct and indirect relationships. Debt is not just a set of discrete numbers. Debt is a web of interactions best understood as ratios—debt/GDP, debt/disposable income, debt/equity, expenditures/revenues, investment/interest rates, and so forth. To cite just one example, the appropriate deficit/GDP ratio will depend in part on the prevailing private saving/GDP ratio and in part on the desired foreign investment/GDP ratio. There are no fixed destinations, inexorable principles, or unchanging goals— just relationships. All is process and change. Debt has its own culture; it is a living system that has its own resiliency. This resiliency is generally underrated, and therefore the effects of bankruptcy are often overrated. How debt is used is often more important than how high it is. This is a significant point. For example, in years past people bought a house and paid it off as soon as they could. The house was an investment and was necessary for basic existence. Today, an increasing number of families are taking out second mortgages or home equity mortgages to pay off credit card debt or for some other purpose—since interest on home mortgages is tax deductible— even though this move places their homes at risk. Such behavior would have been scandalous in Victorian times, or even as recently as the 1950s or 1960s. Not today.

No single theory of debt is very useful,[52] even in understanding public debt, the most studied of all debt components. Nor are we much better today than the Victorians at predicting when private households or corporations are likely to run into trouble.[53] Add to this mix all the new and barely understood debt instruments, such as derivatives—now at the level of *$35 trillion worldwide*—and the whole subject becomes something of a witch's brew.[54]

Astute experts on debt are beginning to compare our private debt behavior to the risks of casino gambling. Ron Chernow in *House of Morgan* says the "Casino Age" began in 1948 and has continued to the present, with the trend steadily intensifying, while James Grant bases his analysis of the most recent bull market on the gambling instinct and finds "unmistakable signs of mutual-fund addiction."[55] Speculation and gambling have always been interconnected, but never more so than today.

In the late 1990s, prosperity appears limitless. For example, Jeffrey Sachs, an economist at Harvard University, reportedly said that the world was standing on the brink of a new Golden Age, with economic growth and rising income at higher rates than ever before in history.[56] Increasingly, we hear talk about the end of the business cycle, the irrelevance of the past, and how inappropriate it is that government authorities should issue cautionary comments about the longest bull market in American history. All these factors provide the current context for debt analysis, a context that is surprisingly euphoric from an historical perspective.

J. Pierpont Morgan used to say: "The first requisite of credit is character." Honesty, integrity, fortitude, consistency, and what Victorians used to call "soundness"—which meant a willingness to pay one's debts as well as the capacity to do so—are also part of the nature of debt, if not its very essence. Individuals do matter—both their honesty and their judgment matter—as we learned when Robert Citron made Orange County go bust in 1994. Citron ended up in jail, and Merrill Lynch & Co. ended up paying $437 million to Orange County to settle the resulting lawsuit. In recent years, Nicholass Leeson, a single rogue banker, brought down Barrings, Britain's oldest merchant bank; and Michael Milken both created and then almost destroyed the junk-bond market in the United States. Without integrity, proper accounting is impossible, and budget targets will not be credible. With regard to good judgment, the U.S. economic expansion of the 1990s is largely built on borrowed money in the corporate and household sectors, just as the expansion in the 1980s was built on government debt. Rising share prices makes all this debt seem unalarming, Louis Uchitelle points out in a recent *New York Times* column; but U.S. corporations have borrowed hundreds of millions of dollars to buy back their own stocks in order to give share prices a boost.[57] Since corporate profits have been falling since 1995 in the G–6 nations (the G–7 minus Italy) at the same time share prices have been rising, slower growth may be in the cards. It is odd—to say the least—to increase corporate and household debt at the same time corporate profits are falling, especially when this game plan got the Japanese into deep trouble in the early 1990s. Surely this is not a "sound" way to run an economy.

There is no single way to define "debt" or "deficit." These simple terms, as indicated above, hide a multitude of definitional problems.[58] Cross-country comparisons can be very misleading if they are not adjusted for country-specific issues, if government assets and net worth are not included in measuring deficit impacts, if long-term comparisons are not in real terms, and if current operating outlays and capital expenditures are not identified wherever possible.[59] Whether to include social security as part of debt analysis presents a special problem. Some believe that only direct liabilities, not contingent ones, should be considered. Others believe that the present value of the expected stream of payments, minus the expected stream of revenues, should be included, with the difference being added to the deficit. Probably the best approach is to measure these things in a variety of ways, depending on what is at issue.

Even limiting our analysis to calculable measurements creates numerous problems. James Grant, in his dour but insightful *Money of the Mind*, writes that debt is a mental construct largely devoid of empirical reality. For example, if people are highly confident about their own personal situation or the era in which they are living, debt has less danger and credit more value than in economically tighter and less confident times. We should be prepared, therefore, to accept numerous definitions and approaches toward understanding debt, insisting only that definitions be as precisely defined as possible and that comparisons be consistent.

Private debt poses additional definitional complications. The character and terms of private debt contracts differ enormously, and debt instruments are complex and large in number. They differ about when and how payments are to be made, or whether they need be paid at all until the final due date. Various options about payment are available: Some contracts are negotiable and some not, some marketable and some not. Most private debt is secured, but some is based only on the faith and credit of the debtor. Some private debts eventually wind up being claims against the government, as in the case with the savings and loan debacle. There are also a host of complicated financial instruments relating to private debt understandable only by experts. These include repurchase agreements ("repos"), which played a major role in the Orange County bankruptcy, and well over a *hundred* varieties of derivatives—caps (a call option on interest rates), swaps (an agreement to exchange cash flows linked to an asset on liability) and much more exotic instruments.[60]

Our economy is by nature two-sided—with both a credit and a debit system. Our money is based on trust; most of our transactions are merely pieces of paper or verbal orders. Short-term debt (e.g., credit cards) has largely replaced money or supplements it, and tends to extend our money supply. Our economy could not function without a well-developed credit system; savings could not be channeled into productive investments; and capital would not be very mobile; hence, growth would be slow. Private debt is both beneficial and dangerous in excess. It is like the fuel that drives our automobiles: carefully controlled, it is one of the wonders of the modern world, but our fiscal instruments, like our automobiles, are powered by extremely flammable material.

The long-term trend of debt among advanced nations is "more." This is particularly true of public debt. Since the 1980s, gross public-sector debt has increased as a percentage of GDP in all the G–7 nations and most of the other industrial nations. Debt increases have been especially large in Japan, Italy, Belgium, and Canada. But even as debt has increased in recent years, concern about it has decreased. The *Harvard Business Review* recently published an article, "Is the Deficit a Friendly Giant After All?"[61] The *Wall Street Journal*, traditionally a fiscally conservative newspaper, has recently taken to calling those who are still concerned about U.S. deficits "debtheads." A very sophisticated and careful analysis in the *Journal of Economic Literature* on the consequences of rising deficits in the United States concluded that there is no peril in the rising public debt and that current levels of debt are essentially without effect, either positive or negative.[62] Most economists do not accept this view.[63] But such messages, especially from very respectable sources, can be beguiling. They encourage people to ignore the issue or put off solutions to a later day.

Virtually all the studies that dismiss or minimize concern over current and rising levels of public indebtedness, however useful they may be as a corrective to alarmist literature, ignore the larger lessons of history and certain factors that cannot be quantified. More useful and insightful than these highly focused and intensely theoretical approaches are the broader studies undertaken by international agencies, such as the World Bank, the International Monetary Fund, and the Organization for Economic Cooperation and Development (OECD). These agencies have been concerned about rising public debt levels for several years, and are still concerned.

Rising public and private debt levels in most, if not all, of the G–7 countries confirm that debt in general has lost its Victorian stigma. The rising inflation of the 1970s encouraged leveraging and going deeply into hock early in life. The good times of the 1980s created a new "Casino Age," in Ron Chernow's words, that has "jettisoned traditions that have ruled Anglo-American finance since Victorian times."[64] These "funny money" periods come and go in history. Charles Kindleberger has chronicled them marvelously in his delightful book, *Manias, Panics, and Crashes: A History of Financial Crises.*[65] No nation is immune to experiencing these excesses from time to time.

The dramatic decline in savings rates suggests that fear of debt is simply not as intense as it used to be. One reason for this decline in savings might be that we no longer have depressions, panics, and fiscal crises with the same degree of intensity and frequency as we did in the age of J. Pierpont Morgan. Another reason for the decline could be that we now have a lender of last resort in the United States in the form of the Federal Reserve System, and an almost worshipful attitude toward its chairman, Alan Greenspan. The existence of the IMF tends to serve the same purpose internationally.

The third major component of debt—after public and private debt—is *international* or *balance of trade* debt, as represented in the balance-of-payments accounts among nations. The trade balance is the difference between exports and imports of goods and services. The difference between exports and imports must equal the difference between national saving and domestic investment. When that figure is negative, the difference must be borrowed from abroad. The United States used to be a lender of funds to other countries; but since the early 1980s, it has had a net current account deficit, largely because of growing public deficits and increased indebtedness in the private sector. From 1988 to 1997 the United States borrowed more than $1 trillion from abroad.[66] This international indebtedness was increasing at an annual rate of more than $200 billion per year in 1998, which was about three times more than all the rest of the G–7 put together. By contrast, Japan had a trade surplus in 1998 of circa $70 billion a year with the United States and the European Union. For some time now, the United States has been the world's largest debtor nation.

Several consequences follow from this balance-of-payments debt. First, the United States is now dependent on savings provided from abroad. This dependency is clear evidence that Americans are not saving enough and that we are "living beyond our means," in the words of the President's Council of Economic Advisors.[67] If foreign lenders were to cut back on their loans to the United States, interest rates would surely soar. Second, chronic deficits on current accounts lessen a nation's ability to influence foreign affairs. Power and influence flow to creditor nations, not debtor nations. Many have pointed this out.[68] A declining manufacturing sector—along with a relatively high level of defense spending—can also lead to imperial "overstretch."[69] Third, a high and persistent trade imbalance generally causes domestic interest rates to rise to attract foreign capital. This increased demand for dollars causes the value of the dollar to rise relative to other currencies, making exports more expensive, putting still greater pressure on the manufacturing sector. Gradually, this demand for dollars is saturated and the dollar falls in value—but the debt remains. As Benjamin Friedman has pointed out, there is not just one debt problem, but two, the federal debt and the national or trade debt, as a result of borrowing from abroad to finance the rising trade deficits.[70] This debt can increase just so long as foreigners are willing to loan us money. But we do not control them, and at some point they will have all the U.S. debt they wish to acquire. At that point, imports of goods that have tended to keep inflation low, and imports of capital that have tended to keep interest rates low, will reverse themselves, and the costs of this "twin deficit" will become more evident. Fourth, apparently the only way to reverse course is to have a recession. During the depths of the last recession, in 1991, the U.S. trade deficit was only $10 billion. Each previous recession also temporarily reduced the trade deficit. Importation tariffs could also accomplish the same purpose, but they are unthinkable in the present climate of opinion.

The Limits of Debt

The key question in all the above is whether current policies and practices are sustainable over the long run, and whether the world should begin to reduce its current levels of debt. How long can debt continue to increase without causing significant harm to important groups? The short answer is that no one knows exactly. And we probably will not know until the pain is already evident. Whether we look at public debt levels and trends, or private debt levels and trends, it is all the same: Neither is sustainable over time if debt is growing faster than income and assets, or revenues and GDP.

A major factor in debt sustainability is public confidence in the future. Popular opinions—about growth rates, interest rates, job opportunities, what the future looks like for the next generation, and whether the public generally believes that their nation is on the upswing or in relative decline—are all relevant to the capacity to sustain current debt levels. The restoration of a high degree of price stability in recent years has made people more optimistic than they were a decade ago. Impressive reductions in the public debt levels of a few nations like New Zealand and Chile have also been encouraging. Finally, in the medium term, global economic expansion is expected to continue at a somewhat lower but still satisfactory pace, according to the IMF,[71] and hence the future looks reasonably promising.

But there are problems. There is broad agreement that rates of public debt are not sustainable in the long run if they are in excess of 60 percent of GDP and are growing rapidly.[72] This is the crossover point for the World Bank and the European Union officials, and is embodied in the 1991 Maastricht Treaty. Technically, public debt sustainability depends on interest rates, the growth rate of the economy, and the ratio of the size of the budget to GNP.[73] It is possible to have much higher debt levels for a long time, but not without some negative consequences, particularly retarded investment and higher interest costs. In the private debt area, market forces generally come into play before catastrophe strikes, forcing cutbacks. Corporations begin to cut back as bankruptcies grow. Households do not generally move beyond a band of historic debt levels for very long. Farmers cut back on debt accumulation when crops are disappointing or when they have overexpanded their credit.

Experience has shown that there are a few fairly reliable signs of debt excess. Put in economic terms, debt is subject to diminishing marginal returns: Beyond a certain level, debt stops delivering financial and social benefits. Peacetime public debt/GDP ratios in excess of 100 percent are a cause for concern. Falling savings rates are another. Rapidly rising interest rates are still another. Tim Congdon, in *The Debt Threat*, focuses on this problem.[74] Congdon describes how virtually everyone wanted to borrow money during the 1970s when interest rates were low; but as those rates went up, what were once modest and serviceable investments became increasingly onerous burdens. Higher real interest rates undermine capitalism by requiring the injection of public funds to bail out highly leveraged and influential debtors. Since real interest rates have started to climb once again, this factor is likely to become increasing salient.

Economic theory gives little guidance on the proper ratio of government debt to GDP. In practice, this ratio will vary over time and across countries, depending on whether a given nation is at war or not, going into a depression or coming out of one, and the general health of the private economy. In general, public debt has risen in tandem with the growing size of the public sector. For the major industrial countries, gross public debt now averages about 70 percent of GDP.[75] In 1970 that figure was 41 percent. The combined effect of rising public debt levels since 1970 has been to raise real interest rates about 1 percent, according to one of the most extensively used fiscal policy models,[76] to cause a 12 percent permanent reduction in capital stock, and a 2 percent reduction of consumption—all of which persist forever! Clearly, these are limiting factors.

Debt-limiting factors in the private sector are harder to evaluate. Of the major nations of the world, Japan has the most private debt. According to the Bank for International Settlements, total debt for Japanese households and firms was 202 percent of GDP in 1993.[77] Debt/equity ratios of Japanese manufacturing firms are also high, but have been falling in the last ten years. Most other nations, including the United States, have private debt levels that center on 100 percent of GDP. Countries where households and corporations rely mainly on long-term loans at fixed interest rates—Japan, Germany, and the United States—are largely insulated from the immediate impact of interest rate increases, but those more inclined to adjustable rates—Italy and Britain—are more vulnerable to rising interest rates. Capacity to fund private debt is also influenced by savings rates. All the G–7 nations have high household savings rates except for the United States and Canada, thus making debt service easier than in those two countries.[78] Interest rates are also low in Japan and Switzerland, which makes their high private debt levels easier to finance, compared to Sweden where both debt *and* interest rates are very high. In the United States, private-sector debt does not appear to be unsustainable near-term, although unprecedentedly low savings rates are a growing concern.

Of even greater concern, going back to public debt levels, are excessive entitlements, well described by Peter Peterson in his 1993 *Facing Up*.[79] Non-means-tested entitlements, which are entitlements people receive regardless of their income, go mostly to the middle class, and represent 45 percent of the federal budget in the United States. Total welfare benefits—that is, all government spending at whatever level for welfare purposes, plus interest—now consume 60 percent of total tax revenue and, by 2003, will take 75 percent under current laws.[80] Peterson is especially persuasive in showing how the elderly are favored in America with regard to credit-based entitlements. Those over age sixty-five receive eleven times more federal funds than do children under eighteen, who of course cannot vote benefits for themselves. In fact, the average couple who retired at sixty-five in 1981 had, by 1998, received back from the government all of their Social Security taxes, all the Medicare taxes they had paid in over the years, and *all* the income taxes they had paid over their entire lifetimes![81] This figure includes the interest the couple could have received had they invested these funds themselves. Clearly, this situation is not sustainable, neither is it moral, for the elderly have the fewest poor of any age cohort in America.[82]

Some say that the government has made a promise to the elderly that cannot now be broken. But the government never promised that the elderly would get back more than they contributed and certainly did not promise that the average person would receive a rebate of *all* income taxes paid into the treasury over his or her entire lifetime. Entitlements run amok was clearly one of Italy's and Sweden's recent financial wake-up calls; it is beginning to be clear that the same thing is true in America. Increased clarity about the problem does not necessarily mean there will be a greater propensity toward taking action, however. Government policy changes, more often than not, occur as a result of interest groups using their political power to achieve their private goals, not because of clarity of understanding. This has been especially true of fiscal matters.[83]

Declining workforce participation is another debt limitation, since workers must not only pay the interest on their own debts but also produce the revenues to support those who have retired. In America for example, 83 percent of all males fifty-five to sixty-four years of age were in the workforce in 1970. By the mid-1990s, only 66 percent were.[84] In fact, at every age level except for those in their early twenties, males are working less than they used to. In contrast, in Japan, 75 percent of males ages sixty to sixty-four were in the workforce in the 1990s, and 39 percent of males over sixty-five were still working. Comparable figures for the United States were 58 percent and 18 percent. Not only do the Japanese save more than Americans, they also work longer. This means that it is much easier for them to service their higher household and public debt. The Germans and the French have even lower workforce participation rates than Americans, but in the case of the French, their overall debt is also lower.

Not so obvious but equally important are indicators of growing debt that have not yet created public concern. Growing household equity debt in the United States, especially in the Northeast, is placing more and more homes at risk if the economy turns down for an extended period. Nor is this a small matter. Home equity debt rose from about $150 billion in 1988 to $255 billion in 1993.[85] The same pattern is true of automobiles, the next greatest household expense. As recently as 1986, 12 percent of all automobile transactions were leases; today about a quarter of all transactions are leases. Over half of all luxury cars are now leased. Home ownership is declining as an economic value to increase current consumption. A consumer can have more things now if that consumer does not pay off the mortgage, or leases rather than owns. There is an interesting paradox here. As the percentage of families in the United States with savings accounts fell from 62 percent in 1983 to 44 percent in 1989, the percentage of all banks offering home equity loans almost doubled. So did the amount of home equity debt.[86]

Finally, two trends related to debt at the state level nicely capture the point that our views about debt are largely shaped by the cultural values that have emerged in recent decades. First, from 1895 to 1963, every state in the United State prohibited lotteries. This law was part of a Victorian values system that discouraged gambling. Today, more than thirty states have lotteries, and more states are considering making them legal. All but two states now have some form of legalized gambling, or "gaming." Gambling, to call it by its real name, is now a $30 billion a year industry, bringing in nearly six times the revenue of the motion picture industry. Second, despite almost universal constitutional or legislative restrictions against state indebtedness, per capita state debt rose from $115 in 1960 to $1,629 in 1995.[87] In real terms, this is about a fivefold increase in the level of state debt. States have simply ignored these legal restrictions by borrowing funds that have no guarantee of repayment. Total state debt was $427 billion in 1995, with $305 billion not covered by the usual "full faith and credit" provisions.[88] States with the highest per capita state debt tend to be in the Northeast; those with the least debt are in the South and the Midwest. State constitutional provisions limiting indebtedness are now largely unenforceable, but states with constitutional or legislative restrictions do appear to have lower levels of long-term spending.[89] In sum, as American cultural values have become more liberal, so have our attitudes toward debt accumulation and risk taking. But as public and private debts have risen, factors that limit debt have also become more evident.

Toward a New Understanding of the Nature of Debt

Dramatic changes generally do not happen quickly in matters relating to debt; they happen slowly, almost imperceptibly, and often without much notice. Metaphorically speaking, comparing debt to what happens when termites invade a house is a better tool for analysis than alarmist rhetoric about "hockey sticks," impending "crashes," or "bankruptcy." Termites eat away quietly and take years to do their damage. So it is with debt. This is why a historical approach is so important in understanding debt. It often takes years to determine the results of policy changes and decades to plot changing social values and mores. Prices rise and fall over very long periods of time, nations rise and fall, but not suddenly, and cycles give up their insights only after several waves have occurred.

A second important methodological tool involves looking at debt from a variety of disciplines and perspectives. Paying attention only to what is numerically calculable misses what is moral. Using economic theory alone runs the danger of ignoring contrary empirical data. Even treating debt in strictly rational terms, as many economists do in discussing the Ricardian equivalence theorem,[90] misses the irrational and the paradoxical, both clearly part of the human condition. Debt is as multifaceted as human nature, as complex as a gene, as unpredictable as the weather. It varies by time and place, by nationality, and by class. Frankly, we simply do not understand some aspects of debt, and some aspects we have long misunderstood.[91] Hence, the more facets of this complex topic we can examine, the better we will appreciate its nature and worth.

Understanding debt is like understanding complex phenomena in Gestalt psychology; debt is more than the sum of its parts. One illustration should suffice to make this point clear. The size of the national debt of various nations is usually distributed along a scale as a percentage of GDP. In 1994, the gross public debt of Italy was 123 percent of GDP, that of the United States was 80 percent, that of Germany was 49 percent, and so forth. Yet, the impact of public debt in these countries did not vary proportionally to their debt/GDP ratios. High public debt in Italy was not as onerous as the 123 percent figure would indicate, because the Italians save more than residents of most countries and therefore have a larger pool of funds to service their debt. They also have a lower than average level of private indebtedness, which enables them to finance their high public debt more easily. Again, we must evaluate the question of sustainability within the national context.

Third, we should be skeptical when dealing with correlations. Many allegedly harmful consequences are assumed to be rooted in debt, especially public debt; examined more carefully, these consequences are not supported by the data. For example, it is often asserted that rising public debt will "crowd out" private borrowers, thereby raising interest rates and retarding investment. If we look at the most sophisticated studies, both here and abroad, a close correlation between public debt levels and interest, inflation, growth, or investment rates is difficult to sustain empirically over the short term—hence the caution about correlations. Deficits do tend to retard investment but after a one- to two-year lag.[92]

We should not conclude that, because statistical correlations are not always possible or do not give a clear signal at the present time, debt levels do not matter. They do. But they often matter in ways different from those we suspect or on a timetable that we cannot precisely determine now. This is an important point that is often overlooked. For example, in a recent book by M. Michael Cox and Richard Alen entitled *Myths of Rich and Poor, Why We're Better Off Than We Think*, the authors persuasively demonstrate that, based on consumption patterns, most Americans are better off than in the recent past.[93] They then go on to say that "the next generation of Americans will be better off than the current one."[94] No one can possibly know this. Standards of living have declined in the past for long periods of time. The fivefold increase in the consumer-debt burden since the early 1970s may not be a serious problem *currently*, but the capacity to fund these debts is largely based on a stock market that has reached historically high prices. A prolonged bear market would very likely lower standards of living for millions of Americans, if not for the majority. The best may not be yet to come. Moreover, public debt levels are considerably understated in many countries because their data do not include unfunded government pension guarantees. When they are included, debt burdens increase dramatically. As mentioned earlier, Italy's gross public debt was 123 percent of GDP in 1990; in that same year unfunded pension liabilities reached 233 percent of GDP.[95] Those experts who issue the *World Economic Outlook* noted in October 1993 that net pension liabilities in all major industrial countries are "at least as large as current debt levels, even under favorable assumptions."[96] Italy will need to borrow heavily in the future to pay these pensions, whether or not there is a correlation between debt and interest rates.

A fourth analytical problem in dealing with debt relates to sophistry. Assertions that all public expenditures are wasteful or that an increase in debt will lead to an increase in national wealth are examples of causal relationships that are superficially plausible but generally fallacious. These sophist claims fall within the realm of special pleading or are deliberately misleading. For example, we often hear that public debt levels are not a problem because "we owe it to ourselves." As early as 1776, Adam Smith spent considerable time in *The Wealth of Nations* discussing public debt; he dismissed the argument that the right hand is merely paying the left hand as "sophistry." "But though the whole debt were owing to the inhabitants of the country, it would not upon that account be less pernicious," Smith wrote.[97] Another example of sophistry from that same era is Thomas Jefferson's preachment that the public debt should expire at the end of nineteen years because no generation has a right to burden those who come after it.[98] Many responsible nations have had modest public debts for generations without noticeably negative effects. Better questions are: What is the debt for? Is it for investment or consumption? Is it sustainable over time? Was it for the payment of a major war, the winning of which provided security for subsequent generations?

To sum up, debt, whether public or private, is neither evil nor good per se. Good or bad consequences depend on a host of factors relating to the reasons for that debt and how it will be paid down, as well as whether the debt in question will be productive or not in the long run.

The Balanced Budget and Emergency Deficit Control Act of 1985 (commonly known as the Gramm-Rudman-Hollings Act) is another example of political sophistry. It had nothing to do with reducing the deficit, only with reducing the *projected* deficit; and when the deficit targets set by that act could not be met, they were simply put off into the future. Congress's passage of sixty-four acts since 1960 to raise the federal debt limit is another example of political maneuvering. These are not debt-limiting acts; they are meant simply to give that impression. Nor are congressional acts to extend the limit of a "temporary" debt increase actually temporary in fact. Almost without exception these "temporary" acts become permanent.

A whole garden of "rosy scenarios" relating to debt accumulation blossomed during the Reagan years. During the 1990s, the more common error was an overstatement of projected deficits. Both scenarios were way off the mark, because deficits simply cannot be projected forward more than a year or two. More recently, the Clinton administration's FY 1999 budget assumes that current budget surpluses will continue for "several decades."[99]

Such a projection is patently absurd; all economic forecasts are very sensitive to a host of unpredictable factors and can change by hundreds of billions of dollars in a single year.

We should be particularly suspicious of debt estimates of major new government programs like health care. The difference between the original estimate and the current cost of Medicare, according to Peter Peterson, is 300 *times* (not 300 percent).[100] Cost overruns are typical in U.S. fiscal history.[101] Perhaps this tendency to underestimate the cost of major governmental programs is a by-product of the persistent American belief that deficits simply do not have serious consequences and can therefore be ignored. If traditional fiscal restraints have largely disappeared, as Buchanan has long argued[102], then cost estimates will likely be taken less seriously and debt will rise. Of equal importance is the diminished credibility of the government as cost overruns become endemic. The government's credibility is crucial so that it can maintain its ability to finance future interest payments.[103]

Placing certain items, for instance, Social Security, "off budget" is another example of what we are emphasizing here. Federal debt really should include unfunded obligations, such as Social Security entitlements, because these obligations are based on a long-term contract between generations and must be paid for at some level. The government recognizes these commitments as a moral obligation—but not as a fiscal liability, because Congress can change the law at any time. It is quite true that Congress has this power; but until Congress *does* change the law, these Social Security obligations ought to be on budget, just like everything else. The great economist Walter Bagehot, in his classic 1873 work, *Lombard Street*, insisted in dealing in "concrete realities" and in describing these realities "in plain words."[104] Following his example, we should call a spade a spade, and put Social Security back on budget. This gesture would have the additional benefit of highlighting the need to gradually increase the age of retirement and to modestly lower the benefits to retirees, so that the system can be maintained without a significant increase in taxes.

Finally, we should be aware of the direction in which the issues under discussion are heading. As the rate of increase of public debt has been declining, concern for the consequences of this debt appears to be fading. Diminished faith in the classical view of debt analysis, typified by James Buchanan, is clearly evident. Currently, balanced budgets in the United States and Canada mean that public debt is a back-burner issue in the media. Elsewhere, the financial crisis in Asia has replaced balanced budgets as the issue of central concern.

General Trends

The nature of "debt" is a complex subject, one infused with technical ambiguities, definitional problems, limited data sources, inconsistent findings, inadequate theory, and overheated rhetoric. We must, therefore, approach this topic with caution and special care.

With this caveat clearly in mind, the following general characteristics and trends appear to be evident in most industrial nations during the past two or three decades:

- The amount of both public and private debt has risen in most nations in recent years, however it is measured. Sporadic attempts to reverse this trend have, to date, been largely unsuccessful. Although the growth rate of government debt has been curbed in recent years, these were prosperous years; and when economies turn down again, we should expect the growth rate of public debt to rise once again.

- The current level of public debt in most industrialized countries gives cause for concern and raises questions of sustainability, especially when unfunded entitlements are included. Efforts to paper over this problem with fiscal gimmickry are growing ever more sophisticated.

- By historical standards, the current level of household liabilities is high in Japan, the United Kingdom, Canada, and the United States, but the level of concern about debt levels is not correspondingly high in these countries. The Asian financial crisis does not appear to have generated greater urgency on this subject.

- Savings rates are declining, especially among English-speaking nations, throughout the world. The decline in savings is greatest in the public sector, but it is also observable in the household sector, particularly in the United States. There is some evidence that the inadequacy of savings is becoming a problem.

- As a consequence of falling savings rates and less than robust income growth rates, real interest rates in most countries are high by historical standards. High interest rates mean that the cost of indebtedness is now also higher than it has been in the past; and when economic cycles turn down again and debt "convulsions" reappear—as they always have in history—debt-service costs could be burdensome. Income and wealth will likely fall.

- The emergence of asset and equity bubbles in recent years has tended to make people feel wealthier than usual, thus diminishing the cause for concern over growing debt. When these bubbles burst, as they inevitably do—and already *have* done in Japan and several other Asian countries—the relative burden of these debts could climb dramatically. Generally speaking, the larger the bubble, the more painful the recovery. When bubbles burst, public confidence can be, and usually is, shattered; once-popular government leaders are often held in contempt.

- Most nations are in the same predicament in handling their growing public and private debt, although Japan appears to be somewhat ahead of the rest because its asset and equity bubbles have already burst. Despite public indifference to the problems caused by growing debt, there is clearly a need for more fiscal prudence and greater budget transparency about public and private credit.

- The moral limits on debt acquisition so evident in the Victorian era and earlier are virtually gone. In their stead, a new "Casino Era" attitude toward private debt appears to be emerging in the United States and the United Kingdom, but not in Germany or Japan. If correct, this new attitude will likely encourage even more indebtedness and financial risk taking, suggesting that current debt-related problems are not merely cyclical, but of a more fundamental nature.

- The danger of not acting on these growing debt problems is substantial. In the United States, the consumer prices bubble that began in the 1950s and expanded to its maximum in the 1970s has burst and is now back at the level it was when it began to inflate. If the global economy now moves from the recent era of disinflation to a new era of deflation, which has already happened in Japan, the burden of both public and private debt could skyrocket.

Just as compensatory spending by governments to address recessions and depressions has limits—most nations are no longer expanding their welfare state initiatives—so, too, does the policy of relying on a lender of last resort. Addressing the problem of excessive and unsustainable growth in indebtedness by granting still more loans with longer payout periods is a policy that may work for a finite period of time, but it is intrinsically illogical and will almost certainly prove dangerous if relied on indefinitely. The point at which IMF bailouts are counterproductive—that is, the point at which countries, large banks, and major corporations should be allowed to suffer the consequences of their own decisions—is receiving only minimal consideration. The well-known lessons derived from the excesses of the welfare state do not appear to have been applied in a serious way to the global debt crisis. Eventually, the welfare state had to be curbed. It is time to do the same thing with debt.

Early Warning Signals of Emerging Crises

Our final topic on the nature of debt raises the question of whether there are reliable methods of predicting when debt becomes unsustainable. Since economists have developed sophisticated, albeit imperfect, indicators of approaching recessions, is it possible to develop similar indicators for approaching public or private debt crises? Probably not at this stage of our understanding, but it is possible to take certain strides toward a better understanding of what causes nations and individuals to get into trouble by getting too far into debt.[105]

First, good signs of approaching difficulties are rapidly rising public or private debt ratios as a percentage of GDP for nations, or the ratio of debt to disposable income for individuals, or the level of after-tax profits as a ratio of corporate debt for corporations.[106] Rising real interest rates in excess of the growth rate of GDP are also a warning sign. The rule of thumb is "what goes up rapidly will likely come down rapidly." Perhaps the best example of this tendency is the stock market. In recent decades, markets that have risen rapidly have tended to fall just as rapidly. Both the Nikkei stock index and urban residential land prices in Japan began to take off in the mid-1980s, but they fell just as rapidly in the early 1990s. The price of the average urban dwelling in Japan reached sixty-seven times average disposable income per head in 1989 when the property bubble peaked. Ten years later housing costs had fallen back to twenty-six times earnings. U.S. housing costs are forecast to be 8.3 times average disposable income per head in 1999.[107] These "bubbles" were indicators of excess. The U.S. stock market "crash" of 1987 was not so severe or so lasting in effect, partly because the previous increase in stock prices was moderate.

Second, an unexpected and rapid increase in real interest rates is a leading indicator of emerging fiscal problems. When interest increases exceed the growth of a borrower's income, debt/income ratios can rise explosively. This is what Tim Congdon calls *The Debt Threat.* His view is that the retribution for the *omission* of proper debt management procedures early on is likely to be greater than the *commission* of those mistakes.[108] Italy is a good example of what we are talking about here. High levels of debt and high interest rates have required the Italian government to roll over its public debt very rapidly, most of it within less than one year. Very little Italian debt is purchased by foreigners, unlike American debt; and a high percentage of Italy's public revenues goes to pay interest costs, thus reducing what is available for other purposes. Monetization of the debt—that is, inflating the currency to reduce the debt in real terms—was done earlier on, but is no longer possible because the Italian public cannily requires a premium before it will purchase government bonds. Italy's income taxes are the highest in the OECD, and its tax resistance is growing; hence, Italy has very limited options for increasing public debt levels. Italy also faces a more serious future than other G–7 nations because it has one of the greatest discrepancies between the tax burden on current residents and future generations, owing to very generous entitlements.

A third leading indicator of excessive public debt levels is the growing share of government resources that must be devoted to debt-servicing costs. The cost of servicing public debts has more than doubled as a percentage of GDP in the G–7 nations in recent years. Net interest payments were 12 percent of GDP in Italy in 1993, whereas they were less than half of 1 percent in Japan. When unfunded pension obligations—which in some countries add up to more than their total national debts—are added to these public debts, the IMF has declared that most of the G–7 nations have unsustainable current budgetary trends and that they should aim for a gradual reduction in their debt ratios.

A fourth leading indicator of excessive public debt occurs when the interest rate exceeds the growth rate of debt. This trend can go on for years, but not indefinitely. Government bond yields, and hence the cost of borrowing, were over 10 percent in the fall of 1994 in Italy, Spain, Sweden, and Australia—all nations with either very high public debt or very low private savings. Given this fact, the IMF authorities are of the opinion that, in all the major European countries, "considerable deficit reductions are necessary."[109] The net public debt of the United States is about average for a G–7 nation; hence, that advice clearly applies to us as well. Additionally, it is widely believed that high public debt levels raise real interest rates globally, thus reducing investment. The IMF considers debt-induced interest rates in excess of about 200 basis points to be a generally reliable sign of debt excess.

Finally, a fifth leading indicator of excessive public debt is falling public confidence in government accompanied with growing tax resistance. Growing entitlements, made possible only because of deficit spending, can raise expectations. If, later on, these entitlements prove to be too expensive and need to be cut back, public resentment can arise. Regardless of where the *quantitative* indicators fall on a continuum, if the public begins to lose confidence in its government, the ability of officials to manage debt will be severely restricted. Tax resistance sets limits to what can be funded, regardless of the worth of that which needs funding. "Americans have always reviled taxes to an extent unparalleled in any other industrial country (which is why, as a share of GDP, our taxes are the lowest in the industrial world)," comments Peter Peterson, former secretary of commerce.[110] In short, growing tax resistance may be a good leading indicator of excessive public indebtedness. Kevin Phillips also discusses this issue in *Boiling Point.*[111] Among advanced countries, fiscal expansion has now reached the outer limits of what is politically possible.

With regard to private debt, market forces seem to be adequate regulators of excessive behavior. Bankruptcy awaits the unwary corporation or individual. Farmers who borrow to excess can and do lose their farms. Households that default on their loans have their purchases on time repossessed. Individuals have to "qualify" to buy a home or a car and are thus regulated at the outset. Default rates and bankruptcy rates are leading indicators of emerging problems in the private sector, but the essential point is that the private sector is essentially self-regulating.

Conclusions

All major industrial countries increased their net public indebtedness as a percentage of GDP from the 1980s to the mid-1990s. Under current policies, this debt is expected to decline somewhat provided that world economic growth rates do not fall below trend. If the Asia crisis widens, as appears likely, debt levels will continue to rise.

Net private debt has also increased as a percentage of GDP in most of the advanced nations during this same period. Private domestic financial debt in the United States has increased as a percentage of GDP by about a third since 1980. In Japan, private nonfinancial sector debt has risen even faster from an even higher base during this same period, and the United Kingdom has seen its private debt rise from well below that of the United States as a percentage of GDP to a position that is now slightly higher.

National savings rates and rates of capital formation have, on the other hand, declined considerably in all major countries during the past two decades. They are unlikely, according to the IMF, to be sufficient to support adequate growth of production capacity, employment, and living standards in the near term. These unprecedentedly high and rising world debt levels and declining savings rates have tended to inhibit investment by raising the cost of funds to finance various public and private projects. As funds saved face higher demand, inflation also has become a greater concern.

This, then is the industrial world's basic problem: rapidly rising debt and declining ability to service debt. This trend is not sustainable over time. For the United States, the problem can be simply stated: Total credit market debt has risen from 174 percent of GDP in 1980 to 261 percent in 1997, an increase of 50 percent. During that same period, U.S. mortgage debt grew from 52.6 percent to 65.3 percent of GDP, and consumer debt grew from 12.6 to 15.3 percent of GDP. Corporate debt was 32.7 percent of GDP in 1980; it was 40.6 percent in 1997. Federal government debt rose from 26.4 percent to 47.1 percent of GDP in that same period. Clearly, the growth of debt has been substantial and across the board in the United States during the past two decades. Obviously, growth rates of this magnitude are not sustainable.

How should we best approach this growing debt problem? Long experience among a variety of countries regarding debt, coupled with careful technical work here and abroad, indicate that the following concepts are very useful in addressing debt problems:

1. Expect the problem to get worse before it gets better. Debts (public, private, and foreign trade debt) will continue to climb, at least in the near term according to the best authorities on this subject.[112] Like Old Man River, they just keep rolling along. In the absence of a major fiscal crisis, little is likely to happen. Requirements for a balanced budget or constitutional provisions mandating such outcomes, at either the national or the state level, appear to be ineffective barriers to deficits. More important are a nation's cultural mores—like Germany's fear of inflation—in reducing debt. Politi-

cal will, rather than budget reform or long-term debt targets, produces the most effective budget strategies. Even then, it is very difficult to sustain or achieve fiscal discipline.

2. There is no *immediate* debt crisis, either public or private or in the balance of payments on current accounts. No major nation is about to go bankrupt, not even Italy. There is no wolf at the door, but there *are* termites in the basement, chewing away. Debts, both public and private, can and will be managed near term—say, for the next ten years or so—but probably not for twenty years without significant changes or a major crisis.

The long-term problem is much more serious. Growing health-care costs, the eventual retirement of the baby-boom generation, rising real interest rates, and the inevitable downturn in the economic cycle will continue to exert upward pressure on the debt levels of most countries. For the United States, the most serious short-term debt problem appears at this time to be rising household debt but federal debt is of greater long-term concern because of unfunded pensions and entitlement commitments; for Japan, it is the banking crisis and unfunded pensions; for the United Kingdom, mortgage debt seems to be the least sustainable; and for Germany, the deficits required by reintegrating the Länder have taken center stage. Italy's problem is more systemic—how to govern itself. At this writing, Canada appears to have mustered the will to directly address its public budget problems better than any other G–7 nation. Among the smaller countries, New Zealand and Chile offer the most encouraging models.

3. An international and interdisciplinary approach produces much better insights than a single-nation, single-discipline approach, especially for public debt. Each nation is different in significant ways, and there are many unseen connections between debt and other matters. Broad-based studies conducted over long periods of time produce the most reliable results.

As Paul Posner and Barbara Bovbjerg have pointed out, the causes of deficits among major nations are surprisingly similar and have become more so as national economies have become more integrated.[113] But each nation responds quite differently to its debt problems, whether public or private, based on its own traditions. Nevertheless, insights and experience gained elsewhere are often helpful in understanding one's own problems. This fact argues for greater emphasis on the historical approach, especially to discover what seems to work and what does not.

4. Rapid changes in debt levels, interest rates, and so on should be watched carefully. "Debt traps" can appear with amazing rapidity as Congdon explains so well in the chapter entitled "The Algebra of Debt Growth" in *The Debt Threat*.[114] On this same point, the downside of bubbles is just as important as the up side. The exhilaration of rising purchasing power funded by

debt can quickly turn into the "yoke" of past commitments. Stock market crashes, recessions, and even depressions can, on the other hand, be very beneficial in restoring equilibrium and appreciation for and acceptance of the inevitable cycles of history.

5. In the long run, unfunded public pensions should be included in public debt analysis. Unfunded pensions are often called the "invisible debt problem." They are deliberately kept invisible because, when unfunded pensions are included, they make the prospect for balanced budgets dramatically worse. This problem will be much more of a burden in the future for Canada, Italy, and Japan than it will be for the United States. Regarding private pensions, only half of all full-time workers in the United States have any pensions whatever,[115] and workers aged twenty-five to thirty-four with only twelve years of schooling have seen their pension benefits fall from 49 percent in the late 1970s to 23 percent by 1992.[116] The pension issue—both public and private—is likely to loom larger in the future.

6. As John Makin and Norman Ornstein have pointed out, the "single most visible residue" of the U.S. failure to balance the federal budget has been the rising sense of disappointment and distaste for politics and politicians, even among politicians themselves.[117] Promising to reduce public debts and then not doing so has led to widespread cynicism, and this cynicism may in part be responsible for actually *increasing* public toleration for debt. If we do not think anything will work, why try? This cynicism about debt reduction has spread to a wide variety of other issues, making politicians here and abroad more unpopular than they have been in decades. In other words, what was once largely a fiscal problem has now become a political problem as well. Profound unintended consequences are clearly a part of the nature of debt.

7. Private debt is a bigger problem, in terms of the amount of indebtedness, than public debt, but the market tends to modify excess in the private sphere early on and rather efficiently. Public debts do not have such an automatic governor. Although private debt could become a larger problem than public debt in the future, this prospect does not seem very likely at present. When we add the other twin—the balance-of-payments deficits—the public problem looms even larger.

8. Rapidly rising public and private debt has probably increased the standard of living for the current generation, but this increase will come to some degree at the expense of subsequent generations. Net national saving (low in the United States) and net capital formation are closely related; hence, high consumption and low savings usually mean high interest rates, reduced growth rates, and a lower standard of living in the future.[118] High debt levels have also probably deferred and diminished growing income inequality, at least in America. It is well known that earnings inequality increased during

the 1980s in large part because there were fewer middle-class jobs in that decade than in the previous one.[119] Without the huge increase in public debt in that decade—which increased federal expenditures—this problem would undoubtedly have been made worse.

9. Experience here and abroad has taught us that the best way to approach the problem of unsustainable debt is to cut spending rather than to increase taxes in the public sphere, and to cut back on consumption rather than going after additional income in the private sector. Several studies have pointed this out.[120]

10. Debt should be coupled with savings, and both should be attached to consumption patterns. Consumption drives the system worldwide—debt is but a means to that end. Savings fall because the desire to consume rises. Undisciplined *spending* is the root problem, not debt. To achieve any long-term change in public and private debt habits, a new and more critical attitude toward consumption is required. If consumption as a percentage of GDP falls, savings will automatically increase. However, trying to increase savings without simultaneously decreasing consumption is folly. Some substitute for the moral restraints of past generations needs to be found, since it is unlikely that any of the G–7 will return to Victorian values.

11. Finally, rather than looking for crises or other sensational happenings, the astute observer will look for cycles and long-term trends. History generally moves in cycles rather than crises, although they too occur now and then. Third World debt cycles occur in long waves every few generations, nations go to excess in public indebtedness from time to time, and corporations and individuals find themselves too deeply indebted and pull back. There is a certain rhythmic pattern in these matters. But there is also an unseen factor that keeps the whole thing from flying apart—a sort of animating ghost in the debt machine. From this perspective, debt is not an entity or a fixed quantity but a series of relationships, a fundamental unit of a larger property.[121] Taking this quantum and more nebulous perspective brings wisdom not available from a strictly quantitative approach. From such a perspective, we do not seek final answers, fixed destinations, or even objective reality—only proximal explanations rooted in unseen and vaguely understood connections. This approach emphasizes the resiliency rather than the fragility of our debt relationships and the need for intuitive awareness as well as statistical sophistication.

I offer these concepts as some *fundamentals* of debt analysis, whether public or private, whether in the United States or abroad. Careful attention to these matters, although not a guarantee to complete understanding, is arguably a necessary prerequisite to the beginning of intelligent analysis.

Chapter 4

Private Debt

"There can be few fields of human endeavor in which history counts for so little as in the world of finance. Past experience, to the extent that it is part of memory at all, is dismissed as the primitive refuge of those who do not have the insight to appreciate the incredible wonders of the present."[1] This is the view of John Kenneth Galbraith, a well-known American economist, after a lifetime of study and nearly thirty books authored on this subject. Charles Kindleberger, an economist who spent his career at MIT and who has authored some fifty books, has a similar view of the relevance of history to financial affairs. In Kindleberger's *The World Economy and National Finance in Historical Perspective*, he maintains that financial crises cannot be explained fully by rational means and that these periodic crises do not teach better behavior.[2]

Why is there a disjunction between history and finance, past experience and private indebtedness? Why is history becoming increasingly irrelevant in making personal financial decisions? A couple of reasons suggest themselves: First, although America is a rich nation by any conceivable measure, Americans are not really rich people. The median household in America in the mid-1990s had a net worth of less than $15,000, excluding home equity.[3] Most American families have zero financial assets, such as stocks and bonds. Even America's richest 20 percent have a net worth not much above $50,000, excluding their homes.[4] For the great majority of Americans, *owning* property is not of great importance, but *acquiring* the use of property is. The observant Frenchman Alexis de Tocqueville pointed out two centuries ago that possessions are largely what define us as individuals and as a people. The difference between acquiring the use of property actually owned by others and owning that property yourself is, of course, debt. Debt is the real currency of success in America, not net worth, and that is why Americans have a lot of debt and little net worth. This emphasis on the consumption of goods, rather than on the acquisition of knowledge or wisdom, has been much commented upon, and is surely one reason for the low importance given to understanding history in America.

Second, Americans are far more religious than others with whom they like to be compared, whether measured by those who believe in a transcendental universe or by church membership. Perhaps this is why they are so optimistic. They tend to believe that in the long run all things will work out for the best. And in the past, they generally have. "Part of being an American is to feel that you deserve more than you have," according to Andrew Hacker, a political scientist and an astute student of American attitudes toward money.[5] But a strong belief that you deserve more than you now have and that the system will provide you with these things devalues history. History does not teach that things will necessarily work out for the best. History teaches that life is fragile, that the only constant is change, and that nations and individuals can fall as well as rise. Thus, this more realistic view is simply not very useful to the leading players in the current American drama.

Is History Irrelevant for Understanding Private Debt?

The widely admired early twentieth-century economist Joseph Schumpeter, like many of his contemporaries, believed that recurrent financial euphoria and manias were a natural feature of the business cycle. Booms were followed by busts as night follows day. One reason for this cycle, according to Walter Bagehot, a former editor of the *Economist*, was because "people are most credulous when they are most happy"—and when much money has just been made.[6] In his classic work, *Lombard Street*, Bagehot despaired of ever correcting this cycle of boom and bust. He felt that "only feeble and humble palliatives" were possible, given human nature.[7]

A special financial jargon has developed in recent years which reflects this human tendency to ignore the boom-bust cycle and make people feel good about the present. As the *Economist* pointed out recently, "Recessions tend to be described by businessmen and politicians as cyclical downturns, while economic booms are never cyclical expansions. This is convenient: bad times are the fault of impersonal economic forces; good times the result of far-sighted human decisions."[8] Stock analysts today almost never tell people to "sell" stock in a falling market. Instead, they tell investors to "hold" what they own. This advice assumes that the down cycle will be brief and that the long-term trajectory of the market will be up. In fact, bear markets last about the same length as bull markets and the long-term trajectory of the U.S. stock market is only slightly upward, in real dollars. For example, in dollars of constant purchasing power, the Dow-Jones Industrial Average (DJIA) in 1982, at the beginning of the current bull market, was just about at the same level it was in 1907. This approach denies the very existence of historical cycles. When markets do fall—as they always do sooner or later—

we are told by reporters that the market is "off" and that there has been a good deal of profit taking that day. Markets are never described as "off" when they rise. Historians have traditionally described financial crises with words like "manias," "panics," and "crashes." Today, these same events are more often called "corrections" or "buying opportunities." As we saw in Chapter 2, palliative euphemisms abound in debt analysis.

Over time, American economic expansions have become somewhat longer and contractions somewhat shorter, when measured in nominal terms—that is, without adjusting for inflation. These nominal trends suggest to the unsophisticated that history is becoming increasingly irrelevant, because the market appears to be climbing ever upward. But in real dollars—dollars of constant purchasing power—that is not the case. The market goes through cycles, ups and downs, and there is very little evidence that there has been much progress in real terms right up to the beginning of the current bull market. Add to this a negative household savings rate and an unusually high level of corporate investment—both fueled by cheap and widely available credit—along with unprecedented gains in equity prices, and one can begin to understand how debt has played a smaller and smaller role in the contemporary American mind-set.[9]

It appears that the United States, if not the world, is in one of its periodic cycles of happy forgetfulness. By the end of 1998, the U.S. economic expansion that began in March 1991 was the longest ever in peacetime. Actually, the U.S. economy has been in a sustained growth phase since 1982, except for a brief recession in 1990–1991. Typically, the longer the expansion, the more people forget the cycles of history and the greater the expectation of never-ending prosperity. After eight years of continued prosperity in the United States—from 1991 to 1999—unemployment was near a historical low, inflation had been tamed, interest rates were falling, and the brief "correction" in the stock market in the fall of 1998 appeared to be over. Many now thought that the business cycle had been dampened, if not rendered entirely defunct. By the end of 1998, consumer confidence was higher than it had been in decades, the impeachment of President Bill Clinton hardly registered on the confidence index, and more than 60 percent of the American public still thought he was doing a good job. Warnings about "irrational exuberance" made by Chairman Alan Greenspan of the Federal Reserve in December 1996 fell on deaf ears. Optimism abounded.

At the same time that optimism was growing in America, historical forgetting was also becoming more evident. Numerous polls over the years have shown that young people were less well informed than earlier generations about history.[10] Adults, for whom there is less excuse, were appallingly ill informed. A *New York Times* poll in 1995 showed that "60 percent of

Americans are unable to name the President who ordered the nuclear attack on Japan, and 35 percent do not know that the first atomic bomb was dropped on Hiroshima. One of every four people surveyed . . . did not even know that Japan was the target of the first atomic bomb."[11] Even serious scholars were beginning to discuss the possibility of the end of the business cycle, and "the end of history."[12] The "end of history" concept began as an erudite article by Francis Fukuyama, an analyst in the U.S. State Department, published in the *National Interest* in 1989. He argued that all societies must follow the American model of consumer-oriented democracy because Western democracy and our current brand of capitalism are the end points of historical evolution. Although life will continue, Fukuyama believes that history has come to an end. A society conditioned by Christian values to believe in the Last Judgment apparently found this idea compatible.

By the end of the twentieth century, America was in a great struggle between memory and forgetting. This struggle came to a head when the Asian crisis broke in 1997.

Prior to the Asian fiscal crisis, world financial conditions were extraordinarily favorable for a continuation of the economic expansion that had begun earlier in that decade. Industrial production was climbing, especially in Asia, inflation was declining, and world growth was above the long-term average. Consumer confidence had been climbing in most of the G–7 nations since the early 1990s, and was especially high in the United States. Long-term interest rates were sharply down, and equity prices sharply up, except in Japan. The number of new jobs created had been very impressive in the United States and Japan, though not in the rest of the G–7 nations, and the rate of increase in public deficits was moderating, again with the exception of Japan. In a word, times were good. "The most vivid image capturing this phenomenon was that invoked famously by Abby Joseph Cohen, Goldman Sachs's irrepressible market strategist: 'Supertanker America,' she called the U.S. economy, a sturdy ship largely immune to the rough seas around the world."[13]

But good times tend to generate excess; and by the fall of 1998, international economic and financial conditions had deteriorated considerably. Recessions had emerged and deepened in Asia. Japan had severe banking sector problems, rising debt, and profound problems with public confidence in its government. Russia's economy was at a level only half what it had been under communism, and Brazil teetered on the edge of financial default. Overall, world growth projections by the International Monetary Fund (IMF) for the near term were well below trend.[14] By the end of 1998, stock market prices had fallen dramatically from their record highs almost everywhere, and by as much as 64 percent in Japan, 37 percent in Austria, and 24 percent in Germany.[15] Among the major nations, only the United States and Australia had stock markets that were still near their record highs.[16] Early in the fall of 1998, Alan Greenspan had warned that the United States could not remain "an oasis of prosperity unaffected by a world that is experiencing greatly increased stress."[17] But Americans apparently took no more notice than they had taken when Greenspan had stated in December 1996 that the stock market was moving into the realm of "irrational exuberance."[18] At this writing (February 1999), the global financial crisis is continuing to grow.

It is widely asserted that imprudent lending and borrowing characterized the buildup to this crisis, preceded by the excessive optimism of investors and borrowers alike.[19] Household savings rates declined in every G–7 nation except France between 1996 and 1998, but they had already been trending downward for the previous ten years in every country except France and the United Kingdom. In Canada, household savings rates had fallen from 9.7 percent of disposable household income in 1990 to 1.7 percent in 1998. In the United States, household savings had fallen from 5.5 percent to below zero in this same period. For all of the OECD countries for which we have data going back to 1980, only four countries—Korea, Norway, Spain, and Switzerland—have saving rates that have *not* declined.[20] Private-sector debt has been increasing for decades in all nations for which we have data, especially in Asia. According to Greenspan, new technology has radically reduced the costs of borrowing and lending across national borders, facilitating a massive increase in capital flows. This increase in capital flows has contributed to rising standards of living worldwide, but it has also facilitated the transmission of financial disturbances to other countries, thus leveraging upward the dangerous consequences of excessive indebtedness.[21] Many Asian countries permitted debt to rise to unsustainable levels which led to a fiscal breakdown. "Once the web of confidence, which supports the financial system, is breached, it is difficult to restore quickly," according to Greenspan.[22] Once confidence disappears, high levels of debt, combined with a weak banking system, pegged exchange rates, and falling demand can turn market corrections into a fiscal collapse. Corporate debt has also increased, albeit at a lower rate. In Asia, large corporate debt burdens have undermined the viability of many well-known firms, and corporate bankruptcies have risen sharply. Why did these "showcases" turn to "basket cases"? According to the IMF and a host of academic experts, excessive corporate sector leveraging, too much short-term private debt, declining rates of return, cronyism, too little regulation of excess production capacity in some industries, and property market bubbles have led to growing fragility in Asia's financial system. Fundamental financial weaknesses that will require profound reforms are now evident in Asia. The fear is that these financial weaknesses will create a "mania" that will spread to the world at large.[23]

This global context is essential for understanding the growth of private and corporate debt in recent years, why this debt has become excessive, and what should be done about it.

The Growth of Private Debt

Private debt has been increasing as a percentage of GDP in all G–7 countries in recent decades. An even greater increase in private debt is evident in those Asian nations that have already experienced a fiscal crisis.

Table 4.1 shows quite clearly that, since the mid-1960s, the nations with the greatest increase in private-sector debt, generally speaking, were also more likely to suffer a financial crisis. Indonesia increased its private debt tenfold from 1965 to 1995 and, arguably, suffered the worst financial crisis of that region in recent years. Malaysia had the second highest increase in Table 4.1, and suffered severely, as did Korea. It appears that a rapid buildup in private debt can create more risk than an already high level of debt that has been adequately funded. Large increases in private-sector debt were also evident over this same period for Singapore, Taiwan Province of China, and Thailand. Indeed, in most east Asia countries, private-sector debt has expanded rapidly.

Debt/equity ratios in the manufacturing sector were also high during the later part of the 1990s. As Table 4.2 indicates, Korea and Japan have had very high manufacturing debt/equity ratios compared to that of the United States, and this, surely, is one major reason both of those countries have greater debt-related fiscal problems than does the United States.

According to the IMF, the debt/equity ratio in manufacturing in Korea was approaching 400 percent on the eve of the Korean financial crisis.[24] It adds that these high and rapidly growing debt levels in the east Asian economies made both the banking sector and the corporate sector more vulnerable to adverse financial shocks. When these inevitable shocks to the financial system appear, they are made worse if the outstanding debt is short term, as was the case in several of these countries. Moreover, some of these Asian countries also relied on family-controlled firms for their financing, not the world credit market, and therefore avoided the discipline that goes with international borrowing. This was particularly true in Indonesia. In Korea the *chaebols*—as Korea's giant conglomerates are called—were given funding preference by the Korean government and had hugely leveraged balance sheets before the Asian crisis began.[25]

Along with a rapid increase in private debt, one generally finds a relative lack of sophistication about financial matters and a lack of commensurate regulatory and supervisory agencies whose mission it is to keep an eye out

Table 4.1

Private-Sector Debt, for Selected Nations, 1965–1995
(as percentage of GDP)

Nation	1965	1975	1985	1995
Japan	81	88	99	118
Germany	57	70	87	100
United States	53	62	68	65
Indonesia	5	21	18	53
Korea	11	35	49	61
Malaysia	13	27	62	85

Source: IMF, *World Economic Outlook*, October 1998, p. 93.

Table 4.2

Debt/Equity Ratios of the Manufacturing Sector, 1985–1995
(in percentages)

Nation	1985	1990	1995
Korea	348	285	286
Japan	252	226	206
United States	121	149	159

Source: IMF, *World Economic Outlook*, October 1998, p. 94.

for excessive risk taking. Nonperforming loans grow, financial institutions come under stress, corruption becomes more egregious and widespread, and the whole financial system is put at risk. Countries that are most successful in dealing with this growing risk allow weak financial institutions to fail, require them to merge with stronger ones, and insist on management changes. Hong Kong, Singapore, and Taiwan did this; Malaysia, Thailand, and Indonesia did not. When banks also lent funds for investment in equities during the upswing of the various bubbles which occurred in Asia at this time, the financial crisis was, of course, made much worse when those bubbles burst.

Many countries have experienced a boom in asset markets, often associated with rising private and public indebtedness. Part of the explanation for this correlation between rising debt and rising asset market prices is that rising debt leads to rising consumption, and rising consumption leads to a feeling of greater euphoria. For example, in 1997, virtually every major country had an asset bubble, defined here as a rise in equity prices of at least

20 percent. Almost every nation also saw a decline in the rate of household savings in 1997 compared to 1996. Why save when so much profit can be made in the stock market? This attitude particularly prevailed in Japan beginning in the late 1980s, with its dramatic real estate and stock market bubbles, but it was also true in the United Kingdom during that same period. In Japan, inflation-adjusted residential property prices increased at an annual rate of 20 percent and 14 percent in the United Kingdom during the late 1980s.[26] These same trends were evident in Scandinavia. Private indebtedness increased in the United States less rapidly, in part because it did not experience such dramatic increases in asset prices during that era. In those nations with high or rapidly rising debt, real interest rates also tend to be high, and the financial system tends to be more fragile.[27] Often forgotten in the heady days of rising equity prices is the fact that these bubbles eventually burst, and the downside of the market is almost as severe, and almost as long, as the rise in market values that preceded the crash. In Japan, the effects of the asset price collapse are still being felt nearly a decade later. One suspects that the effects of declining savings will have the same long-term impact. It will take years for personal and corporate balance sheets to climb back to historical trend lines.

Some Consequences of Rising Household and Corporate Indebtedness

Private debt data are more readily available for the United States than for any other country; hence, we shall focus our attention there first. Private debt is defined as credit market debt at face value or par, owed by households and business organizations as found in the "flow of funds" accounts published in the *Federal Reserve Bulletin*.[28] Private nonfinancial debt in the United States, which excludes borrowing by financial institutions, governments, and foreigners in U.S. credit markets, has been rising steadily as a percentage of gross domestic product (GDP) since World War II. In the early 1950s, private debt represented about 50 percent of GDP; by the early 1970s it had reached 70 percent, and in 1998 private nonfinancial debt reached 125 percent of GDP.[29] Both businesses and households have increased their indebtedness at about the same rate, except in recent years, when corporate debt has been relatively flat. By international standards, U.S. corporate debt is relatively low as a percentage of GDP, whereas personal debt levels tend to be on the high end of the international scale.[30]

This rather large increase in private debt in the United States since World War II has often been cause for alarm among journalists, particularly during the economic downturn of the mid-1970s. Many articles appeared at that time denouncing what *Time* magazine called "the magic world of Buy Now, Pay Later."[31] Credit card debt seemed to be the primary concern at that time, although consumer credit actually increased only modestly. The big increase came in mortgage debt during the 1980s. Economists, on the other hand, have not been much concerned about either the rise in either consumer debt or corporate debt. When private debt is measured as a percentage of tangible assets, a much less alarming picture emerges. Measuring private debt this way makes it possible to tell whether corporate or household net worth is increasing or decreasing. During the 1970s, debt surged but assets grew even faster.[32] During the 1980s, the reverse was true, and debt ratios decreased, both for households and for businesses. The reason for the increase in the debt/assets ratio during the 1980s was a sharp deceleration in asset values. Business failures soared, and both corporations and households reduced their debt exposure.

Was the decade of the 1980s a "decade of debt" in the private sector? Between 1980 and 1990, U.S. private domestic nonfinancial debt increased from 106 percent of GDP to 132 percent of GDP, about twice the rate of asset increases. Such rates are obviously unsustainable; hence the negative phrase, "decade of debt," is at least partially justified. On the other hand, U.S. corporate net debt/fixed assets ratios were relatively low by international standards during the 1980s; and although they did climb during that decade, corporate debt/asset ratios climbed only back to the level they had reached during the 1960s. Even during the late 1980s, when the decade of greed was supposedly at its height, corporate debt/fixed assets ratios were higher in Canada, Germany, France, and Japan than they were in the United States.[33]

Personal bankruptcies and mortgage foreclosures increased in the 1980s in the United States, suggesting excessive debt, but not as rapidly as in other countries. What did increase very rapidly in many countries, beginning in the mid-1980s, was home mortgage debt. It rose in the United States from about 45 percent of disposable income in the early 1980s to 65 percent by the early 1990s. Home mortgage liabilities rose even faster in the United Kingdom during the same period, however.[34] The British increase is also much more worrisome because most houses in the United Kingdom are financed with floating-rate mortgages, and changes in the interest rate are passed along to the debtor within a month or two.

Overall, the above data suggest that Americans in the 1980s were not especially greedy. Corporate debt, however measured, was relatively flat, both by our own historical standards and when measured against the other G–7 nations. Farm debt actually declined as a percent of GDP, and nonfarm, noncorporate debt was also little changed. Households increased their mortgage debt considerably, but that was mainly because the price of housing climbed rapidly. Consumer debt was little changed. Some feared that the level of private debt during the 1980s would cause the next recession, which arrived in 1990, to be more severe. That did not happen. Others felt that the subsequent recovery would be more sluggish. That *was* true by historical standards. But the U.S. recovery came earlier and moved further than was the case in other G–7 nations. In any event, trying to set objective empirical standards for when private debt becomes a serious burden is very difficult to do.

Market forces appear to govern household and corporate delinquency rates and default rates quite effectively during good times. But as time goes by, consumer credit as a percentage of disposable personal income tends to rise, often quite rapidly. Good times make people overly optimistic and more inclined to take risks. In 1998, consumer credit as a ratio to after-tax income reached 21 percent in the United States, the highest on record.[35] Credit card loans with payments that are thirty days or more overdue also reached record highs from 1995 onward. When the inevitable recession arrives, consumers are invariably overextended and are forced to cut back. Corporate debt in the United States grew from 32 percent of GDP in 1980 to 42 percent of GDP in 1998. Businesses also tend to go deeper into debt during good times and are forced to pull back in harder times, when bankruptcy petitions rise. Corporate restructuring, rather then corporate greed, is probably a better description of what happened during the 1980s. In this instance, the economists rather than the journalists and the filmmakers have the better case.

Corporate Debt

There has been a steady but modest increase of U.S. corporate indebtedness as a percentage of GDP since World War II. Nevertheless, corporate debt/GDP ratios in recent decades have been lower than they were in the 1920s and 1930s.[36] Measured as a percentage of corporate output rather than GDP, corporate debt has increased much faster, particularly during the late 1980s. By this standard, corporate debt rose from 70 percent of corporate GDP in 1960 to 100 percent in 1975, and then rose another 20 percent by the early 1990s, only to fall back to about 110 percent of corporate GDP in 1993.[37]

Compared to other G–7 countries, U.S. corporate debt is rather modest. Only the United Kingdom has had a lower corporate debt/GDP ratio since the mid-1960s, or a lower corporate debt/profit ratio, for most of those years, or a lower corporate debt/net asset ratio.[38] Generally speaking, English-speaking countries are less inclined to leverage their corporate debt than other G–7 countries, particularly when compared with France, Japan, and Germany, where there is a closer connection between banks and corporations.

Most economists would probably agree that measuring corporate debt as a ratio of net assets is the best indicator of financial fragility and long-term solvency.[39] On this basis, six of the G–7 countries—data for Italy are not available—have corporate debt/net asset ratios that are very similar to U.S. ratios, falling somewhere between 40 and 60 percent. In the 1960s and 1970s, the ratio was higher for Japan, and, during the 1980s, it was somewhat lower for the United Kingdom; but over the long term, corporate debt ratios are converging among the industrial nations. During the 1960s, corporate debt and corporate assets in the United States grew at about the same rate. During the 1970s, assets grew faster. During the 1980s, debt grew much faster than assets, partly because perceptions of rapidly rising prices and low real interest rates indicated that leveraging could be very profitable. Following a relatively brief period of leveraged buyouts, mergers, and takeovers, U.S. corporations began to rein in their debt in the mid-1980s. With the coming of the recession of the early 1990s, U.S. corporations instituted a dramatic reduction in their leveraged positions in response to a decline of their net worth, according to the President's Council of Economic Advisors.[40] Increased foreign competition and widespread corporate downsizing contributed to this debt reduction. With recovery well under way in North America by 1994 and expectations for strong recoveries in Japan and Europe, this downward trend in corporate debt in the United States and in the rest of the G–7 began to reverse itself. In recent years, corporate debt ratios in the United States have been relatively flat.

Many observers believe that current levels of corporate indebtedness are excessive, and are dangerously exposed to changes in interest rates. This concern varies by country. In Germany, all corporate mortgage debt is based on a fixed-interest rate; in Britain only 5 percent is.[41] U.S. corporations have about 80 percent of their mortgage debt in fixed-interest loans. Corporations in Germany, France, Canada, and the United States are less exposed to interest rate changes than corporations in Britain, Japan, and Italy. Others believe that the overall level of corporate debt is excessive because it has led to an unsustainable boom in asset markets, is inadequately adjusted to the common risks of doing business, or makes the economy particularly vulnerable to a recession. A few scholars believe that excessive corporate debt in one sector will lead to a "contagion effect," where a debt-induced downturn in one sector will spill over into other sectors.[42] The Senate Banking, Housing, and Urban Affairs Committee made a careful analysis of these issues in 1991 and concluded that corporate debt in the United States had grown somewhat more slowly than noncorporate debt since 1970, and that, although short-term debt as a ratio to total debt has increased, short-term debt compared with short-term assets has remained fairly constant.

With regard to corporate debt ratios, which are widely used by financial analysts to measure excessive debt, this committee made the point that there are no standard rules about which ratios should be used, when they should be used, nor which values or levels of debt can be said to establish when a corporation has crossed the threshold of debt excess.[43] In short, there are no agreed-upon theoretical guidelines or clear historical experiences to tell us when corporations have gone too deeply into debt. That can be determined only with hindsight. Nevertheless, the worldwide slowdown in industrial activity since 1995, especially in Asia, and emerging crises in Russia and Brazil raise the possibility that current levels of corporate debt may become a problem if the world enters a recession or if several equity markets turn down and stay down for a long period of time.

This discussion leaves us with corporate solvency and bankruptcy ratios. Business failures in the United States averaged about 35 per 10,000 per year during the 1970s. The business failure rate then began to rise in the early 1980s, and peaked at 120 per 10,000 in 1986. The rate then fell back to 65 in 1989, but rose again during the recession of 1992 to 109 per 10,000.[44] Since that time, the business failure rate has moved gradually upward. This rate over time has been very similar in the United States, Canada, and the United Kingdom, and somewhat similar in France.[45] Business failures are expected to climb in Japan and Asia, however, as their excessive debt levels are more fully addressed.

Business failures in recent years in the United States have been especially high in the textile, apparel, and transportation equipment industries, where foreign competition is significant. Failures tend to be lower in the service industries, which is an increasingly large part of the economy. Debt/capital ratios are higher than average in the travel, food processing, aerospace and defense, and electrical utilities industries. Debt/capital ratios tend to be lower in the computer industry and in insurance.[46]

A liberalization in U.S. bankruptcy laws in 1978 may be a significant factor in the increase in business failures, as well as increased corporate debt. Overall, E.P. Davis, a British economist, in his authoritative *Debt, Financial Fragility, and Systemic Risk*, concludes that there is a strong correlation between increasing corporate debt and rising default rates in all the G–6 countries (he did not include Italy), except in Japan and, to a lesser extent, in Germany.[47] Davis also concluded that although levels of debt vary by country, that does not necessarily mean that risk varies similarly. Structural differences in a country's financial system make for different risks with the same level of debt. Heightened competition, innovation, liberalization of lending, and globalization of corporate activity appear, to Davis, to be the main reasons for the increase in corporate indebtedness among industrial nations, rather than profligacy.[48]

Finally, does the amount or the mix of U.S. corporate debt ratios adversely affect a nation's competitive position? Japan and Germany are clearly the major economic competitors with the United States. With a far smaller population, Germany exports almost as much as the United States does, and Japan exports more per capita than does the United States. Japan's trade balance is growing positively and was about $120 billion in 1998; the U.S. trade balance is growing *negatively* and was minus $230 billion in that same year.[49] Germany's trade balance was about $75 billion in 1998. These figures are expected to worsen for the United States and to improve for both Japan and Germany.[50]

What is the impact of corporate debt on this crucial competition? Table 4.2 compares key corporate debt factors for Korea, Japan, and the United States. Although these data are only for one decade, these corporate debt ratios do not change very much over time, as demonstrated in at least two of the cases in Table 4.2. That said, since the mid-1960s Japan clearly has the highest corporate debt as a percentage of GDP, and in recent decades both Germany and Japan have corporate debt/equity ratios that are more than twice as large as those in the United States.[51] The corporate debt/profit ratio is also much larger in Japan and somewhat larger in Germany. But in terms of debt as a ratio of net assets, perhaps the best measure of exposure, the striking thing is the similarity of this ratio among the three nations.

There appears to be little reason to believe that corporate debt levels in the United States are hampering the country's competitive position against Japan and Germany. The United States is the largest exporter in the world; and the signing of the North American Free Trade Area (NAFTA) treaty and the Uruguay Round of the General Agreement on Tariffs and Trade (GATT) in 1994 has reduced, and probably will continue to reduce, international trade barriers, thereby strengthening the U.S.'s trading position in the future. On the whole, corporate debt/capital ratios in 1997 in the United States looked quite healthy, particularly when compared to the corporate situation in Japan. U.S. corporate debt/capital ratios were high (over 40 percent) in the food distribution industry, financial services, and in the entertainment industry, however. Corporate debt levels also appeared reasonable in the United Kingdom.[52] This optimistic view is further supported by international indicators of business confidence. Business leaders in the United States have demonstrated much higher levels of confidence since the early 1990s than those in the United Kingdom, Germany, France, and most certainly Japan.[53]

The corporate debt picture is much cloudier in Japan. Japan's "controlled-risk capitalism" model, which Japan has followed for several decades, quite early removed or limited a substantial part of the risk of corporate debt inherent in other capitalistic countries. Over the years, banks became too lax in their loan policies, and speculation based on easy credit led to a stock market and asset bubble which collapsed in 1990. Economic growth has been sluggish ever since. Deregulation in the financial sector will likely make Japanese corporations more conservative in debt accumulation in the future, and their impressive prowess in the manufacturing sector will likely keep them competitive in international markets. The debt problem in Japan has more to do with Japanese banks than with Japanese corporations.

Household Debt

There have been rising levels of individual debt in all G–7 countries in recent years. Individual debt includes household debt, farm debt, and nonfarm, noncorporate debt. Since farm debt has been falling in recent years as a percentage of GDP, and nonfarm noncorporate debt has been essentially flat, we shall be concerned here primarily with household debt and, under that title, primarily with consumer and mortgage debt.

The primary reason for the rise in household debt in all the major nations can be related to the rise in consumption. As a percentage of GDP, consumption in the United States in the mid-1950s hovered around 68 percent; by the mid-1990s, consumption had risen to 74 percent.[54] From what limited data we have, it appears that the U.S. rate of consumption is the highest in the G–7 by a significant amount.[55] Not only has consumption increased as a share of GDP, but it has also increased faster than personal disposable income.

Among the reasons for this rise in consumption in the United States is a fall in real average hourly earnings and median family income beginning in the early 1970s, especially in the construction and retail sectors of the economy. Corporate downsizing, which generally results in lower wages for those who are laid off but find work elsewhere, earlier retirements, declining union membership, and pay raises below the rate of inflation for many workers in the services sector, are other reasons for the rise in consumption and the decline of savings. In response to declining real wages for males, more and more females entered the workforce to make up the difference in family income. For example, in 1970, about half as many adult women were in the labor force as men. By 1997, that figure had climbed to over 80 percent. Women began to marry later, have fewer children, and have them later in life. Nevertheless, real family income remained relatively flat after the early 1970s. The share of total household income received by the bottom four quintiles actually declined from 1975 to 1997, whereas the top 5 percent of households rose from 15.9 to 21.7 percent.[56] Although data do not exist to prove that this also happened in other G–7 countries, the reasons for what happened in the United States appear to be related to worldwide trends. In any event, if families wanted to continue to increase their level of consumption, to achieve the "American dream" of an ever-rising standard of living, there was only one way to do it—go deeper into debt.

Table 4.3 shows an increase in household liabilities in the G–7 nations as a percentage of personal income for all countries, and especially for Italy and the United Kingdom. Although Italy's rate of increase in household indebtedness since 1980 is by far the largest, its base was so low to begin with that this rate seems less impressive, particularly when one knows that Italy has very stringent down-payment requirements and a very high saving rate. More striking is the doubling of household debt in the United Kingdom, which is in keeping with its skyrocketing mortgage debt mentioned below.

Common sense would suggest that when households dramatically increase their indebtedness, their savings rates are likely to fall. Indeed, that is what has happened in all seven countries (see Table 4.4). The largest drop in household savings between 1980 and 1997 was in Canada, although the United States reduced its household saving rate to below zero in September 1998. The lowest savers in today's world are the English-speaking countries. This point is reinforced when one knows that the Australians and the New Zealanders also save less than the non-English-speaking G–7 nations do. The anomalies in the last two tables are these: Italy has low household liabilities but very high savings; Japan has high levels of debt and savings; and Germany has very low household debt but average savings.

Another consequence of increasing household indebtedness, at least in the United States, is a marked decline in the amount of equity in owner-occupied housing. Traditionally, Americans have paid off their home mortgages as soon as they could; and as recently as 1980, equity in owner-occupied housing amounted to 73 percent of total value.[57] By 1994, when data ceased to be gathered on this subject, equity in owner-occupied houses had fallen to 57 percent and was trending sharply downward. Falling home equity is a worrisome trend and will be a very big issue when the next serious recession arrives. Along with falling equity, the homes that have been purchased have gotten bigger, have more bathrooms, have more sophisticated wiring, and are therefore more expensive in real terms than they have ever been. In short, as wages have stagnated, Americans have bought ever bigger and ever more expensive homes and cars. This can be done only by increasing debt. Houses used to serve as an automatically growing savings account for American families. That is no longer the case. Americans not only save less than they used to, they also have less equity in their homes. In other words, they want the "American dream" they feel they deserve, but they no longer can afford to pay for it.

E.P. Davis, in *Debt, Financial Fragility, and Systemic Risk*, examined the

Table 4.3

Household Indebtedness in the G–7 Nations, 1980–1995
(as a ratio of personal income)

Rank	1995	1980	% Change
1 Japan	13	0.77	47
2. United Kingdom	1.10	0.57	93
3. Canada	1.09	0.87	25
4. United States	0.99	0.77	29
5. France	0.68	0.62	10
6. Italy	0.33	0.08	312
7. Germany	0.17	0.15	13

Source: OECD, *Economic Outlook,* June 1994, p. A62; and December 1997, p. A63.

Table 4.4

Household Savings Rates in the G–7 nations, 1980–1997
(as a percentage of household disposable income)

Rank	1997[a]	1980	% Change
1. France	13.6	17.6	−23
2. Italy	11.7	23.4	−12
3. Japan	1.2	17.9	−37
4. Germany	11.0	12.8	−14
5. United Kingdom	10.8	13.4	−19
6. United States	4.0	8.8	−55
7. Canada	1.4	13.6	−90

Source: OECD, *Economic Outlook,* December 1997, p. A297.
[a]OECD estimates.

household debt data for all the G–7 nations, except Italy, between the mid-1960s and 1990. He found rising levels of personal debt/income ratios as well as rising personal debt/asset ratios.[58] In recent years, this upward trend in personal indebtedness is evident in the debt/GDP ratios as well. One reason for this rising indebtedness is booming stock markets. Rapidly increasing stock holdings and stock prices have become the current equivalent of a savings account. In the 1970s, about 20 percent of Americans owned stock; in 1998 roughly half of all Americans held stock in some form. As the U.S. stock market began to rise, beginning in 1982, more and more Americans began to believe that they were becoming richer; hence, the belief in the need to save declined. In fact, they *were* becoming richer, and by 1997, the long bull market had helped boost the household net worth/income ratio to record levels.[59] But this newly acquired wealth based on equities is much more precarious than traditional wealth based on home ownership. By late 1998, record household debt did not appear to be a great strain on American households; but if the United States were to move into a long bear market, greater-than-average hardships could occur because far more

Americans own stock. Another concern is that, even with a rising equity market, baby boomers are not saving sufficiently for their retirement and either will have to retire later in life or have less income in their retirement as a consequence. This is less of a problem in other countries, where stock ownership is less and savings are larger.

Breaking down household debt into its major components, it is clear that consumer credit has risen dramatically in recent years. In the United States, for example, consumer credit amounted to less than 10 percent of disposable personal income in the mid-1950s; by the late 1980s it had risen to 20 percent. The consumer credit/income ratio in 1997 reached 22 percent, the highest on record.[60] Some see this rise in consumer debt as a continuation of a long-term trend; others believe consumer debt goes in cycles and that the current level of consumer indebtedness will therefore be self-correcting. Virtually all experts, however, believe this situation bears close scrutiny.

Rapidly rising personal bankruptcy rates have given rise to even greater concerns. Personal bankruptcy rates began rising in the late 1970s and early 1980s; at the same time, productivity began to slow and real income growth went flat. Bankruptcy filings rose from 349,000 in 1984 to 1.4 million in 1997.[61] These were years of record employment, rising nominal incomes, and dramatically rising equity prices, so there would have been little reason to expect climbing bankruptcy rates during this period. Nevertheless, bankruptcy filings leaped as much as 960 percent from 1984 to 1997 in Massachusetts, 886 percent in New Hampshire, and 746 percent in Maryland.[62] The largest increases were in New England and Florida; the smallest were in the upper Midwest.[63] Some believe that this increase in the bankruptcy rate is closely related to the increase of credit card use. But the amount of debt based on credit cards of those who go bankrupt is a relatively small fraction of total indebtedness. More importantly, much of the increase in bankruptcy filings has occurred among middle-income consumers, and most of those who file are between the ages of thirty-five and fifty.[64]

The average American now has eleven credit cards, up from seven in 1989.[65] The number of credit cards in circulation increased 34 percent between 1988 and 1994, the number of transactions increased 55 percent, and the overall value of credit card transactions increased 98 percent.[66] Credit card use increases with income, and credit card debt has increased for all income groups, although the average indebtedness for lower-income groups has increased faster than debt for upper-income groups. Perhaps the main reason for the explosion in credit card debt is an extraordinary high level of consumer confidence, the highest sustained level since the 1960s.[67] This is truly an age of high expectations despite slow growth in wages, rapidly increasing inequality, and falling hourly and weekly wages for full-time male workers. Even in "good times," inequality is rising—not every year, to be sure—but the trend toward greater stratification is clearly evident.[68] While jobs are becoming less stable and less equal, personal indebtedness is rising, especially for those in lower economic classes. Strikingly, in the English-speaking world—where the increase in inequality is the greatest—the decline in savings is also the greatest.

Overall, what this means is that less skilled and lower-income workers have been experiencing declines in real income for many years in the United States. Simultaneously, they have increased their indebtedness as a percentage of their income more than upper-income workers. The rise in inequality was largest in the United States and in the United Kingdom, precisely where the decline in savings has been the most evident. Extreme financial fragility now marks both countries. It would not take very much of a decline in the economy to create financial stress for millions of working-class families. This situation does not touch readers of the *Wall Street Journal*, whose average income is a bit over $200,000 per year; but growing income inequality is a very basic reality for the bottom two quintiles and an increasing concern for those in the middle.

Credit card use varies widely by country. By far the heaviest users are Americans, 66 percent of whom had at least one credit card in 1995, and 56 percent of whom had a continuing balance.[69] Ninety-seven percent of Americans who earn over $100,000 per year had a credit card in 1995—the latest year for which data are available—and a median unpaid balance of $2,100 per month. Credit card debt, which was $240 billion in 1990, is projected to climb to $677 billion by the year 2000, according to the *Nilson Report*, which tracks credit card usage.[70]

Credit cards are almost unknown in France. Germans have the next lowest credit card usage, with only 13 percent of the adult population using them.[71] Germans much prefer debit cards, which deduct payments directly from the user's bank account. Moreover, 90 percent of Germans who use credit cards pay their bills fully at the end of the month. Canadians have the most credit and debit cards per head, Italians the fewest. Overall, Europe and Japan remain more cash-based in their purchases than do Americans.

Mortgage Debt

All available data indicate that mortgage debt has gone up in every G–7 nation since 1980.[72] There have been particularly large increases in the United States and the United Kingdom, beginning in the late 1970s in the United States and the early 1980s in the United Kingdom. The magnitude of the increase is truly impressive. In the early 1960s, home mortgage debt represented a bit over 30 percent of disposable income in the United States; in

1991 it was well over 60 percent. In the United Kingdom, the rate of increase was even faster, from less than 20 percent to nearly 80 percent. One positive consequence of this rising debt is that the British now own about 70 percent of their homes, up from 30 percent in 1950. On the downside, home mortgage debt is also riskier in the United Kingdom, since most homes are financed by floating-rate mortgages. Home mortgage debt is much more modest in Japan, reaching "only" 48 percent of disposable income in 1992.

Delinquency rates on conventional home mortgages in the United States are between 2 and 3 percent and have been trending downward since the mid-1980s.[73] VA and FHA delinquency rates are much higher, reaching 7 and 8 percent, respectively in 1997. Unlike conventional mortgage delinquency rates, Veterans Administration (VA) and Federal Housing Administration (FHA) delinquency rates are trending upward, as are foreclosure rates. Total mortgage debt outstanding in 1997 in the United States was $5,277 billion, or 65 percent of GDP.[74] In 1980 total mortgage debt was only 53 percent of GDP, indicating a substantial rise in mortgages in recent years. The loan-to-price ratio has also been increasing, even though mortgage interest rates have been falling. There does not appear to be much concern among U.S. government or private financial agencies that existing home mortgages can be serviced, despite rising delinquency rates for VA and FHA loans. A stock market crash or a major recession could change this view substantially. Comparable mortgage data for other countries are not readily available.

Why Has Private Debt Increased So Rapidly?

There are a number of reasons why private-sector debt levels in all of the major nations have been rising.

- First, life-cycle trends have favored an increase in family debt. For example, the baby-boom generation (born between 1946 and 1964) in the United States created a bulge in housing and consumer credit demand. In 1998, this population cohort was between thirty-five and fifty-two years of age, peak debt-accumulation years. These baby boomers should be decreasing their debt beginning in the early years of the next century. People are also living longer and staying in debt longer. For example, 25 percent of Americans between the ages of sixty-five and seventy-four still have mortgages or home equity loans, something their parents would never have tolerated. Growing debt among the elderly will offset somewhat the decline in baby boomer debt.
- Second, beginning in the late 1970s, a large number of countries initiated a process of financial deregulation and liberalization that increased

access to credit markets by both households and business enterprises.[75] Low-income, high-risk households that could not get credit in the past could now get loans, often substantial ones.

- Third, as private savings declined, the level of private debt had to rise to finance a continuous or rising level of consumption. Rather than live within their incomes, households all over the industrial world assumed that the high rates of economic growth in the 1960s would continue into the 1980s and 1990s and that the high rates of inflation that existed in the 1970s would also continue. Neither trend did. Growth rates fell and inflation declined almost to zero, leaving households with highly leveraged indebtedness and a shrinking capacity to fund it.

- Fourth, heightened competition among commercial banks led to more leveraged transactions, derivative packaging, and new instruments of debt liability. More people were offered credit, especially unsecured credit, and more people took advantage of these offers. In the United States and the United Kingdom, real estate loans increased as a percentage of total loans as real estate rose in value.[76]

- Fifth, there has been a sharp increase in the United States in home equity loans. The Tax Reform Act of 1986 phased out deductions on consumer debt, but exempted home equity debt. Consequently, homeowners increased their home equity debt from 5 percent of home mortgages in 1977 to 13 percent in the early 1990s, and to 22 percent in 1995.[77] Rather than paying off the mortgage, more and more Americans used the equity in their homes to finance consumer goods, especially automobiles and trucks. In 1997, 50 percent of home equity lines of credit were used to buy vehicles or to take a vacation.[78] Conceivably, auto loans can now be extended to ten or fifteen years by this method of finance. More ominously, an increasing number of Americans are putting their homes at risk to take a vacation that they could not afford otherwise. This new way of buying vehicles and taking vacations is not concentrated among the less well-off or the poorly educated. On the contrary, home equity loans tend to be made on more expensive rather than less expensive homes, to people with middle- to upper-middle class incomes, and to residents in the eastern and southern parts of the United States, rather than in the West.[79]

- Sixth, banks in the major industrial nations may have become more risk-tolerant, according to E.P. Davis.[80] Banks can now pass on more debt in securitized form to other institutions in the form of derivatives and other financial instruments created in recent years.

- Seventh, the 1980s were, for most industrial nations, years of optimism and consumerism with its attendant "me generation" attitude.[81] Debt normally rises under these conditions.

These reasons need to be placed in the context of how Americans perceive themselves and how debt fits into their general attitude toward the world and life. Here symbols are important. They can serve as a launching platform toward further illumination, if not pushed too far, and pull a lot of loose ends together. Times Square, the Place de la Concorde, Piccadilly Circus, and the Berlin Wall are all symbols that, in their turn, have illuminated the essence of what is important at a given time, or the fundamental concepts that lie at the very core of a given civilization. What symbol best illuminates America today? I would argue that it is the shopping mall. Consumerism permeates American society like nothing else; it is the very soul of the typical modern American. Life in America today is mostly about consumption, whether one is working to buy goods and services, or is retired and enjoying the fruits of one's efforts. Shopping, watching TV, reading newspapers, going to the movies, and even studying at the average college or university are activities that are essentially involved with consumption. Americans invented the shopping mall and the credit card to go with it.

Americans admire success more than anything else, and they measure success largely by what they are able to consume. A good recent example of measuring success by how much we consume is M. Michael Cox and Richard Alm, *Myths of Rich & Poor, Why We're Better Off Than We Think*. The thesis of this book is that Americans are better off than others because they consume more. Rising debt levels are of no concern to the authors. Such views have a long tradition here. Thorstein Veblen saw "conspicuous consumption" as one of the major driving forces of the American character a hundred years ago in his *The Theory of the Leisure Class*. Earlier in our history, America stood for democracy and for freedom. But in the 1998 election, 119 million eligible Americans did not even bother to vote, and virtually all polls show that Americans are most satisfied when the economy is booming. Even a presidential scandal does not affect the president's standing with voters, so long as they have the ability to consume to their usual standards. Granting the importance of the shopping mall as a symbol of modern America makes it easier to understand why savings rates have been falling and indebtedness has been rising. Americans instinctively move toward those things which will enhance their ability to consume, and that surely includes increasing debt.

Conclusions

- Growth in private-sector debt, which includes corporate as well as household debt, as a percentage of GDP, has been rapid in recent years in all of the G–7 nations, and in most other industrial nations of the world. Private-sector debt is very high in Japan—about 200 percent of GDP in

1993 according to the Bank for International Settlements—and above the G–7 average in Germany and Britain. The United States, Canada, and France have average private-sector debt levels—around 100 percent of GDP—and Italy's debt is well below average.

- The primary reasons for the rapid increase in private indebtedness have been increased investment by corporations and increased personal consumption by households. A decrease in savings rates, especially in the English-speaking world, has been a consequence of this increase in consumption. Excessive buildup of private debt to finance asset accumulation has had significant adverse consequences in Japan and Asia generally, including stock market crashes, deep recessions, and fears that financial turbulence would spread throughout the world.

- Credit has been liberalized almost everywhere, especially consumer credit; and deregulation has made credit easier to get. Nations have varied considerably in accepting these new trends. Americans, Canadians, and the British appear to have liberalized their credit markets the most—Germans, French, and Italians the least. Except for Japan, which traditionally has comparatively high levels of corporate debt and is now dealing with a financial crisis, there does not appear to be a major problem among the G–7 nations with regard to corporate indebtedness. Corporate debt levels vary widely among nations, partly because of the role banks play in corporate finance, and partly because their market systems differ.

- Household debt as a percentage of disposable income has risen substantially in all the G–7 nations since the mid-1980s, except for France and Germany. In 1998, the household debt burden was highest for Japan and lowest for Germany. Household savings ratios have fallen for all these countries, except for Germany and the United Kingdom, where household savings have been flat. Savings by households in Canada and the United States have plummeted to zero or below zero in recent years. A combination of consumerism, optimism, and rising stock markets appears to be driving savings rates downward.

- Booming equity markets in recent years may have persuaded many households that investing in the market is a better idea than investing in savings. In any event, a sharp downturn in the economy, or a bursting bubble in equities, would place many of these households in serious financial jeopardy. American households appear to be especially at risk on this front because they have experienced the longest peacetime bull market in their history and because their savings rate is the lowest since the 1930s.

- Americans use credit cards far more than any other people, followed by Canadians and the British. Indeed, the credit card is an American invention. Increases in credit card indebtedness have occurred in all regions and all income groups in the United States. The French and Germans are the least inclined of the G–7 nations to use this form of credit. Credit card debt carries extremely high and rigid interest rates and is therefore very profitable for lenders.

• Personal bankruptcy rates have climbed rapidly in recent years in Canada, the United Kingdom, and the United States—once again, precisely where personal savings rates have declined the most. Greater acceptability of bankruptcy, liberalization of bankruptcy laws, and increased advertising by bankruptcy lawyers are among the main factors pushing bankruptcy rates upward. Personal debt is still not looked upon very favorably in Europe and Asia, and most countries still offer severely limited protection to debtors. There has been no systemic private debt crisis yet, but lending practices tend to grow lax during long periods of growth, especially while stock markets are rising rapidly. Good times bring on a tendency to disregard uncertain, low-probability, high-risk hazards. This has clearly happened in Japan and in Asia generally. There is no guarantee that a private debt crisis could not happen in other nations as well. In history, equilibrium is the exception, not the rule. The greatest danger in the private-debt sector is that people in general, and exuberantly confident Americans in particular, have forgotten this historical lesson.

Chapter 5

Public Debt

The rapid increase of public debt in industrial countries during the past two decades is *historically unprecedented in peacetime.* In 1970, the major industrial countries regularly tracked by the Organization for Economic Cooperation and Development (OECD) had an average gross public debt of 41 percent of the gross domestic product (GDP); by 1997 that figure had almost doubled.[1] The average increase for the smaller sample of G–7 nations was almost exactly the same, from 42 percent of GDP to 80 percent of GDP. Even more worrisome is the fact that in all of these countries the population is aging, thus exacerbating budgetary pressures because of rising pension and health-care commitments, neither of which are even modestly funded. The public debt problem is, therefore, far bigger than simply balancing current budgets.[2]

Most of these nations have had only limited and temporary success in placing their public indebtedness on a downward trajectory. Typically, budget deficits have been reduced for a year or two but then go into deficit again. Even in relatively prosperous periods, from 1991 to 1996 for example, all the G–7 nations increased their net indebtedness.[3] Nor are the G–7 nations expected to do much better regarding debt reductions in the near future, even assuming a high level of prosperity and even assuming that all these nations carry out their announced intentions in their budget documents, which they surely will not. As life expectancy continues to grow and fertility rates continue to decline, the elderly will make up an ever-larger proportion of the population, requiring massive expenditures for health-care and retirement benefits. Even though some nations have recently balanced their budgets, the health-care problem lies just over the horizon and the unfunded retirement problem is not far behind.

Experts from across the political spectrum believe that the current policies that have led to this rapidly rising indebtedness are not sustainable.[4] Furthermore, all agree that there is no quick fix to the public debt problem. More thoughtful students of the public debt problem also believe that the crisis is not merely a fiscal one but a social and cultural one, as well. Hence, the global debt bomb is ticking in the public sector as well as the private sector. But the problem is much greater in the public sector because rapidly rising public pension deficits could soon consume the entire savings of the developed world.[5]

Adding to these budgetary worries is a worldwide trend of falling savings—especially public savings—coupled with slower economic growth.[6] Since the early 1990s, savings rates in the United States, the European Union, and Japan have fallen by about 2 percentage points of GDP from the average of earlier decades. This 2 percent figure might not sound like much, but savings are the source of investment, and investment has also dropped worldwide by the same amount. According to the International Monetary Fund (IMF), virtually all this dissaving came in the public sector.[7] Private savings rates have not changed much, except in English-speaking nations, where savings rates have fallen dramatically, nor are they expected to change much in the near future. Saving and debt are closely linked, since savings fund debt, and the reasons for the decline in savings are clearly related to the reasons for increasing indebtedness. Debt can also be funded by creating money—which the Federal Reserve can do and does from time to time—but money creation can lead to inflation—and usually does.

No country seems to have escaped this fiscal challenge of rising public indebtedness for more than a few years, and some have seen dramatic increases in their net public debt levels since 1994. Among the G–7, only Italy, Canada, and the United States have seen decreases in their levels of public debt since 1994, but those decreases were modest, and are likely to be reversed early in the next century as unfunded health-care and public pensions become an acute problem. Italy will experience a pension crisis right after the turn of the century; the United States and Canada will feel the pinch about twenty years later. Nor is this bleak picture expected to change much in the near term. Only Canada, as of late 1998, appears very likely to see a significant decrease in public indebtedness by the turn of the century.[8] Small decreases in public debt by the year 2000 are also likely in the United States, Italy, and the United Kingdom, assuming those economies stay strong.[9] But in the long term, all the G–7 countries except the United Kingdom are facing a serious public debt problem of unprecedented magnitude. Peter Peterson, chairman of the Council on Foreign Relations and deputy chairman of the Federal Reserve Bank of New York, puts the problem succinctly: "Official projections suggest that within 30 years, developed countries will have to spend at least an extra 9 to 16 percent of GDP simply to meet their old-age benefit promises. The unfunded liabilities for pensions (that is, benefits already earned by today's workers for which nothing has been saved) are already almost $35 trillion. Add federally funded health care, and the total jumps to at least twice as much."[10]

Prior spending commitments in virtually all these nations have such a grip on their budgets that it is likely to become even more difficult to pay down these public debts as time goes on, according to several experts.[11] There is little support for tax increases anywhere; hence, increasing pressure is being placed on reducing entitlement spending to accommodate rising indebtedness. Some countries have made significant progress in reducing public indebtedness—Ireland and New Zealand, for example—but only Britain among the G–7 nations saw a significant fall in public indebtedness between 1970 and 1998. Unfortunately, the downward trend in public indebtedness in Britain was reversed in the 1990s. Of the G–7, Canada and the United States appear to be in the best position presently to reduce their public debt in the near term, largely owing to strong economies; Japan appears to have the greatest long-term debt problem, largely owing to its aging population and sluggish economy.

As Table 5.1 indicates, gross public debt measured as a percentage of GDP has increased in all G–7 countries since the 1980s. Gross public debt is expected to increase near-term in Japan, stay about the same in Germany and France, and fall in the rest of the G–7 according to the IMF. Looking only at gross public debt suggests, therefore, that the public debt problem is being addressed at least moderately in all of the G–7 except Japan.

When net debt is used to measure public debt levels a different picture emerges (see Table 5.2). Net debt (gross debt minus any social security surplus) is used here because it comes closest to the correct measure of government net worth that should be used to calculate sustainability, according to the IMF. Table 5.2 shows that by far the greatest net public debt is to be found in Italy, the least in Japan. Since the 1980s and forecast to 2003, the largest increases in net public debt will occur in Japan, because of its popped equity and asset bubble, and in Germany, because of reunification. Net debt levels in the United States have risen moderately during the past decade and are expected to decline near-term. These data do not include net public pension liabilities. In several G–7 countries, pension liabilities exceed current net debt. The United Kingdom and the United States have the lowest pension liabilities, measured as a percentage of GDP; France, Germany, and Japan have the highest.[12] If both net debt and net pension liabilities are included, France and Germany are the most indebted nations in the G–7; the United Kingdom is the least.

Near-term IMF estimates of gross public debt trends indicate a downward projection, except for Japan. Gross debt is used here because it is more

Table 5.1

IMF Near-Term Forecast of Gross Public Debt in the G–7 Nations, 1981–2003
(as a percentage of GDP)

Nation[a]	1981–1991	1997	2003
Italy	83	122	104
Japan	68	99	138
Canada	65	96	67
United States	52	63	41
Germany	41	61	58
France	31	58	57
United Kingdom	50	55	39

Source: IMF, *World Economic Outlook*, October 1998, p. 28.
[a]Ranked according to 1997 data.

Table 5.2

IMF Near-Term Forecast of Net Public Debt in the G–7 Nations, 1981–2003
(as a percentage of GDP)

Nation [a]	1981–1991	1997	2003
Italy	76	115	99
Canada	33	67	43
Germany	21	52	49
United States	37	51	33
France	23	48	47
United Kingdom	42	48	31
Japan	20	18	48

Source: IMF, *World Economic Outlook*, October 1998, p. 28.
[a] Ranked according to 1997 data.

commonly used in public debt calculations and plays an important role in financial markets. Gross public debt, for example, is substantially larger than net debt in Japan, and considerably larger than net debt in Canada, but only somewhat larger in the other G–7 nations. On this basis, Japan is by far the most likely nation to be severely indebted in the near term, followed by Italy. The United States and the United Kingdom appear to be the best off.

These IMF projections are very optimistic and should not be accepted uncritically. The estimates are based on official intentions, that is, that all the G–7 governmental proposals submitted to the various legislatures will be adopted, that the various economies will continue to grow, that there will be no recession, that budget caps will hold, that taxes will not be significantly reduced, that no wars will occur, that inflation will not begin to rise again, that the economic and monetary union in Europe will be successful, and that interest rates will stay low.[13] With deteriorating financial conditions, rising financial turbulence, and world economic growth projected well below trend growth, such assumptions are rosy indeed.

Using different and perhaps more reasonable assumptions about the future, a dramatically different outcome is possible for public deficits in the coming years. Assuming that the U.S. GDP growth rate falls by 1 percent beginning in 1999, that unemployment climbs by 1 percent, that corporate profits fall from their high levels of recent years, and that real interest rates move upward a percentage point, the U.S. Office of Management and Budget (OMB) estimates that the U.S. federal deficit could climb to $150 billion by 2003.[14] This $150 billion deficit figure also assumes that there is no recession prior to 2003, even though the United States is overdue for one. But if it is further assumed that the longest bull market in U.S. peacetime history comes to an end sometime before 2003, that defense spending increases, that more Americans retire because of recent stock market gains—thus increasing social security outlays—and that deflation is a possibility, this $150 billion deficit figure could go much higher. Finally, what if foreign investors, who bought 34 percent of the total U.S. debt held by the public in 1998, decide to sell some of their holdings—say about $200 billion worth a year, which was about the rate of increase in foreign purchases of U.S. debt from 1995 to 1997? Then a very different picture emerges. Were that to happen, interest rates could climb rapidly, and the American economy could go into a severe recession.[15] The point is that near-term public deficits in the United States are just as likely as budget surpluses.

Extended surpluses in other G–7 nations are not very promising either, despite positive balances presently in some of these countries. All these budgets are extremely vulnerable to economic downturns. Typically, budget estimates are off by hundreds of billions of dollars, depending on the state of the economy. More importantly, although the *official* short-term forecasts are very encouraging, the long-term *historical* record is not. Aging populations in all these countries will affect these forecasts profoundly because of a declining workforce, earlier retirements, declining savings rates, and rising health care costs. On this point there is little dispute. For example, in 2030, 20 percent of the U.S. population will be over age sixty-five; in 1998 that figure was 12.8 percent. An aging population is the ticking time bomb that, more than anything else, will affect public spending in future years; and rising health-care and social security demands will be the key challenge to attaining budget surpluses.

This chapter will briefly address the major economic, political, and historical factors that have led to the rise of public indebtedness in the major industrial nations; what we can say with some confidence about the positive and negative consequences of this rising indebtedness; which nations seem most likely to deal effectively with this public debt problem; and what the long-term prospects are for reversing these trends.

The Causes of Rising Public Indebtedness

Rising public indebtedness has surprisingly similar causes among nations, as Paul Posner and Barbara Bovbjerg have pointed out, and these causes have become more similar as national economies have become more globally integrated.[16] For 150 years before the Great Depression, central budgets were significantly unbalanced only in time of war. During World Wars I and II, public deficits shot upward, as they always did in wartime. To a lesser extent, this also happened in the Great Depression, especially in the United Kingdom, Canada, and Japan. These wartime deficit spikes were thought to be temporary, and even World War II debt began to evaporate as a percentage of GDP a few years following the end of hostilities. Large, governmental deficits, or large and growing public debt ratios, were simply not part of the human experience prior to the 1970s. As we saw in Chapter 2, peacetime debt was widely considered immoral, and almost all nations made a concerted effort to balance their budgets following an emergency.

Given this long history of modest public debt/GDP ratios in peacetime, it is all the more striking that public debt ratios began to creep upward in the 1970s, widening dramatically after 1980. The main reason for this increase in deficits and public debt was the rapid expansion of public entitlements, especially public pensions, medical care, and income transfer programs. During the 1960s and early 1970s, many nations dramatically expanded their welfare programs and undertook new entitlements, assuming that the rapid economic growth rates of earlier decades would continue. Public support programs became more generous and more widely available. Unemployment benefits and the minimum wage increased. In some countries, unemployment benefits reached two-thirds of the average wage, contributing to structural unemployment by discouraging people from seeking work. The ratio of workers to nonworkers also declined in the 1970s, requiring either higher taxes or larger deficits to make up the difference between what had been promised and what could be funded from tax revenues. Taxes dramatically increased in the major industrial countries—from an average of 28 percent of GDP in 1960 to 44 percent in 1994.[17] Nordic countries increased their taxes even more; but even countries with low taxes—like Japan and the United States—increased their taxes by about the same ratio. Nevertheless, government expenditures increased more than tax revenues; hence, large deficits began to be a staple of the new fiscal order. Growing tax rates caused growing tax resistance among taxpayers and some distortions in the labor market.[18] As a consequence, taxes were not increased sufficiently to cover more rapidly growing expenditures; hence, annual deficits and growing public indebtedness began to be the norm. As a result, between 1980 and 1995, the average gross public debt of the industrial nations grew from about 40 percent of GDP to about 70 percent.[19]

Unfortunately, at the very same time public entitlements were increasing, the capacity of the state to fund these commitments was declining. Why was this so?

1. Productivity (that is, worker output per hour) began to slow down in most of the major nations in the early 1970s and has not improved much since then, for reasons that are not entirely clear.[20] This decline in productivity reduced the rate of growth of GDP.

2. Manufacturing employment as a share of total employment also began to decline—almost continuously in most advanced economies—beginning in the early 1970s.[21] Higher-paying manufacturing jobs (including overtime) were replaced by generally lower-paying service jobs, which meant less government revenue from taxes. Median real hourly wages for men in the United States have declined since the 1970s.

3. Changes in the structure of the labor force, at least in the United States, can account for some of the decline. Many young and inexperienced workers entered the labor force for the first time in the 1970s, thus reducing productivity. Conversely, many more experienced workers left the workforce. The average age of retirement in America in 1950 was sixty-eight, in 1998 sixty-three.[22]

4. As per capita economic growth rates began to decline (by about 0.5 percentage points below the level of the previous hundred years), income disparities also began to rise, particularly in the United States.[23] This condition put increasing pressure on government budgets to redistribute income downward by raising taxes on the wealthy and by raising entitlement expenditures, compensating citizens who were not experiencing a rise in their standard of living. Commitments and goals established during the more prosperous 1960s to create and to expand public programs now became more costly and harder to achieve. Special interest groups determined to preserve these new rights made reform almost impossible.

5. New government regulations raised the cost of doing business almost everywhere. These regulations added expense, lowered profits, and as a result, also lowered tax revenues.

6. Public spending was increased across a wide spectrum of nations on

the presumption that the unusually high economic growth of the 1950s and 1960s would continue indefinitely.

7. Personal saving rates in the United States began to fall in the early 1980s and have continued downward ever since. Falling savings may indicate growing optimism, or simply an effort to maintain living standards when income is falling. Median family net worth also fell between 1989 and 1995, suggesting that families were willing to be more dependent on the government in the event of a serious economic downturn. For these reasons, most people, including most experts, were slow to recognize that a new era of lagging economic growth and more rapidly growing public debts had arrived. In fact, most people have still not recognized this new era of slower growth, accompanied as it is by the need to reduce their expectations of what government can realistically afford to provide for them.

Highly desirable government programs that were affordable in the 1960s became more generous, more generally applicable, and more taken for granted as time went on. Among these programs were increases in social security, Medicare, and Medicaid, and a variety of income support programs. The public wanted more, and politicians found it almost impossible to set limits on voter expectations.[24] One of the major reasons politicians were unsuccessful in their efforts to reduce expectations and rein in spending is that large budget deficits simply did not appear to have any negative consequences.[25] Try as one might, it was difficult to show a clear statistical connection between rising debt and interest rates, inflation, and a host of other things.[26] This lack of certainty regarding the actual consequences of deficit spending provided support to those who advocated greater entitlement spending because the perceived cost to voters was unclear or very distant. In the absence of these limiting and sobering factors, public programs became entrenched, interest groups hunkered down for the long haul, and "the yoke of prior commitments"[27] became the driving force that caused budgets to skyrocket. As a consequence, there was a general disintegration of the fiscal rules and principles which had governed public spending for generations.

Germany and Japan simply ignored requirements for a balanced budget. Politicians who tried to balance the budget in the United States were often punished. Every effort to reduce the deficit seemed only to increase it until very recently. Promises to reduce the deficit led only to growing cynicism toward and alienation from the government itself when these promises to balance the budget were not kept.[28] Even though taxes increased substantially, revenues from these increased taxes did not change much as a percentage of GDP. The result was substantial budget deficits from the early 1970s to the late 1990s. When domestic savings were insufficient to fund government borrowing, funds were secured from abroad by raising domestic interest rates. As a consequence, real long-term world interest rates have risen in comparison to those in the pre-1980s.

The largest increases in G–7 government spending in the past two decades have been in income transfers to assist the less well-to-do and interest expenditures; the largest cuts, especially for the United States, have been defense spending. In the United States, the Office of Management and Budget estimated in 1994 that federal entitlement spending at that time would impose a net tax burden on future taxpayers equal to 93 percent of their lifetime incomes, unless these commitments were changed.[29] Obviously, commitments at that level are impossible to maintain. According to Toshihiro Ihori, a professor of economics at the University of Tokyo, Japan's increasing public debt was caused by an expansion of its social security system; oil price shocks; and an agreement with the United States to become, along with Germany, a "locomotive" for the rest of the globe, pulling the world's economic train.[30] In Europe, spending growth is largely related to the transformation of what was once a social safety net for the deserving few into universal government benefits. Increasingly generous unemployment benefits in Europe that last for long periods have also contributed to growing public indebtedness, according to the IMF.[31] Fewer workers now support an army of unemployed—reaching as much as 12 percent of the workforce in Germany, France, and Italy by the late-1990s. A large and growing share of the European population, again according to the IMF, is simply no longer participating in economic production.

Rising real interest rates are another reason for growing deficits. It simply costs more to finance debt nowadays because the demand for funds is greater. The traditional ruse of inflating debt away by allowing inflation to climb and paying off debt with inflated currency is now much more difficult because increasingly sophisticated government bond buyers insist on a risk premium. Globalization of the financial market has also allowed some countries, like the United States, to borrow more funds from abroad—from Japan, for example—thus increasing their debt leverage over what it might have been if all these funds had to be raised in the home market. Again, 34 percent of the public debt of the United States was owned by foreigners at the end of 1997.[32] About half of it is held by foreign central banks.

A final reason deficits have grown so rapidly in recent years is the growing number of senior economists and political scientists, especially in the United States, who believe either that deficits do not matter very much or that we have grossly overrated their importance. This view is best expressed by Arther Benavie in his recent and lucidly written book *Deficit Hysteria: A Commonsense Look at America's Rush to Balance the Budget.* Benavie views deficits as either "a blessing or a curse, depending on how the government spends the borrowed money."[33] Used for investment, rather than consumption, a constant deficit of, say, 3 percent of GDP is preferable to a balanced budget, as Benavie sees it. Nor does he see an upper limit for the debt–GDP ratio—it is simply a matter of national preference. According to Benavie, most of the reasons for concern given by those disturbed over rising public debt are simply "myths."[34]

A sustained argument among economists on the technical subject of Ricardian equivalence, which attributes no effects at all to public deficits, found a significant number, though many fewer than a majority of adherents, among economists, during the early 1990s.[35] Major and influential newspapers and journals, like *Fortune Magazine*, *Business Week*, and the *Wall Street Journal*, have also downgraded the deficit as an important public policy concern in recent years. The *Wall Street Journal* has for some time been more concerned about the size of the government than about the size of the deficit.[36] In fact, its editors have derisively dismissed those who are concerned about balancing the federal budget as "debt heads," a less than flattering reference to the Grateful Dead.[37] The editors of that journal have long viewed the move to balance the budget as a recipe for increasing taxes, and therefore have editorialized against a balanced budget. *Business Week* even runs articles encouraging Americans to save less and spend more.[38] This attitude is being expressed at a time when private savings are hovering around 0 percent of personal disposable income. When traditionally conservative journals no longer advocate a balanced budget, and even encourage greater indebtedness, it is not surprising that ordinary people are no longer much interested in reducing public indebtedness.

The usual defense of falling personal savings rates is that the United States is awash in savings from other sources, namely corporate earnings, state surpluses, and the meteoric rise in stock values. Net investment from overseas is also touted as a substitute for American savings. It is even argued that Americans should be the world's "buyer of last resort," an idea based on the concept that the International Monetary Fund is "the lender of last resort," keeping a weak global economy afloat. In short, it is one's patriotic duty to spend everything and save nothing. Such advice does little to convince Americans that public deficits are to be taken seriously. Finally, it is argued, often with some smugness, that Wall Street's strong bull market has pushed household net worth to record levels and created public surpluses. So, why worry? In reality, U.S. household net worth as a percentage of disposable personal income has actually declined from what it was in the early 1980s, and U.S. family net worth in constant dollars has declined from what it was in the late 1980s.[39] The large budget surplus of 1997 is also largely owing to one-time events, not to a fundamental shift in fiscal policy. The $70 billion surplus in

1997 is probably the high point of U.S. government surpluses for the fore-seeable future, according to J.P. Morgan analysts, because lower capital-gains tax rates kick in thereafter.[40]

Some Consequences of Rising Public Debt

The rapid increase in public indebtedness all over the world has given rise to an enormous literature focusing on the possible negative consequences of rising debt. Large public debts have been given as "a major cause of recessions, unemployment, inflation, high interest rates, trade deficits, gyrations in the dollar, and virtually any other unsatisfactory aspect of economic performance."[41] Not only has the debate on this topic grown more varied and intense, it has also grown more incoherent, according to Daniel Shaviro, a professor of law at New York University and author of *Do Deficits Matter?*[42] one of the most erudite and persuasive books on this subject in recent years. Different authors have different political and economic agendas, and they often talk past each other or engage in intemperate harangues. I take an especially cautious approach on this topic, focusing only on consequences that appear to have wide support among the experts, both here in the United States and abroad, both now and over long periods of time.

It is also important how public deficits are measured, especially over time. In this study, the *deficit* refers to the governmental deficit and includes state and local surpluses or shortfalls, depending on the years in question. I give debt data in real terms to correct for inflation when measured over time. Because the United States does not have a capital expenditures budget, although most European countries do, it is not usually possible to separate the operating budget from the capital expenditures budget, but I take this problem into account where possible. Domestic saving rates, both public and private, will be included in this analysis along with the deficit, because nations have widely different capacities to fund their deficits based on whether they have high or low savings rates. Nor does this chapter include a built-in bias for lower deficits. Deficits can be either too low, as was the case in the United States during the Great Depression, or too high, as seems to be the case in Italy today. Alan S. Blinder, a professor of economics at Princeton University and an authority on this subject, has written that there are worse things than a deficit—such as a recession.[43] My position is that what is worse than either recessions or depressions is the massive loss of what the founders of the American constitution called "civic virtue." A society which is cut loose from its ethical and moral roots runs the risk of losing its freedom, whatever its level of public indebtedness. Leadership, the founders believed, was essentially a matter of character. "The whole art of government," said Jefferson, "consists of being honest."[44] Better to have honest government and high deficits than low deficits and dishonest government.

This chapter focuses attention on seven major consequences of high public indebtedness—areas where a substantial number of experts are in general agreement about what these consequences are. It should be stated clearly at the outset that our capacity to understand these issues is more an art than a science, and this is true whether from the perspective of statistical analysis, fiscal theory, or long-term historical trends. I have chosen these seven consequences to reflect the results of what is best understood about public debt, avoiding naive and trivial questions that have already been resolved, or that appear to be impossible to resolve at this time. Finally, it is important going into this discussion to have an appropriate mind-set, to be able to relate to this debate in ways that will produce maximum understanding. To this end, it is important to keep in mind at every turn that deficits and debt are a gamble. When we go into debt, we are gambling that we can eventually pay off that debt or, if not, that we can continually roll over the debt to satisfy the interest payments. Public debts are like a giant Ponzi scheme. A Ponzi scheme is named after Charles Ponzi who, in the early 1920s, set up a swindle in which a quick return on his initial investment was paid out of funds from new investors who were lured into the scheme by large profits realized by the earlier investors. Ultimately, as always, the scheme ran out of suckers. It works as follows: (1) new investors must continually be lured into buying government bonds to fund the debt, thus joining the original gamblers, and (2) the debt managers gamble that they will not go beyond the point where the scheme will spiral out of control and fall of its own weight, a point that is always unknown. In theory, public debts need never be paid off and can go on forever. Historically, it does not always work out that way. With these cautions in mind, we may now discuss the more enduring consequences of rising public indebtedness. Here are the six most basic of all questions that, in my view, can be raised about public debt:

1. Is the Ricardian equivalence theorem, which argues broadly that it is irrelevant whether the government raises taxes or incurs more debt to pay for increased spending, correct? That is, do deficits *really* matter? John Maynard Keynes argued that, during a depression, if government increased its outlays without increasing taxes, people would feel richer and therefore spend more. This increased spending would lead to more employment and more rapid economic growth. Keynes believed that people were generally irrational and myopic on these matters.[45]

During the 1970s, Robert Barro, a professor of economics at Harvard University, challenged Keynes's view by arguing that the general public was more rational than this: People understand that unfunded expenditures mean higher taxes in the future and will take steps in the present to lessen the future tax burden on their children. In other words, Barro believes that deficit spending has no clearly measurable economic first-order effects on the economy.[46] Barro thus captures the essence—much oversimplified—of Ricardian equivalence, first introduced by David Ricardo in the early 1800s.

The Ricardian equivalence theorem is very controversial. Ricardo himself later rejected it. As Shaviro points out, it is more cited, admired, and studied than accepted.[47] It assumes a degree of public and individual altruism and farsightedness that is difficult for historians to document anywhere. It is more "an elegant intellectual exercise than a plausible description of reality."[48] Barro himself thinks that public deficits are not very important because clear and persuasive correlations cannot be established between deficits and their alleged consequences; and on this point, there is much more agreement. Barro also believes that the intensity of argument on this issue is based more on what one believes the size of the federal government should be than the size of the deficit. Surely he has a point here. Nevertheless, the preponderance of research supports those who say that, while there may be some tendency for private citizens to compensate for changes in public indebtedness, this relationship is quite modest, at best.[49]

We next turn to the alleged impacts of deficits and public indebtedness, beginning with those which have received the most attention:

2. Do rising public deficits increase real interest rates? There is little direct empirical evidence that budget deficits *clearly* increase interest rates over time. A simple example makes this point. A comparison of the gross government debt to GDP ratio in 1997 for countries in the European Union with the long-term interest rates in those same countries shows that only three of those fifteen countries with higher than average gross debt have higher than average long-term interest rates.[50] About half of the empirical studies on this question say that budget deficits increase interest rates; about half say they do not.[51] When it comes to claiming connections between debt and interest rates, we should be very cautious, even skeptical.[52]

This is not to say that there are no connections, however. There probably is a slight income redistribution between those who pay taxes and those who own government bonds and receive the interest on those bonds, but the effect is small because government bonds are largely held by government agencies and large institutional investors who represent a wide spectrum of the public. Moreover, rising public debt may have a significant impact on *global* interest rates which exceed the impact on individual nations. There is only a limited total of savings (personal, business, and government) in the world; and when the great majority of nations collectively increase their demands for credit, interest rates are very likely to increase within the global system. This phenomenon seems to have happened recently. Real interest rates have risen worldwide in recent years, and rising deficits very likely have been at least partially responsible for this upward bias. Some International Monetary Fund staff studies suggest that this run-up in world debt may have increased real interest rates *globally* by 1 to 2.5 percent of GDP, or more.[53]

3. Do large and persistent public deficits "crowd out" competing private needs for credit and investment? There has been a dramatic increase in the government's share of credit markets all over the world. William Simon was the first to point this out when he was Richard M. Nixon's secretary of commerce.[54] More recently, Francis Cavanaugh, an economist and a former senior career executive responsible for debt management policy advice in the U.S. Treasury Department, has shown that the share of the U.S. credit market required to finance federal programs has reached as high as 89 percent of available credit (in 1992) and has risen from about 15 percent in 1965 to more than 50 percent in recent years.[55] A simple illustration makes this clear. In 1995, net federal borrowing from the public to pay for the deficit was $171 billion. Net guaranteed borrowing—for government housing and urban development loans, for example—was $26 billion, and net borrowing for government-sponsored enterprises—such as for federal home loan mortgages—was $158 billion, for a total of $356 billion. This figure represented 50 percent of total net borrowing in the domestic, nonfinancial U.S. credit market that year. Since the government has first call on the credit available, this means that the government "preempted" one-half of all available credit that year.[56]

This federal borrowing both facilitates and crowds out private investment. It facilitates investment by offering government-assisted loans which might not otherwise be forthcoming—by guaranteeing student loans that go bad, for example. It encourages investment in small business, agriculture, and education beyond what the market unaided might support. It crowds out other competing investments to the degree that they cannot compete with these federal agencies. By shifting default risk to the government in these areas, it also reduces market discipline, much like events that played out on a grander scale in the savings and loan (S&L) debacle.

While reducing risk to individual investors, Cavanaugh rightly suggests that the risk to the economy as a whole may be increased in a recession.[57] Remember, the federal government preempted 89 percent of the U.S. credit market at the height of the last recession in 1992. Credit was much tighter that year than it otherwise would have been, absent government credit needs. Because these government-sponsored enterprises are not "on budget" (that is, they are not accounted for directly in the annual budgetary process), they raise concerns about the long-term viability of the U.S. credit market.

On the negative side, the "crowding-out" theory assumes that, if interest rates rise substantially, large deficits will crowd out private investment. But this theory is weakened by the lack of evidence that deficits do in fact raise interest rates. Moreover, given our global economy and capital mobility, the availability of funds elsewhere might blunt the impact of rising debt in a particular country.

Another factor also needs to be mentioned here. As the federal government has increasingly involved itself in the economy and the social lives of its citizens, its long-term responsibilities and net financial liabilities have increased. The largest component of these liabilities is federal debt held by the public, which amounted to $3.7 trillion in 1996. Federal pension liabilities added another $1.6 trillion. Federal insurance and other liabilities brought the total that year to $5.6 trillion.[58] Back in 1960, federal government liabilities amounted to 0.7 percent of GDP; in other words, government assets were larger than government liabilities. In 1980, the net liability figure was −10.4 percent of GDP, and in 1996 government liabilities had risen to −41.6 percent of GDP. This rapid increase in the scale of net government liabilities is worrisome. If this rate of increase continues, the connection between deficits and interest rates and "crowding out" will likely become much stronger. How much stronger?

4. Do large deficits today place a burden on future generations who will have to pay higher taxes tomorrow? There is no question that using debt to fund current expenditures is very much like deferring tax payments to some future time when interest and principal come due.[59] Citizens simply agree to pay for these expenditures later, rather than at the time they are made. Since the average maturity of a U.S. government bond is about six years, and the median about three years, the length of time into the future we are talking about is really quite short, because federal debt is rolled over rapidly.[60] Since total debt owed is generally not paid down—or at least for most G–7 countries it is not paid down for very long—rising public debt is a very long-term phenomenon. Public indebtedness can rise rapidly—to fund a war for example—but it seldom declines rapidly.

Whether one generation is "burdened" by another is a complex question. Long-run and short-term effects need to be considered. Whether the burden is to be placed on individuals or on the economy as a whole and whether to use traditional methods or newer "generational accounting" methods are only two of the considerations in this debate.[61] Which government expenditures should be financed by taxes and which by debt is also a problem. How to measure the benefits of spending on national security, law and justice, roads, education, and other public matters that benefit individuals, while deducting the cost in taxes and interest payments on public debt that represent a cost for individuals, is also a problem for which there is no clear answer. What we "owe" to our grandchildren, both morally and as grandparents, is also a difficult question to answer. Surely we owe something to future generations; but since, historically, later generations have almost always been richer than earlier generations, it is almost impossible to say precisely what that obligation should be. Finally, the tax lag has to be measured against the assets these taxes have purchased, both directly and indirectly. It is not the size of the national debt so much as the uses to which that debt has been put that matters. A national debt that financed a major war, for instance, might be much more defensible than a national debt that merely increased consumption.

Perhaps the most sophisticated approach to understanding the burden shift problem is the "generational accounting" method. Generational accounting is used to assess the distributional implications from one generation to the next, based on changes in fiscal policy. Generational accounting methods "seek to answer the question of how much each generation would pay in net taxes—that is, taxes and contributions paid minus transfers received—if fiscal policies were to remain unchanged," according to the IMF. "The difference between the lifetime net tax rates of newborn and future generations provides an indicator of the sustainability of present fiscal policies."[62]

Laurence Kotlikoff, professor of economics at Boston University and an international expert on generational accounting, has shown that the dominant trend of federal policies since the 1950s has been to transfer wealth from younger to older Americans.[63] The older generation is able to do this because it has more political power than the younger generation; hence, there is a clear case of burden shifting. IMF studies show that for the United States, Italy, Norway, and Sweden, today's young workers will have to pay $200,000 to $300,000 more in taxes over their lifetimes than they will receive in benefits, under current policies.[64] Such a wide disparity in tax burdens and benefits suggests that burden shifting is inequitably high. Should current policies continue for some time, future taxes could reach prohibitive levels for future generations.

The generational accounting approach has severe limitations, however. It imposes heavy data demands, requires a single discount rate for all generations, requires accepting certain assumptions on the impact of a wide range of taxes, and leaves out intergenerational benefits from public consumption and capital expenditures.[65] Nevertheless, this approach is instructive and gets to the heart of the burden-shifting problem. More significantly, this method of accounting suggests that the higher the public debt, the greater the generational unfairness. Italy's very high public debt coincides with a very high level of generational unfairness, for example, whereas the U.S. debt, at its more modest level, coincides with more modest generational inequity.[66] The real unfairness of this generational burden is widely recognized, but there is little movement to do anything about it. Increasingly, the young realize what is happening to them—that they are engaged in the giant Ponzi scheme described earlier—and have lowered their expectations accordingly.[67]

I now turn from the impact of public debt on future generations to the impact of that debt on other governmental activities.

5. Are public budget deficits significantly related to balance of payments or trade deficits? Put somewhat differently, do we really have a "twin deficit problem"? Do deficits crowd out exports and turn otherwise solvent nations into international debtors?

Balance of payments is a statistical term indicating the flow of money in and out of a nation. The *current account balance* is the net balance on trade and services plus remittances, such as social security payments to a citizen living abroad. Logically, when taxes are deferred to future generations, current consumption should rise. People feel wealthier than they really are; hence, they consume more than they really should. The increase in demand drives up prices and interest rates domestically, and the increase in interest rates attracts foreign capital seeking higher returns here than can be had abroad. The capital inflows make our currency appreciate and our exports more expensive. Our exports then fall from what they might have been had they been cheaper, and our balance-of-payments deficit rises. Thus, it might be argued that a large budget deficit can cause a large trade deficit.

Foreign capital enters the country to make up the difference between domestic saving and investment, or to make up the difference between what a country can afford to buy and the bonds its government must sell to finance the deficits. In other words, governments borrow to fund the excess of imports over exports. When foreigners buy government bonds, this is a loan to the seller of those bonds. When foreigners buy more goods and services than we buy from them, this, too, is a loan because these excess goods and services must eventually be paid for. In the meantime, the difference between our imports and exports raises the balance-of-payments account.

Net foreign borrowing in the United States has gone up year after year, from a *positive* balance on current account of $2 billion in 1980, to a *negative* balance of about $150 billion a year by the late 1980s, to more than $200 billion in 1998.[68] In 1998, foreigners held 34 percent of U.S. federal debt, up from 15 percent in 1985.[69] Increasingly, foreigners are also funding U.S. interest payments because Americans—households, businesses, and government—save too little to finance their own budget deficits. For the same basic reason, our trade deficits continue to rise—that is, we continue to import more goods and services than we export, and we pay for these additional imports over exports by borrowing. Both public deficits and private balance-of-payment deficits are rooted in the same national psychology: buy now and pay later.[70] Both have the same result—increasing indebtedness.

Rather than public deficits causing trade deficits, both seem part of the same national tendency—to consume more now and to defer payments to a later time. This pattern is supported by the lack of a clear causal relationship, either in the United States or abroad, between public deficits and trade deficits over long periods of time.[71] There does seem to have been a causal relationship in the United States during the early and mid-1980s, however. Increased budget deficits were followed by increased balance-of-payments deficits. As Benjamin Friedman and Alan Blinder have written, the United States went on a consumption binge during the 1980s. "We threw a party, to which . . . the wealthy were especially invited."[72] We did not invest this borrowed money, we consumed it. Hence, when the bills come due, we shall have a reduced standard of living as a consequence, assuming always that the funds borrowed did not on balance actually increase the rate of economic growth from what it otherwise would have been. Since our rate of growth has been quite sluggish in recent years, that does not seem likely.

It is commonly agreed that the federal debt need not be paid off, that it can be managed indefinitely. This is not true of foreign debt. At some point, foreigners may begin to think that they have sufficient exposure in their American portfolios and begin to withdraw their funds. Or they may begin to worry about repayment or a devaluation of the dollar. Such a loss of foreign investor confidence could prove to be painful, at least in the short term. Closer to home, if income inequalities continue to grow, and jobs for the unskilled continue to suffer from technological change and foreign competition, our trade deficit might become a political symbol for increased trade protection sentiment. This historical backlash has occurred before, particularly during the 1930s.

In the long term, nations deeply in debt tend to lose their political clout and their moral leadership. Those best prepared to face the future have modest debt, high savings rates, and impressive and productive investments.[73] Just like families and individuals, nations can lose their way, overextend themselves, default on their debts, or appear about to do so, and hence become social and political outcasts.

In summary, two things can be asserted about the relationship between deficits and our growing balance-of-payments problem. First, rising public indebtedness and rising debt-generated trade deficits have most likely increased the standard of living for the present generation. While the relationship between budget deficits and trade deficits is not strong, it does appear to be somewhat stronger than the relationship between rising deficits and inter-est rates—and much stronger than the relationship between deficits and Ricardian equivalence. Second, although budget deficits have been declin-ing among some of the G–7 nations because of the longest peacetime expan-sion in decades, trade deficits are not. Nations with large trade deficits prior to these falling deficits have large trade deficits now.[74] If these trade deficits continue to rise as a percentage of GDP, whatever their cause, at some point they will likely become unsustainable and could contribute to a very hard landing. Being an international debtor nation is very much like being a do-mestic debtor nation: Neither situation is very desirable.

Finally, we turn to the subject of the unintended consequences of rising public indebtedness. Historically, such consequences are almost never antici-pated, but they often have the greatest impact of all.

6. Does steadily rising public indebtedness eventually lead to myopic and hence unsustainable budget policies? In other words, is there something spe-cial about prolonged and ever-rising debt that inclines nations over time to go to excess, to do foolish things? On the one hand, the answer seems to be yes. Virtually all authorities believe that rising budget deficits can lead to "fiscal illusion."[75] This phrase simply means that we think we are richer than we actually are. Fiscal virtue—that is, paying for increased expenditures by increased taxes or decreased expenditures elsewhere in the budget—has not been popular since at least the 1970s, and in the United States for an even longer period of time.[76] In the late eighteenth and early nineteenth centuries, Adam Smith and David Ricardo argued that debt financing "tends to make us less thrifty—to blind us to our real situation."[77] These illusions also in-cline us to try to shift the resulting future tax burden onto others and away from ourselves. Hence, engaging in debt finance over a long period of time can make those who do so not only less cautious, but less moral as well.

More recently, this idea has been put forward by Nobel Laureate James Buchanan and the Virginia School of Public Finance where Buchanan and many of his colleagues are located. In the 1970s, Buchanan and Richard Wagner argued, especially in their *Democracy in Deficit: The Political Legacy of Lord Keynes*, that the federal government was a "Leviathan" whose pri-mary purpose was to maximize revenues, either by raising taxes or by accru-ing debt. Buchanan and Wagner assert that politicians manipulate the system deliberately to maximize their power, including devaluing the value of gov-ernment bonds by creating inflation.[78] In short, fiscal illusion is both a cause and a consequence of government financed debt in democracies.

Both the classical economists and the more recent Virginia school of debt finance have been roundly criticized for their views. The Virginia school, it is argued, has overestimated Keynes's influence on government policy, has failed to show a close relationship between deficits and inflation, and has not developed a systematic theoretical basis for its conclusions. Critics further argue that increased government spending does not necessarily increase the size or the power of the bureaucracy—the size of the U.S. government, for instance, has been slowly shrinking for several years at the very same time the budget has been exploding—and that the conclusions of the Virginia school are excessively influenced by their conservative political views.[79] Nevertheless, the basic idea that deficit spending reduces *perceived* long-term costs is sound.

As Alan Blinder has pointed out, excessive concern with public deficits can actually be harmful to long-term public investment strategy, resulting in the underfunding of public infrastructures like roads, bridges, airports, and waste treatment facilities.[80] If all new and valuable programs "raise the deficit" and therefore should be resisted, then the discredited "leviathan" argument returns to the discussion of public policy in a different guise, and public policy can be rendered myopic.

But there is an even greater danger than fiscal illusion: Do politicians have an innate tendency to act selfishly—not just unwisely—or in ways that are counterproductive over the long term, when it comes to debt finance? A growing body of literature suggests that politicians do tend to favor larger deficits the longer they serve. This is because the more money Congress spends, the more campaign funds a member of Congress can attract for his or her reelection.[81] But the public is an active partner in larger deficits. The basic problem is that the public, whether in the United States, the United Kingdom, or Germany, says it wants a balanced budget, when in reality it wants only the *appearance* of one. What the public really want is government programs and subsidies that benefit themselves and their interest group without raising taxes. For Democrats this means a continuation of welfare spending and entitlements; for Republicans it means continued efforts to lower taxes, especially for the wealthy. These are the core political positions of both parties and are not affected by deficit reduction measures, including the most recent effort in 1998.[82] Polls consistently show that a balanced budget is high on the list of desired goals, but both polls and election results show more clearly that this goal becomes less desirable if it means raising taxes or cutting expenditures. John H. Makin and Norman J. Ornstein note that at no point in recent history did anything near a majority of Americans indicate a willingness to solve the deficit problem if cutting deficits meant cutting spending or raising taxes.[83] The result is that politicians have created a long list of deficit gimmicks that have the appearance of reducing the deficit but, in fact, increase it.

Some of these smoke-and-mirror tricks are quite ingenious. For example, elected officials of both parties propose *temporary* cuts in tax rates or increases in spending that they know, going in, will not be temporary; they move billions of dollars "off budget" so that the programs removed will not count toward an unbalanced budget; and they include social security *surpluses* that are legally committed to the social security program to offset deficits elsewhere. Budget mavens also propose seven-year plans to balance the budget in the future, thus avoiding a two-year plan which would require actual expenditure cuts or tax increases in the present. Politicians, with strong public backing, propose constitutional amendments that would take years to pass, and whose spending limitations could be easily avoided. They also take middle-class entitlements off the table at the beginning of the budgetary process when everyone knows that, without addressing these entitlements, no lasting spending reductions are really possible. Almost habitually, politicians of both political parties favor "rosy scenarios" over more realistic assessments to make budget balancing easier, take personal credit for budget reductions that result almost entirely from economic growth, and seldom pass a budget in a timely fashion. Each year Congress goes through the charade of passing a debt limitation measure; each year it raises the debt ceiling to allow for desired expenditures. There have been sixty-eight of these charades since 1960.[84] Both the president and Congress back-load budgets by concentrating huge *promised* spending cuts in the final year or two of the budget cycle, and front-load tax cuts, especially for the wealthy.

If this judgement seems harsh, remember that the largest tax three-fourths of Americans pay is the social security tax. This tax has *never* been reduced. Most recently, Congress passed a line-item veto for the president so he could better control spending. President Bill Clinton did cut a few billion dollars out of the budget in 1997, only to have Congress add virtually everything back in again.

These budgetary gimmicks are not especially alarming to the American public—who probably find them quite amusing—because the nation's citizens are willing, if not eager, to participate in these fiscal games. For example, the much-heralded 1998 budget, balanced after thirty years of deficits, occurred primarily because of an unusually long economic expansion and special one-time revenue-enhancing measures, not because of a major change in entitlement spending. In fact, that same year, Congress immediately voided its self-imposed spending caps, passed emergency spending measures without any emergency, and engaged in the usual chaotic and expensive deal cutting that ate up one-third of the budget surplus within the first year.[85]

In other countries, fiscal gimmicks are less in evidence, but that is because, until very recently, growing deficits generally failed to attract significant public attention, even when those deficits and public debt levels exceeded those in the United States by a wide margin.[86] The primary reason for Europe's greater tolerance for public deficits is the much greater commitment to social spending and government intervention in the economy. Fiscal gimmicks are, for the most part, an American phenomenon, rooted in the public's modest desire to appear to be prudent, while at the same time accommodating a much more intense desire to enjoy expanding benefits without raising taxes.

This point is strengthened by the fact that the same Ponzi game—with all its smoke and mirrors—has been evident at the state level for several decades now. Forty-nine states have some kind of limitation of state deficits; forty-three have constitutional requirements to do so. But fewer than one-third have any kind of an enforcement mechanism if the government does, in fact, fail to balance its budget.[87] In hard times, many state and local governments simply shift general fund obligations off budget, as Congress has done, or raid their employee pension funds. Nor are such tactics a recent phenomenon. Since the turn of the century, state constitutional restrictions on deficit spending have resulted in little more than lip service to earlier fiscal norms.[88] Budget gimmicks are now, and have been for a long time, as American as apple pie.

Summary

- The rapid increase in public debt in the industrial world since 1970 is historically unprecedented in peacetime. From 1970 until 1998, average gross public debt doubled, from about 40 percent of GDP to about 80 percent of GDP. This increase in public indebtedness is especially worrisome because of aging populations and very large and unfunded pension commitments. In Japan and Europe (except for Britain), populations are aging faster, birth rates are lower, and social welfare benefits are more generous. The looming public debt crisis promises to be more acute there than in the United States and Canada.
- The primary reason for the increase in public deficits and expanding public debts during the past two decades was the rapid expansion of public pensions, social spending, and government transfer programs. Approved with the best of intentions in good economic times, these programs gradually became more generous and more widely available, and were fiercely defended against cutbacks. Governments found it politically expedient to fund the increased revenues required to finance these programs by increasing debt rather than by increasing taxes, and instead of cutting back the programs.
- At the very time these entitlements were increasing, the ability of the state to fund them was decreasing. Productivity began to slow in the

early 1970s, growth rates declined, the percentage of workers in highly paid jobs in the manufacturing sector dropped, and more people left the workforce—either to become semipermanently unemployed or to take early retirement. As more and more nations turned to debt finance, competition for available credit increased, as did real interest rates. Because these trends were not well understood, willingness to increase taxes was limited, but rapidly rising rates of inflation made investors supersensitive to traditional methods of financing deficits by inflating them away. Globalization of capital markets also helped low-savings nations like the United States to borrow abroad and to run up larger deficits than they had in previous decades.

- Paradoxically, as public debt grew, academic concern for the negative consequences of rising debt declined. Persistent deficits and rising public debt levels were thought to have few measurable consequences. A preponderance of the evidence shows, however, that when public debt exceeds a certain level of GDP—the Maastricht Treaty sets this point at 60 percent—negative consequences begin to be evident. Some of these consequences—although much debated—are rising real global interest rates, some "crowding-out" of competing needs, some burden shifting from older to younger people, and possibly some increase in trade deficits. Virtually all experts believe that high and continuing deficits and rising public debt lead to "fiscal illusion" and growing cynicism about government, both about the government's capacity to meet the needs of its citizens and about its basic honesty.

- In recent years, the prospects for lower deficits and perhaps even lower debt levels have brightened, especially in the United States, Canada, and the United Kingdom. Whether this is a temporary phenomenon, as has been the case in the past, or a truly new direction in public finance, will be the subject of the final chapter.

Outlook for Public Spending Balance

The Near-Term Outlook

The International Monetary Fund is projecting a general improvement in the fiscal balances and debt levels of the major industrial countries from 1998 to 2003.[89] I am defining this same period as the "near-term" outlook for the purposes of this discussion. The IMF's projection is based on official budgets that have been passed or are expected to pass, and it assumes that these nations will really do what they say they will do. On this very optimistic basis, general government budgets were balanced in the United States and

Canada in 1997 and are expected to be balanced in the United Kingdom by 2000. Germany, France, and Italy will continue to have unbalanced budgets during this period, but their debt levels are projected to be lower than in 1998. Japan's public debt is expected to rise dramatically, from 99 percent of GDP in 1997 to 138 percent of GDP in 2003.

The assumptions upon which these forecasts are based are highly questionable, especially for the United States. For the United States, the IMF is assuming that the spending caps outlined in the Balanced Budget and Taxpayer Relief Acts of 1997 will be honored, that promised and very difficult spending cuts in the final two years of the annual budgets will in fact occur, that no recession will appear until after 2002, and that the emerging crisis in social security and Medicare funding will be both addressed *and solved.* The IMF further assumes that the plummeting deficit estimates—the Congressional Budget Office (CBO) windfall that unexpectedly appeared on the horizon—which that office admits it does not fully understand, will not reverse themselves in later years, and that the new educational entitlements passed in 1997 and 1998 will not expand faster than expected—even though every other entitlement in recent years has done so. It is further assumed that the bull market, already the longest in peacetime history, will continue, despite its growing volatility and sharp market drops, both in the United States and in other countries. More ominously, the IMF does not see any significant connection between the emerging fiscal crisis in Southeast Asia and budget deficits in the United States.

There is, thus, good reason for extreme caution in accepting these estimates. Skepticism is justified because the U.S. deficit actually *will increase* in the first year of this budget cycle, and there are no penalties if these deficit targets are not met.[90] More importantly, the historical context of recent budget-balancing efforts was ignored, as was the deliberate and full-bore push by both political parties to keep the budget from balancing itself through unanticipated rising revenues. The real story was the rush to cut taxes—and especially capital gains taxes—by Republicans; and the rush to increase spending—especially spending for education—by the Democrats, once it became clear that the United States might "achieve" a balanced budget by simply doing nothing. Both political parties in reality abhor the idea of actually passing an honestly balanced budget; but both love to take credit for appearing to be the champions of fiscal austerity, in keeping with the pattern of recent decades.[91]

In reality, both sides have reason to be ashamed of the fiscal year 1998 budget, as the *Economist* pointed out at the time the budget was passed.[92] The 1998 budget agreement will actually make it harder to balance the budget in the next century, not easier. The tax cuts are back-loaded so that tax cuts for capital gains, estate taxes, and new retirement accounts explode in five to ten years. The loss of revenue is very large—from $600 billion to $700 billion. The entitlement problem was not addressed, and the usual horse trading tilted the final result in favor of our better-off citizens. Predictably, the budget agreement did not address the growing obligations of government-sponsored enterprises, or the long slide in savings.[93]

On the whole, the 1998 U.S. budget agreement was a pyrrhic victory at best and probably contributed to the problem more than it helped solve the problem. The *Wall Street Journal* labeled it "pathetic."[94] The *New York Times* more generously called it "a small-bore achievement" and predicted that it would lead to even higher deficits early in the next century.[95] House Minority Leader Richard Gephardt, perhaps the agreement's most prominent critic in the House, stated that the budget agreement "sacrifices tomorrow's hopes for today's headlines."[96] Predictably, the American public liked the budget agreement; it was full of righteous rhetoric but had little substance and required no suffering. Actually, if the trust funds (which are already legally committed to future retirees) are excluded, the U.S. budget will not be in surplus in 2002; it will be in deficit to the tune of about $45 billion, and *total* federal debt is projected to rise from 1998 to 2003.[97]

In the meantime, deficits—minus social security trust fund surpluses—are expected to continue at 3 percent of GDP level, about where they were in 1996.[98] More significantly, leaders of both political parties are beginning now to plan how to spend these alleged future budget surpluses, and the will to make promised future spending cuts is already beginning to erode. In early 1999, a large contingent of health-care lobbyists were beginning to confront Congress on the need to revise the 1998 budget agreement to increase health-care expenditures. Robert Reischauer, a fellow at the Brookings Institution in Washington, D.C., and a former director of the Congressional Budget Office, thinks that this erosion is likely to intensify. Reducing the national debt is good policy but bad politics, he sagely observes.[99] Historically, when good fiscal policy runs up against bad politics, the latter usually wins. For all the reasons cited above, it seems unlikely that the United States will actually see a balanced budget in 2002, despite the recent political hoopla and despite the more sober and analytical projections of the IMF.

A much brighter picture emerges in Canada. "Once famously spendthrift, Canada is the new star of sober public finance," declared the *Economist*.[100] Canada is the first G–7 country to actually achieve an honestly balanced budget, a goal it reached in 1997. "No other major country's leaders can boast of such fiscal virtue, or so large a swing to it so swiftly achieved," the editors continued. Excellent economic growth, dramatic public spending cuts, and, more importantly, a change in Canada's fiscal culture, are the primary reasons for this enviable outcome. The government scrapped five-year plans, which allowed the postponement of hard decisions, and instead instituted two-year plans. Total spending was actually reduced, not just the *rate* of spending, as was the case in the United States. Public hearings in major cities were held on fiscal issues, creating broad voter support for the hard decisions; provincial governments were brought on board and expected to adjust to the new reality. Canada is projected to have a 2 percent surplus fiscal balance by 2003, according to the IMF, and there is every reason to expect it will also achieve that goal.[101]

A growing belief that public-sector deficits do not lead to economic growth, but do increase risk, was also evident in Canada in recent years. Free medical care at the provincial level, very generous unemployment insurance, high debt-service costs, and bloated public corporations pushed Canada's public debt—measured as a percentage of GDP—to just below Italy's in 1992. By then, a majority of Canadians had come to believe that their standard of living was threatened by excessive public spending. They were ready for austerity. After years of relative public bliss, Canadians had come to a day of reckoning.[102] They were ready for a sea change in their budgetary thinking and in their approach to politics generally. Evidence that this major change has indeed occurred makes it reasonable to believe that Canada will continue to balance its budget in the near term. Although Canada's gross public debt reached 100 percent of GDP in 1996, it is expected to fall to about 67 percent of GDP by 2003. When budget surpluses occur, they will be used to reduce the national debt and to cut taxes, or to increase social spending for the neediest.

The United Kingdom is also expected to balance its budget by 2000, according to the IMF.[103] Britain's rate of unemployment is very low by European standards, the bargaining power of trade unions has been reduced, unemployment payments are also quite low, and hiring and firing laws were liberalized in recent years. Thus, growth prospects are good, and government revenues should be adequate to meet budgetary targets. Germany, France, and Italy are all expected to continue to have deficits well into the new century,[104] primarily because of continued high unemployment and already high deficits. When the long-awaited take-off of the eastern German economy arrives, Germany will very likely join those nations with a balanced budget. Japan is expected to make the least progress of the G–7, with an IMF projected deficit of 2.7 percent in 2003. For some years Japan has experienced below-trend growth, and it is difficult to gauge the strength of its recovery. Confidence remains low and stock market prices soft; economic difficulties in Southeast Asia and South Korea have raised new concerns. By late 1998, the Japanese government had not yet convincingly detailed the policies by which it intended to reach fiscal balance, and public confidence in the Japanese government remained low. Given the long-term banking crisis in Japan, the financial future of Japan appears less than promising.[105]

In the near term, the goal of 3 percent deficits or less set out in the European Monetary Union (EMU) agreement is likely to be reached in Germany, France, and even Italy. These countries have been given a specific goal and a short timetable; but each nation has cooked the books—at least to some degree—to qualify for original membership, largely by making temporary adjustments. Once in the EMU, there are penalties for backsliding, but there are also rather large loopholes for avoiding such penalties.

Assuming that there is no worldwide recession, the overall deficit picture looks somewhat encouraging for the G–7 nations in the near term, except for Japan. The IMF projections show that net debt—that is, gross debt less financial assets such as social security surpluses—should begin a downward trend in the United States, Italy, the United Kingdom, and Canada, and should not increase much in Germany and France from 1998 to 2003.[106] Clearly, the seriousness of the public debt aspects of the global debt bomb have been widely recognized. But long-ingrained habits of fiscal irresponsibility, weak empirical evidence that large deficits really are harmful, and powerful interest groups, especially the elderly, in all these countries suggest that these recent, positive trends may turn out to be temporary.

The Long-Term Outlook

The long-term outlook for fiscal balance in the G–7 nations can be approached on three different levels. First, and perhaps the easiest to understand, is the need to reduce spending commitments for the elderly, particularly in the area of pensions, health, and welfare. As populations in the industrial world continue to grow older, increasing entitlement outlays for those who are retired at the expense of those who are still working becomes less and less defensible. A modest increase in the age of retirement, modest reductions in benefits, and perhaps a modest increase in the social security tax would go a long way toward solving this problem in the United States. But these proposed changes—however modest—are strongly resisted by the elderly almost everywhere. Short of a major crisis, there appears to be little reason to believe that "the yoke of prior commitments" will be lifted very soon.

Second, evidence of growing public frustration among the middle and lower classes of all industrial countries toward their governments continues to accumulate.[107] Governments are failing to address adequately the problem of growing inequality, which is partly financed by annual deficits, and many believe that some kind of crisis will also be necessary to bring about lasting change here. The usual medicine for addressing this problem, a growing welfare state, is everywhere in retreat, at least rhetorically. These trends suggest that it is getting harder, not easier, to solve the public debt problem, thus ensuring that the global debt bomb will continue to tick.

Third, and clearly the most difficult, is the need for a serious change in public attitudes toward debt, from one that is comfortable with *managing* growing public debt to one that insists that this debt be paid down, perhaps to half its present level.[108] Only then can a radical break with the past be expected to succeed. These three scenarios will be discussed in turn.

The long-term good news is that there is widespread agreement among scholars and public officials that present public debt levels are not sustainable. This is a truly major achievement, since these debt levels have been growing generally (that is, with only brief interruptions) since the 1930s. Consequently, most of the OECD nations and all the G–7 nations have announced plans for what they call "fiscal consolidation," which really means eventual public debt reduction. The first major step in that direction was the passage of the Maastricht Treaty of 1991, which requires that gross government debt should be no more than 60 percent of GDP and annual budget deficits no bigger than 3 percent of GDP for candidate countries seeking admission into the European Monetary Union (EMU), which was created on January 1, 1999. Named after the city in the Netherlands where it was signed, the treaty is an agreement by European governments, later ratified by referenda, that shifts the focus of monetary decisions from nation states to a central European authority. The Maastricht Treaty also established a central bank for the European Union in Frankfurt, modeled after the German Bundesbank, with the purpose of having all the member nations march to the same drummer with regard to currency and debt. Once in the EMU, countries can be fined up to one-half of 1 percent of their GDP for not abiding by these guidelines, or at least moving toward them. The Maastricht Treaty and subsequent IMF and World Bank initiatives are encouraging because they were the product of elite government agencies and world-class statesmen with long and deep experience with these fiscal matters who were willing to lead out on these issues, rather than merely reflecting public opinion or only market forces.

The bad news is that the emerging commitment to balance the budget is rapidly eroding in the United States among policy makers and the public alike. Beginning in 1997, deficit reduction plans were quickly turned into self-congratulations over short-term deficit declines that were largely created by unexpected growth in public revenues, not rigorous spending reductions or tax hikes. The uninformed could get the impression that fiscal balance has been achieved. Indeed, President Clinton, in his budget message to

Congress in February 1998, declared that his budget for that year had brought "an era of exploding deficits to an end."[109] The fact of the matter is, as they say in Washington, the biggest deficits are yet to come because of an aging population and prior commitments to assure unprecedented benefits to the elderly.

The Congressional Budget Office made a long-term study of the U.S. budget outlook in March 1997.[110] Over the next thirty-five years, the number of people age sixty-five and older will double, while the number of people age twenty to sixty-four will increase by only 20 percent. At the same time, people are living longer. In addition, the baby-boom generation will soon begin to retire and claim benefits as well. The high birth rate during the baby-boom generation was followed by a much lower birth rate in the baby-bust generation. As a result, the labor force will begin to shrink relative to the retired, reaching a standstill between 2020 and 2030. This increase in the "elderly dependency ratio" will cause public expenditures to boom, thus increasing the deficit and the total level of debt.

The CBO projects that the U.S. debt held by the public will grow from 50 percent of GDP in 1996 to 75 percent in 2020, then to 158 percent in 2035 and, finally, to a staggering 267 percent of GDP by 2050.[111] The cost of such benefits is expected to rise from 8.4 percent of GDP in 1996 to about 16 percent of GDP in 2030, largely owing to the open-ended entitlement programs in Medicare and Medicaid. The increase in this debt level can be attributed to just four programs: social security, Medicare, Medicaid, and interest on the national debt. Delaying action on reforming these programs by just five years will increase the cost of resolving these problems by about 15 percent, according to this CBO study. A twenty-year delay will drive the cost of solving this fiscal problem about 60 percent higher.[112]

Solving the deficit problem in the United States is not difficult in terms of what needs to be done, *provided the public will agree to a few modest proposals*. A small reduction in the level of social security benefits, an increase in the age for retirement by a few years, and a reduction in the cost-of-living formula would largely resolve the problem. Nor is there much controversy about how to go about resolving the problem. Solving the Medicare problem would be much more difficult. Congress could increase the age of eligibility, reduce the number of people who are eligible for Medicare benefits, collect a higher percentage of the costs from beneficiaries, or limit the growth of the program to some fixed figure, say 4 percent per year. Clearly, the age of eligibility would have to be increased, perhaps to age seventy. Some costs could be shifted to hospitals and to doctors, as the 1997 budget did. The long-term problem is not what to do. The long-term problem is whether the American people have the will to do it. At this point, there is little reason for much optimism.

The net present value of public pension liabilities to 2050 for the other G–7 countries looks dramatically worse, except for the United Kingdom and Canada. (Net present value is the difference between projected primary expenditures and revenues of public pension funds, adjusted for net asset position.) Italy has the largest problem. State pensions in Italy are extraordinarily generous and allow some people to retire in their forties![113] Thus far, the pain of the modest reforms that have been put in place has been inflicted on those under forty-five. Currently, anyone can begin retirement at age fifty-three. Germany, France, and Japan also have a much greater pension problem than the United States. Because those three countries are under considerably greater fiscal stress than the United States—primarily due to high rates of unemployment—reform will likely take longer and require greater sacrifices.

Again, the public debt problem is not lack of solutions. For example, raising the retirement age in Italy to sixty-seven, where it will be in a few years in the United States, could completely close the pension liability gap there.[114] A blend of solutions—emphasizing fiscal rectitude, lowered expectations of what government can do, more personal responsibility for retirement income, and somewhat reduced benefits while still preserving the social "safety net"—is probably the wisest approach in all these countries.

Long-term, what is needed to address the global public debt problem seriously and continuously is a sea of change in public psychology. Unusually good years following World War II created a belief in continued prosperity. Based on that belief, new entitlements were established throughout the G–7 community. In 1970, the U.S. Supreme Court ruled that uninterrupted receipt of public assistance is a *property* right, based on the due process clause of the Fourteenth Amendment, and takes precedence over the state's need to conserve fiscal resources or balance its budget.[115] Thereafter, entitlements became almost as sacrosanct as freedom of speech or freedom of worship. The consequence, according to Peter G. Peterson, is that "most retired Americans today receive two to five times more in social security benefits—and at least ten times more in tax-free Medicare benefits—than what they and their employers contributed, including the interest on their contributions."[116] No country can sustain such largess over an extended period of time, yet no country seems to have been able to resist the entitlement seduction. In many countries, net pension liabilities exceed their current national debt. One cannot, therefore, expect to solve the long-term public debt problem without at the same time solving the even larger long-term unfunded public pension problem—thus making the need for a change in public thinking the *sine qua non* for balance.

Such a change would include a shift from the notion that the market is responsible for life's misfortunes, and that we are therefore entitled to public assistance when we fall short of our expectations, to the recognition that personal responsibility becomes the primary emphasis. This change in public attitudes and social norms will undoubtedly occur eventually, because it will be driven by inexorable fiscal pressures, but entitlement reform is presently timid and piecemeal. To shift gears to a faster and more fundamental level of reform will probably require some mind-concentrating fiscal crisis. In such cases history has been more than happy to oblige.[117]

Chapter 6

Disarming the Debt Bomb

The financial crises that erupted in East Asia in 1997 were rooted in excessive debt based on imprudent lending and borrowing. This pattern was especially true of Japan's economy, which developed an equity and asset bubble that burst in 1990. As these debt crises spread to other countries, especially Russia and Brazil, they helped to trigger a sell-off in equity markets worldwide in the summer and early fall of 1998. As a consequence, the volume of world trade decelerated sharply, and global growth was projected to recover only moderately.

Although all G–7 stock exchanges had recovered from their brief market downturns by the end of 1998, considerable uncertainty remained about the near-term outlook for growth and debt sustainability, with substantial downside risk. The strength of the eight-year U.S. economic expansion—from 1991 to 1999—facilitated a positive adjustment in countries affected by these debt crises, since the United States had served as a buyer of last resort of goods produced in Asia and in Europe which could not be sold there. This willingness came at a high cost to the United States, because foreign purchases had caused an expanding current account deficit. This current account deficit is expected to reach almost $300 billion in 1999, almost double the $155 billion deficit of 1997.[1] A sixteen-year bull market, interrupted only briefly in 1987 and 1998, continued to move upward to historic highs in 1998. But extraordinarily high prices for stocks and price earnings ratios in the technology sector that defy common sense made the stock market in the United States very vulnerable to a market crash. A slowing world economy, declining corporate profits, zero household savings, and a rapidly rising current account deficit raise the possibility of a spreading debt crisis in 1999 and the new millennium beyond.

This chapter briefly examines the historical evidence for cycles, because many people (although not many economists) are coming to doubt their existence, especially *debt cycles*. Here I describe the primary characteristics of debt cycles and offer some indicators of vulnerability and spillover effects when debt levels reach unsustainable levels. The Minsky-Kindleberger model guides this analysis. Finally, both short-term and long-term projections of public and private debt levels in the G–7 will round out this chapter. I conclude that the debt bombs that have already gone off in Asia need not necessarily go off with the same explosive violence in the Americas and in Europe but that there is growing evidence—especially over the long run—that the debt contagion will spread.

Historical Cycles

Historians have long known that there are observable patterns in the economic development of nations. To name just a few: Economic growth rates tend to fall within fairly predictable ranges over time. Developed economies usually grow more slowly than developing economies. World export market shares for the major industrial countries have remained relatively constant over many years. The share of manufacturing employment has fallen in all industrial societies, while the share of employment in the services sector has risen. International per capita income levels and productivity rates appear to converge over time. Recessions and depressions, which themselves have observable patterns, occur in every economy. Advanced capitalist societies are very similar with respect to their overall rates of social mobility. History is rife with banking and exchange crises, and some kind of financial crisis has tended to appear at roughly ten-year intervals for the past 400 years. Much has been written about the cyclical rise and fall of nations, why some nations are rich and others are poor, the rise and fall of presidential reputations, cycles of wars and violence, and so forth. Without some continuity in these cyclical fluctuations, there would be no point in studying history.[2]

Cycles are also well documented in economic studies. Among these, perhaps the best known are those that relate to the alternate expansion and contraction in overall business activity in all free-market industrial countries, although these cycles are not uniform in frequency, amplitude, or duration. Nevertheless, patterns can be observed every forty months or so in these economies, again about every ten years and, some believe, in a long-wave cycle every fifty to sixty years.[3] Financial crises have been a topic of perennial interest, especially with the rising rate of bank failures in recent years and the series of international debt crises that began in Mexico in 1982. In recent years, Hyman Minsky's writings on "money-manager capitalism," a new stage of capitalism that has emerged since the 1970s, document our society's greater reliance on debt, speculation, and short-term financing, with a greater resultant financial fragility.[4] In the current era of money-manager capitalism, mergers, acquisitions, and leveraged buyouts play a much larger role in the business cycle, as does the stock market. According to Minsky, capitalism evolves, and in the current stage, debt and speculation play a much larger role in the overall economy than in the past. Financial crises rooted in excessive indebtedness are therefore more likely to occur than in the past.[5]

In recent years, doubts have arisen regarding some of these time-tested historical cycles. Most prominent perhaps has been the doubt cast on the stock market cycle. Historically, the Dow Jones Industrial Average (DJIA) rises and falls in real terms in a fairly predictable pattern: what goes up, comes down—and at approximately the same rate. As a result of a confluence of factors, U.S. stocks had, as of June 1999, climbed to unprecedented levels. Bulls had had a heyday; bears had declined almost to extinction. Warnings in late 1996 of "irrational exuberance" by Alan Greenspan, chairman of the Federal Reserve Board, went unheeded. Many began to think that the business cycle, and more especially the cycle of debt and default, had been reduced to a ripple rather than a wave. Steven Weber in 1997 argued that cycles were getting shorter and milder, that the world was moving into a fundamentally new era—one in which traditional cycles were anachronistic. This dampening of the business cycle had been caused, Weber believed, by the globalization of production, easier credit, more flexible employment, more effective governmental policy, emerging markets, and improved technology. Services, less cyclical than manufacturing, now dominate all advanced economies; union membership is in severe decline, thus limiting strikes; and the increased use of derivatives now spreads risk so broadly as to largely prevent fiscal surprises. Weber concludes by agreeing with those who assert that a new era has arrived and that financial "bubbles" are a thing of the past.[6]

Others go even further and have begun to argue that a new "golden era" has arrived and that historical patterns of centuries-long duration are no longer relevant in today's society. Among them are U.N. Secretary General Kofi Annan and Joseph Steglitz, chief economist for the World Bank.[7] Essentially, this new view is based on the belief that several trends are converging to generate a global economic growth wave at a level twice the recent trend line of 2 percent per year. In fact, in 1997 the International Monetary Fund (IMF) predicted that real world gross domestic product (GDP) growth would top 4 percent annually from 1997 to 2002.[8] Growth rates at that level for that long are unprecedented in recent decades. Those who believe in this new golden era also believe that private investment will soar and globalization of markets will continue unabated. In their view, technological innovations have muted the business cycle and world stock markets are not overvalued, nor are they excessively leveraged by indebtedness. If this new era has really begun, then of course the relevance of history is at best questionable, and the possibility of finding significant leading historical indicators of major debt crises is considerably diminished.

Debt Crises

To evaluate the accuracy of the golden-era thesis, we must examine its relevance to the more focused topic of *debt crises. The New Palgrave Dictionary of Money and Finance* defines a *debt crisis* as "any situation where a debtor is unable to service the interest and/or principal as scheduled, . . . imperiling the financial health of its lender or lenders."[9]

The term "debt crisis" is widely used to describe various financial phenomena, but most financial crises are debt related. Earlier in this century, debt crises were commonly associated with Third World nations and their inability to service their loans from commercial banks. In more recent years, debt crises have usually related to Latin American nations and a few others who have had similar problems in repaying loans.

A more generic term relating to a debt crisis is "financial crisis." Most financial crises have excessive debt as a major component. *Palgrave* defines a *financial crisis* as "a sharp, brief, ultra-cyclical deterioration of all or most of a group of financial indicators—shortterm interest rates, asset (stock, real estate, land) prices, commercial insolvencies and failures of financial institutions."[10] A financial crisis is characterized by a rush out of financial assets and into cash. According to the *Palgrave Dictionary*, whether financial distress ends in a financial crisis depends on a variety of factors, including the fragility of the earlier extensions of credit, the speed of the reversal of expectations, the disturbance to confidence produced by some financial accident, and whether the debtor believes he or she will be rescued by a lender of last resort. Economists have paid little attention to these financial crises until recently, perhaps because, as economist Martin Feldstein has written, there were so few crises between the Great Depression and the 1980s, and because most of them are difficult to model formally.[11] Historians have paid even less attention to financial crises since the Great Depression, in part because the interests of most historians have not been centered on economic or financial history.

According to Paul Krugman, professor of economics at Massachusetts Institute of Technology (MIT), himself an accomplished authority in the field, the most influential economists who have written on financial crises in recent years are Hyman Minsky and Charles Kindleberger.[12] All three of these experts strongly believe that there is "a single crisis story"[13] and that it is a mistake to try to subdivide the field into different kinds of fiscal crises—

industrial, commercial, banking, or what have you. Kindleberger based his theory of financial crises on the work of Hyman Minsky, who, in turn, took his cues from Irving Fisher, one of America's foremost economists in the early decades of this century. Fisher believed that the business cycle is best explained by two key factors: excessive indebtedness and deflation. The upswing in the business cycle is precipitated by some external event that provides new and wonderful opportunities for profit. These new opportunities encourage speculation for capital gain; and most of this speculation is debt financed, which, by increasing the money supply, raises the price level. This process continues until debtors cannot service their debts and begin to liquidate their assets. If the debt crisis is sufficiently widespread, prices begin to fall and a recession, or possibly even a depression, is created, unless monetary authorities step in to reinflate the economy. Once recovery begins, the process repeats itself.[14]

Minsky believed, following John Maynard Keynes, that capitalist economies were cyclical. Capitalism is in a permanent state of disequilibrium because no one can know for sure where it is moving, and this lack of knowledge leads to a cycle of booms and busts. As the economy moves toward the peak of the cycle, the financial structure becomes more fragile because the upswing was financed largely by debt. Wall Street and stock markets play a major role in this process. Minsky believed that this process was inevitable but that booms and busts did not simply need to be endured. Although government spending and the central bank could not do away completely with cycles, they could modify this pattern.[15] If government could modify the downside of the business cycle, Wall Street could modify the upside. Increasingly, Wall Street provided the funds for a new stage of capitalism, "money-market capitalism," and with the growing influence of Wall Street as a provider of capital, the Federal Reserve's power to regulate the market is diminished. According to Gary Dymski, an economist at the University of California, Riverside, "Minsky feared another profound financial and economic collapse in the near future, especially because financial firms are becoming ever freer from regulatory oversight and hence more likely to create situations requiring even more massive centralized interventions."[16] Minsky expressed his concerns about a possible collapse in 1994; I assume what he meant by "near future" means some time within a decade following his statement. The stock markets of the world play a much larger role today than they used to because business leaders have become increasingly sensitive to the market's valuation of their firm. Margins of safety in indebtedness have decreased as debt ratios have increased and short-term financing has been emphasized. Mergers, acquisitions, and leveraged buyouts have also increased as fund managers have focused on near-term profits. According to Minsky, the world financial system is becoming increasingly fragile as it became more international, and a market crash—such as happened in Japan—is therefore increasingly likely.[17]

Kindleberger's contribution to Minsky's financial fragility theory is rooted in Kindleberger's acute focus on the critical stage, the point at which confidence is lost and the crisis begins.[18] Euphoria is followed by uncertainty and apprehension, which may be followed by panic. Warnings of excessive indebtedness are almost always futile, and the process seems to take on a life of its own. The causes of a debt crisis vary widely, but they often include sharply rising interest rates, balance-of-payments deficits that have gotten out of hand, rising bankruptcies, the beginning of deflation, the return of foreign capital "to its usual habitat," or the failure of a "great house" or corporation.[19] It is impossible to rank these causes of debt crises in any particular order, nor is it likely that a set of indicators could be used in most cases to predict a debt crisis.[20] What these indicators actually indicate is *vulnerability* to a possible debt crisis. In other words, the larger the number of historical indicators of financial distress in the past, the greater the risk for a given nation of experiencing a debt crisis in the present.

In addition to Kindleberger's list of variables, the IMF has found that the following indicators of excessive debt are also germane to a general understanding of why financial crises occur: the level and duration of public deficits and debt, the level of government consumption, the rate and duration of private-sector credit growth, the degree of financial liberalization, the level of short-term foreign indebtedness, changes in equity prices, the amount and quality of nonperforming loans, as well as the rate of growth of GDP and the level of unemployment.[21] Long periods of sustained high expectations and euphoria render a nation especially vulnerable to debt crises, particularly if accompanied by loose monetary conditions, an overheated economy, and bursting asset or price bubbles.

No combination of these indicators of vulnerability to a debt crisis can capture the complexity of any given situation, in part because of unique political events, unfathomable emotional attitudes and investor sentiment changes, and the surprising power of contagion. Debt crises are inherently unpredictable. Rather than trying to predict these crises, it is more useful, as the IMF has pointed out, to identify the kinds of weakness that render nations, corporations, and households vulnerable to these crises. This section attempts to do so. The important thing to remember is that our economic system is vulnerable to financial crises, that the financial sector is especially fragile, that busts follow booms more often than not, and that a long period of euphoria and rapidly growing equity bubbles have rendered the industrial world especially vulnerable to a new debt crisis.

Are Debt Crises Likely to Intensify?

In 1980, total credit market debt in the United States amounted to $4.7 trillion, or 174 percent of GDP. Credit market debt had been at approximately that level of GDP for several decades. Even during World War II, the level of total debt had not risen much higher.[22] By 1998, that $4.7 trillion figure had shot up to $21.7 trillion, or 257 percent of GDP.[23] This 47 percent increase in the debt/GDP ratio in just eighteen years is unprecedented in this century, except for the period of the Great Depression. Nor is there any solid evidence that this upward trend of increasing indebtedness is about to reverse itself.

Each year the United States adds more than a *trillion* dollars to its public and private outstanding debt account, which represents a growth rate of debt in excess of 10 percent per year. Excluding about $500 billion of foreign debt held in the United States and another $5 trillion owed by the financial sector, we are still increasing our debt burden by about 7 percent per year, while our economy and personal income since 1990 have been growing at a rate just over 5 percent per year. Obviously, this rate of debt increase is unsustainable, which means that the possibility of a debt crisis in the United States is increasing.

What makes this situation even more ominous is that rising debt trends can be observed in almost all industrial countries. It is well known that gross *public* debt/GDP ratios have risen dramatically in the G–7 nations since 1980. In 1980, the G–7 public debt/GDP ratio was 42 percent; by 1998 that figure had nearly doubled, having risen to 79 percent.[24] Similar increases occurred in most other industrialized countries. What is not generally known, even by some experts, is that private-sector debt in most of the G–7 nations has also risen, albeit not quite so dramatically (see Table 6.1).

Interestingly, the largest percentage increases in private debt have come in the largest countries, with only France holding the line. In public indebtedness, Japan and Italy have experienced the most rapid increases since 1980, with only the United Kingdom ratios remaining constant.

The Public Sector

Public debt levels have ballooned over the past two decades of relative peace and prosperity and appear to be unsustainable given current policies.[25] By the mid-1990s, all of the Organization for Economic Cooperation and Development (OECD) countries were experiencing deficits except Norway. By 1998, five of the G–7 nations had deficits, and most of the other advanced economies were running deficits as well.[26] The increase in gross public debt

Table 6.1

Increases in Private Sector Domestic Credit in the G-7 Nations, 1980–1997
(as a percentage of GDP)

Nation	1980	1997	% Increase
Germany	72	105	33
United States	36	65	29
Japan	87	112	25
Canada	45	69	24
United Kingdom	106	121	15
Italy	39	51	12
France	80	79	–1
G-7	66	86	20

Source: IMF, *International Financial Statistics,* for the years indicated, line 32d, "Claims on the private sector."

as a percentage of GDP from 1970 to 1998 has been greatest in Japan (558 percent), Germany (233 percent), and Italy (193 percent).[27] The United Kingdom actually decreased its gross public debt from 82 percent of GDP in 1970 to 52 percent in 1998, and the United States experienced only a modest increase in public debt by G–7 standards, from 45 percent in 1970 to 59 percent in 1998.

Adding to the growing debt picture the fact that private savings rates have declined in the advanced countries, from 20.9 percent of GDP in 1976–1983, to 18.9 percent of GDP in 1998—a substantial change in matters like this—reveals that the likelihood of a debt crisis is further increased. At the same time, there is growing concern about unfunded public and private pensions. For many industrial countries, net pension liabilities exceed current overall national debt. The largest pension liabilities are in France, Germany, and Japan; the smallest is in the United Kingdom.

From the above data, it is clear that all the G–7 nations and most of the rest of the developed world have a serious and growing debt problem, either in the public or in the private sector.[28] It is true that the United States and Canada have *temporarily* balanced their *public* accounts, but only when social security revenues are included and when the looming deficits in Medicare are excluded. In the United States, this temporary balance in the public sector is more related to strong economic growth than to a deliberate and publicly supported program of debt reduction. In fact, ever since the budget surplus became known, politicians in both political parties could hardly wait to break the spending caps that were put in place to create the surplus in the first place. Moreover, the statutory public debt limit is scheduled to climb every year as far as the eye can see. When the economy turns down once again, it is almost certain that the pattern of deficit spending will reemerge. Moreover, the ratio of *private* debt to GDP is increasing faster in both Canada and the United States than in most other G–7 countries, indicating that there has been no basic change in public attitudes toward debt in those countries. By early 1999, financial turbulence was increasing in Europe and Asia, as recessions deepened in Asia and the Russian default played itself out. Increasingly, socialistically inclined governments were returning to power in Europe and in Asia, suggesting an increase in welfare spending and growing indebtedness. Persistently high unemployment in major European countries suggests that government deficits will not go much below the 3 percent of GDP targets set by the Maastricht Treaty. Brazil's currency default in early January 1999 also puts Latin America at greater risk. Clearly, too much uncertainty and downside risk is evident in the world economy to have any confidence that the public debt problem in any of the G–7 countries has been solved in the long run.

The growth of public debt in the industrial world has been much studied,[29] and no single theory can explain why this growth has occurred.[30] All experts agree, however, that serious and prolonged deficits were rare in industrial countries, except in wartime or other extreme circumstances, until recently. These deficits widened dramatically after 1980, even while taxes were being increased. According to the IMF, government expenditures in industrial countries jumped from an average of 28 percent of GDP in 1960 to 50 percent in 1994.[31] Since 1994, the size of the government sector in most industrial nations has been modestly reduced, except in Japan. The really big increases in government spending over these years came in transfers, public pensions, and interest payments. General government net financial liabilities (assets minus liabilities and including Social Security) in the OECD more than doubled from 1981 to 1998.[32] In short, government debt has grown rapidly virtually everywhere since the 1980s, although the rate of increase in debt accumulation has moderated somewhat in recent years in those economies that are strong.

Whether debt crises will intensify or modify depends to a large extent on what caused the rapid growth in public debt in the first place. There are several schools of thought on this issue, and several reasons for this increase in public indebtedness. According to Richard Musgrave, one of the world's leading experts on public finance, the basic reason for this increase in government spending is the general belief, dating back to the Great Depression, that unemployment is an inextricable part of capitalist economies, and therefore governments must intervene to stabilize the situation and keep unemployment low.[33] Increasing government spending is the only way to combat this problem, although in recent years, tax cuts have become the dominant approach. Both approaches, of course, increase debt. The view that capitalism is inherently flawed and that governments must intervene in a massive way has been particularly strong in Great Britain and France because of their core of long-term unemployed workers.[34] Another reason for sharply rising public deficits is the assumption, widespread until recently, that rapid economic growth—at rates experienced in the 1950s and the early 1960s—would continue indefinitely. New programs could, therefore, be funded by growth. But world economic growth rates did not continue at the 1950s–1960s level; they fell in the 1970s, and have remained below that earlier trend to the present. In late 1998, the IMF projected world growth rates to remain below trend for the foreseeable future, with considerable downward risk.[35] Hence, governmental promises made in flush times to increase entitlements on a massive scale could not be financed from continued economic growth after world growth rates began to slow in the early 1970s.[36] In short, increased entitlement spending has been responsible for increased public debt. Still another reason for accelerating deficits, at least in the United States, was that the high corporate profit rates of the early Cold War years did not continue after 1970; corporate tax rates declined, thus decreasing tax revenues from that important sector of the economy.[37]

Over time, social benefits have become more generous and more widely available, and special interest lobbies have arisen to protect these benefits. A growing share of the population are also no longer participating in the workforce—retiring earlier, taking part-time positions, or entering the workforce later—hence shrinking the tax base. Meanwhile, beginning about 1980, real interest rates began to rise sharply in the G–7 countries; at the same time, debt began to explode and net private savings rates began to decline.[38] Rising real interest rates raised the cost of debt finance substantially. In the distant past, governments could have financed this increase in debt by simply printing money or by deliberately creating inflation. But, as the IMF has pointed out, supersensitive investors quickly understood this political trick and exacted a risk premium for purchasing government bonds.[39]

Rather than lowering their expectations of what governments should provide as the capacity of governments to provide these services declined, and rather than raising taxes and lowering expenditures to deal with this growing debt problem, voters in virtually all industrial countries became even *less* interested in cutting spending than they had been before and more adamant against raising taxes. I have raised this point earlier in a different context, but it is worth repeating here. As John Makin and Norman Ornstein, both associated with the American Enterprise Institute in Washington, D.C., have pointed out in their insightful book *Debt and Taxes: How America Got into*

Its Budget Mess and What to Do About It, the U.S. government tried to address this growing public debt problem—never quite successfully because of minimal public support. The public, on its part, grew more alienated and more cynical. As promises were made to balance the budget but not kept, the public lost faith in the government's ability to deal with fiscal problems.[40] At no point, Makin and Ornstein argue, did anything near a majority of Americans indicate a willingness to solve the growing public debt problem from 1980 on, if solving that problem meant reducing benefits or raising taxes.[41]

Failure to balance the budget was almost guaranteed because Congress was unwilling to reverse the relentlessly growing rate of increase in entitlements, especially for Social Security and Medicare. The voters would simply not tolerate a serious reduction in their benefits. This was true even though the share of the credit market required to finance these federal programs reached nearly 90 percent of the U.S. credit market in the early 1990s.[42] Nevertheless, President Clinton's fiscal year (FY) 1998 budget did get passed; and because of a strong economy, the United States had a balanced budget (including Social Security surpluses) by 1998. But the spending caps, first introduced in 1990, almost immediately started to crack; and through a myriad of accounting gimmicks and fee increases, discretionary spending started up once again.[43] Still, unlike certain other G–7 countries, the United States was able to modify the growth rate of its public debt *because of a growing economy.* Consequently, by 1998 the net public debt/GDP ratio for the United States was about at the midpoint for the G–7 countries.

Growing unemployment in Europe and Japan has also encouraged more deficit spending, particularly in those countries where unemployment benefits replaced a very high share of previous earnings and where core unemployment appears to be intractable. The oil price shocks of the 1970s also precipitated recessions and slowed growth in those countries without their own oil supplies. Until these very high and rigid unemployment rates in Europe come down, we can expect continuing fiscal deficits there.

Sadly, even dramatic legislative attempts to balance the budget have been effective only when times are good. Germany and Japan, for instance, have legal requirements for a balanced budget; but in recent years, the rate of growth of public indebtedness in both Germany and Japan has been much faster than in the United States, which has no such legal requirement.[44] Productivity slowdowns in most industrial nations since the 1970s, something virtually all nations were slow to understand, have also increased the number of citizens in need of government relief, putting pressure on welfare agencies to increase spending. Finally, the increasing integration of world capital has made the selling of government bonds abroad easier for countries that have maxed out their borrowing capacity at home, thereby continuing to raise debt levels that without this international source of capital would not have been possible.

But perhaps the single most important reason public debt has exploded in recent years is the absence of any clearly related consequences to nations that have very high levels of public debt. For years, Italy's net public debt/GDP ratio has been twice as high as that of the United States, without any clearly related negative consequences for Italy. Conversely, *reducing* public deficits, where that has occurred, has also had very small positive consequences.[45] For a public—whether here or abroad—that has not felt strongly about public debt since the 1930s, the absence of any major public debt crisis *anywhere* in the G–7 during the past six decades has only confirmed the public's growing belief that debt levels really do not matter much. This is an important point. It suggests that some sort of economic or fiscal crisis might be necessary to convince the public and their governments to make the tough choices necessary to start public debt levels on a downward course.

Herbert Stein has written that budget-balancing ceased to have any important influence on fiscal decisions in the United States as early as 1964.[46] Writing in his inimitable style, Stein says he believes balanced budgets are now given "only ritual obeisance" and national goals to balance the budget are merely "totemic goals."[47] The fact that the U.S. budget is currently balanced *according to official estimates* is largely owing to a strong economy; maintaining that balance is extremely vulnerable to an economic downturn.[48] "Much recent political rhetoric has consisted of self-congratulation over short-term deficit declines," Alan J. Auerbach, an economist at Berkeley, has observed, "but long-term projections continue to tell a very different story."[49] To get long-term balance—that is, to really address the projected growth in Medicare, Medicaid, and Social Security—a truly balanced budget "would require a permanent 54 percent reduction in Medicare, relative to baseline (1997); a 58 percent reduction in all government spending other than Medicare, Medicaid, and Social Security; or a 47 percent increase in collections from individual and corporate income taxes."[50] In short, the United States is far from having a truly balanced budget in the long term, and there is little evidence that the public is ready to address this problem seriously. Politicians know it. That is why they pose as guardians of the current federal surplus and then fall all over themselves to spend it.

Efforts to balance government budgets in other countries have been sporadic and never successful in the long term, with the possible exception of New Zealand.[51] Of the major nations, Italy is the country to watch, since Italy's net public debt in 1998 was 112 percent of GDP, by far the highest of the G–7.[52] Canada, among the G–7 group, appears to have the best chance for long-term public debt reduction. Canada's gross public debt fell from

101 percent of GDP in 1996 to 92 percent of GDP in 1998. No other G–7 country has achieved so large a swing toward paying down its debt nor achieved it so swiftly. Canada did it by changing its fiscal culture. High levels of public debt were recognized as a major problem; the Canadians were persuaded to address this problem realistically; and the Canadian government set realistic, two-year goals to achieve their targets. The key was to change the public's mind-set toward debt and to set the government on a path of absolute decline in program spending.[53]

These, then, are some of the major reasons for the explosive growth of public debt in the G–7 and other major nations since the early 1980s, and what has been done to address this problem. Overall, the reasons for the growth of public debt are deeply rooted in social norms. Debt increases have been politically popular, international in scope, and increasingly intractable. Although the increased debt ratios have caused some alarm, in most nations, attempts to reduce rising public debt trends have been sporadic, piecemeal, and timid. Some progress has been made in reducing the increase in public debt and stabilizing debt ratios in Europe and in North America, but efforts to reach these goals were based more on spending cuts than on significant fiscal reforms, and on temporary spending limitations and governmental investment cutbacks, rather than on a change in direction. Most efforts, moreover, have been directed at reducing the rate of increase in public indebtedness, rather than reducing the amount of debt itself. Given the pension crisis that is looming and the declining ratio of those who are working to those who are not, much greater emphasis should be placed on actually reducing public debt levels. Since political resistance to this kind of fiscal reform is likely to be significant, an early and gradual beginning is indicated. Ultimately, major fiscal reforms are called for in most industrial countries, including a substantial reduction in persistent unemployment in Europe.

There appear to be serious risks that these reforms will not be achieved. Equity bubbles have emerged in most G–7 countries, world growth rates are declining, corporate profits are softening, and high labor costs and entrenched entitlement systems have depressed job creation. More ominously, the unfunded pension problem has not been seriously addressed anywhere. In most G–7 countries, with Canada as the exception, the approach to the public debt problem has been ad hoc adjustments rather than fundamental reform. Although President Bill Clinton made debt reduction the centerpiece of his 1999 policy agenda, it is by no means clear that he speaks for a majority of Democrats or that this policy is more than a maneuver to block Republican tax cuts. Republicans clearly prefer tax reductions to debt reductions, and the American public has not been serious about debt reduction for at least a generation. Therefore, continuing if not growing debt crises in the public sector appear likely.

The Private Sector

Turning now to the private sector, and examining the United States first, it is abundantly clear that private debt ratios have been growing steadily and rapidly since the end of World War II. In 1950, private nonfinancial debt as a percentage of GDP was just over 50 percent; by 1998 that figure had risen to 124 percent.[54] Debt in both the corporate and the household sectors rose substantially over these years, but more rapidly in recent years.[55] Clearly, private debt—like public debt—has become a much more significant part of all our lives.

The reasons for this increase in private debt are varied: First, there was a marked acceleration of debt by all kinds by borrowers in virtually all sectors of the economy. This across-the-board increase suggests a common and powerful motivation: a determination to telescope future income into present consumption. Second, corporations shifted more toward debt and away from equity to finance their growth, and shifted to short-term rather than long-term debt—suggesting a shorter corporate time horizon.[56] Third, some have argued that tax changes favoring debt enlargement during the 1980s encouraged debt increases. There is very little evidence for this, however.[57] What does seem to have been influential in the rise of corporate debt, both in the United States and elsewhere, was the creation of easier credit rules, along with heightened international competition, innovative financial instruments, and uncertainty about where debt peril became excessive.[58]

There is no consensus on whether U.S. corporate or personal debt levels at the present time are excessive.[59] On the one hand, household and corporate debt have risen since the 1950s as a percentage of GDP; on the other hand, so have household and corporate assets. The asset/debt ratios of household debt and of corporate debt in 1980 and 1997 are roughly the same.[60] This measurement suggests that debt levels are not excessive. But much of the recent buildup in assets is based on the extraordinarily high bubble in the stock market. In the early 1980s, the U.S. stock market capitalization as a percentage of U.S. GDP was about 40 percent; in 1998 that ratio was approaching 160 percent, twice what it was in 1929. Clearly, the equity market now plays a much larger role than it ever has in the past. If the stock market remains high, private debt levels as of early 1999 do not seem exorbitant. But by all historical measurements, the stock market is overpriced and in the advanced stages of a bubble. Should the market crash, currently high private debt levels will likely prove to be very burdensome. A sharp and prolonged downturn in the market could demonstrate that the United States has too much capital investment based on too much corporate debt and that corporations have been creating an "investment bubble" comparable to the stock market bubble of recent years.[61] For example, in 1998 corporate American was on a "borrowing binge" comparable to that of the late 1980s, adding debt at an annual rate of 11 percent for the first three quarters of 1998.[62] U.S. corporate debt now represents 43 percent of GDP, near the highest level since 1960. Forty-one percent of all new bonds sold were "junk bonds," or bonds rated below investment grade.[63] This appears to be a risky course when one-third of the world's economies are in recession or are experiencing markedly slower growth and when the IMF is projecting world economic growth at only 2.2 percent for 1998 and 1999, a "deceleration of global growth to levels not seen since the pronounced world slowdowns of 1974–75, 1980–83, and 1990–91."[64] Even though U.S. corporate earnings are healthy, an amber light is flashing. It could turn to scarlet and trigger alarm bells if the market turns down.

But even if corporate debt were not currently excessive, James Medoff and Andrew Harless, a Harvard professor and a Harvard-trained consultant, argue that current levels of corporate debt have high levels of interest cost that have led to too much downsizing, declining real wages, more layoffs in recessions, and growing employment insecurity.[65] Historically, businessmen typically go through periods of excessive borrowing followed by periods of retrenchment. One cannot know with any certainty when excess borrowing has occurred until after the fact. Since none of the theoretical models regarding corporate debt can predict when a country's corporate debt level is excessive, appropriate debt levels are a matter of judgment. However, in such circumstances, ordinary intuition suggests that it is better to be prudent now than sorry later.

Consumer debt ratios have advanced at a somewhat faster rate in the United States during the 1980s and 1990s than overall private debt. Marked increases in mortgage debt as a ratio of income during the 1980s was clearly a factor in the rise of household debt. One reason for this increase in mortgage debt was that the percentage of white home owners increased over these years. Another is that the average size of the home increased, as did the amenities that went with it. Still another is that the median sales price of new privately owned one-family houses rose dramatically—especially in the Northeast—as did the median sales price of existing single-family homes—especially in the West. In 1970, the median price of a new home was $23,000; in 1995 the cost of the same home had risen to $134,00.[66] Despite the fact that home buyers increased their average monthly mortgage payments from 24 percent of their disposable income in 1976 to 33 percent in 1997, they had no choice but to increase their indebtedness even more. A final reason for increasing household indebtedness is that more Americans now have credit cards than ever before, and the ratio of those who pay off their monthly balance on those credit cards has dropped. Nearly 70 percent of cardholders under age forty-four had a balance after paying the previous month's bills in 1995.[67]

There is widespread concern that credit card debt in the United States is too high. Rising bank card delinquencies and rapidly rising personal bankruptcies support this view. During 1995, banks mailed out 2.7 *billion* preapproved credit card solicitations, according to the *Wall Street Journal*— about seventeen offers for every adult in the country of working age.[68] That year also saw record credit card delinquencies. This delinquency rate varies by bank: very large and old-line banks, like Citicorp (now Travelers Group, Inc.) and Chase Manhattan, have low rates of delinquency, whereas newer and smaller banks, like First USA and Bank One, have higher rates.[69] This rapid increase in credit is reminiscent of the same situation in the 1920s. New entrepreneurs, out in the hinterlands, without much education, and uninitiated in the more esoteric aspects of risk, were the Michael Milkins of that era.[70] Much the same attitude existed in the credit markets of the 1990s.[71] Because credit card debt is extremely profitable for banks and because bankrupt individuals have almost no problem getting credit again, there is little likelihood that this situation will change until a crisis occurs. Banks will have to lose money—and a lot of it—before they become persuaded to change what has been a very profitable credit venture.

A new life-cycle theory of consumption developed by Franco Modigliani, suggesting that people should live so that all of their assets will have been extinguished at the time of their death—thus leaving nothing to their descendants—appears to have taken hold of the public mind during the 1980s and carried over into the 1990s.[72] Two-fifths of Americans over sixty-five have a net worth of less than $30,000 in excess of the value of their homes. The average person over sixty-five, after a lifetime of work, has accumulated less than $70,000 in debt-free assets (beyond the family home).[73] Such an attitude focuses on the self, rather than on linked generations, and on consumption, rather than on acquiring net worth. "He who dies with the most toys wins" is the motto produced by this kind of thinking—even if it requires leaving the children with a mountain of debt. This "die broke" attitude fixes the mind on dissipation and on using up everything that has been built up in previous generations. It uncouples us from both the past and the future. In my view, it is a truly horrifying idea. We have gone down that road before—during the late 1920s—and we should know better. The party atmosphere and the quest for personal gratification that characterized that era had its consequences. Those who were hurt the most by the Great Crash of 1929 seemed to have been those most afflicted by fiscal myopia—the thousands of small speculators with dreams of easy wealth who were buying overpriced stocks on margin. Modestly talented people with a profound conviction that their speculations will be attended by unlimited rewards in which they were meant to share are the typical speculators in all eras.[74] Although they are the greatest sufferers, it is characteristic of such people that they have little concern either for the future or for the lessons of the past.

Whether this trend toward ever-increasing private debt will eventually lead to a debt crisis is controversial. Many journalists are concerned about rising levels of personal debt; many economists and bankers are not. To illustrate: economists tend to focus on the ratio of debt to assets rather than debt to GDP, since assets indicate an ability to repay debt. During the 1960s and 1970s, household assets grew faster than household debt; but during the 1980s and early 1990s, the reverse was true.[75] By 1995, nearly three-fourths of all American families were in debt, and nearly a third of those over seventy-five had some debt.[76] U.S. businesses increased their debt/asset ratio in the 1960s, decreased that ratio in the 1970s, and then increased it once again in the 1980s. Corporate debt distress was higher in the 1980s than at any time since the 1930s.[77] Corporate bankruptcy filings have fallen in the 1990s, however, and delinquency rates are also low. Conversely, U.S. personal bankruptcy filings per capita have tripled since 1980.[78] Personal bankruptcy filings have risen in all states, not just a select few. Clearly, it is a growing national problem.

Journalists find these trends in personal indebtedness newsworthy and alarming.[79] Economists, on the other hand, are more circumspect.[80] For example, although U.S. credit card debt is soaring, many people now use their credit cards for routine payments to gain enticing extras—such as airline miles—and pay off that debt monthly. Moreover, when assets are taken into account, particularly the rise in the stock market during the mid- to late 1990s, the ratio of consumer debt to assets is not causing unusual strain.[81] However, were the stock market to dive, or merely go down for several years in real terms in its normal cyclical fashion, overextended consumers would feel considerable pressure. It is anybody's guess how serious the consequences might be.

Turning to the other nations of the G–7, it is clear that corporate debt levels in the United States are, on the whole, lower than elsewhere. Corporate debt/equity ratios since the 1960s have been lower in the United States than in all the G–7 except Italy, for which there are no comparable data.[82] France and Japan have the highest debt/equity ratios. The United States also has the lowest corporate debt/GDP ratio of the G–7; Japan's is by far the highest. The United States has the second lowest corporate debt/profit ratio in the G–7. It may be, however, that default risks are not any higher in Japan and Europe because there are closer links between corporate borrowers and their lending banks in these countries, according to economist E.P. Davis.[83] Moreover, a modest increase in the rate of bankruptcy among smaller, newer firms may be a sign of a healthy and growing economy; hence, relatively small increases in corporate bankruptcies should not be alarming. Also important is the fact that, since 1992, growth in industrial production in the United States has been faster than in any of the other G–7, thus making debt repayment easier.[84]

Regarding private debt trends in recent decades in the G–7, it appears that the main factors for generally increased indebtedness are: financial deregulation, loan liberalization rules, increased competition among lenders, falling or flat real income for most people, downsizing (resulting in lower incomes for those laid off), unrealistic expectations, and rising competition from Third World countries. In recent years, private debt levels have been too high in several Asian countries, including Japan; and a debt crisis was the result. Whether private debt levels are too high in the other G–7 countries will depend on what happens in the future. Since stock market bubbles have emerged in almost all the G–7 countries, it is likely that at some point these bubbles will burst. When that happens, we should expect serious private debt crises to be one of the results. In the United States, an overvalued stock market, virtually no private savings, a consumer-driven spending boom, and a growing current-account deficit point to the same conclusion: American families are increasingly at risk. The U.S. economy is more vulnerable to a stock market crash than other G–7 countries because shareholdings are much greater in the United States than in other nations, because America's equities bubble has risen faster and further since 1990 than any other G–7 bubble, and because consumer confidence is higher in the United States than elsewhere.[85] A bursting stock market bubble followed by a recession would clearly present a major problem to most American households.

How Can We Defuse the Global Debt Bomb?

A series of "little" debt bombs have already gone off in Southeast Asia, Korea, Japan, Russia, and Brazil. What began in 1997 as a currency crisis in Thailand developed into full-blown economic recessions in southeast Asia and elsewhere, toppling governments in several Asian countries and fomenting serious social upheaval in Indonesia. The unexpected default on some of its foreign debts by the Russian government in August 1998, along with the devaluation of the ruble, shocked investor confidence all over the world, and was the precipitating cause of the demise of Long Term Capital Management (LTCM) in the United States. LTCM was a hedge fund for a small number of very wealthy and highly sophisticated investors, structured, according to

Alan Greenspan, to avoid regulation.[86] Its failure threatened a fire sale of assets in the amount of "hundreds of billions of dollars," according to William J. McDonough, president of the Federal Reserve Bank of New York.[87] The scale of the potential impact of the failure of LTCM led to the creation—with the prodding of Federal Reserve authorities—of a consortium of private bankers and investment houses to bail out LTCM.

Looking back, it is clear that very high and rapidly growing debt levels in Asia, the failure of Japan to resolve its nine-year, $500 billion debt crisis, and multi-billion-dollar subsidies by the International Monetary Fund have caught the attention of the financial world. Two views seem to be emerging. One, represented by George Soros, who heads Soros Fund Management, the founder of a global network of foundations dedicated to supporting open societies, believes that the global capitalist system "is coming apart at the seams."[88] Soros thinks that the capitalist system is inherently unstable and given to excess, and he has little faith in the IMF's ability to manage these emerging crises. Soros also believes that market forces are producing chaos and that the increasing financial crises are caused by an unsustainable expansion of credit. Soros's proposed solution is the establishment of a new international agency to cope with these crises, an agency he calls an International Credit Insurance Corporation. This agency would convert debt, which cannot be paid, to equity. He also believes that the world has moved into a bear market and expects stock prices to go much lower, eventually leading to a worldwide depression.[89] In some ways, Soros is today's Minsky. As he sees it, capitalism is unstable by nature, money managers have too much power, there is too much debt, there is too much faith is the free market, and there is too little commitment to civic virtue.

The other view, perhaps best represented by the IMF, maintains that the capitalist system goes through bouts of excessive optimism followed by episodes of excessive pessimism. These inevitable fluctuations make all countries prone to crises. Governments need to recognize the volatile nature of the system by establishing specific policies to cope with these crises, but the world does not need any new institutions—only more effective policies. Keep the system and its ideology, only make it work better, is the basic IMF position.[90]

This section analyzes these two positions and appraises three approaches to solving the global debt crisis: (1) managing debt crises as they arise, (2) letting the market take its course, and (3) changing fundamental values. Each of these three approaches has its strengths and weaknesses, but most of the focus today is on the first approach: debt management. This section will argue that it may be time to move on to the second and third ways of dealing with the global debt crisis.

Debt Management

Given the debt crises that have occurred in recent years, there is broad agreement among the major industrial countries that better debt management is called for. The current emphasis is on reducing the frequency of debt crises or, when a debt crisis cannot be prevented, on reducing its cost. This approach assumes that the system itself is not in need of significant modification, nor are any new institutions or major changes in direction necessary. All that is called for is better management of the system that we already have. Critics of this approach sometimes call this "muddling through." Despite this somewhat pejorative appellation, muddling through has had a long and respectable history in Anglo-Saxon countries.

Those who take the "manage-the-debt-better" approach to the debt crisis include the IMF, the World Bank, the OECD, the scholarly community, and most government officials and governmental agencies. Corporate leaders, although they are generally less concerned about this issue, also tend to fall into this group. The public at large, it is safe to say, is little concerned with any of these approaches.

The debt managers, to give this group a generic name, take the position that more financial data are needed and that financial accounting should be more transparent. They advocate internationally comparable accounting standards and proper assessments for the management of risk, in order to enhance market discipline. They much prefer openness in international capital flows to restrictions on capital flows, the solution imposed in Malaysia. The debt managers are seriously concerned about the level of public debt—believing that public debt should not exceed 60 percent of GDP and that deficits should not rise above 3 percent of GDP except for brief periods—and emphasizing the importance of a nation's willingness to tighten fiscal policy when necessary. Overvalued exchange rates, excessive government ownership of the means of production, and high current account deficits are also to be kept under close surveillance. Unsustainable booms and busts in equity and asset prices are to be avoided by making governments and corporations more aware of the risks involved, and by issuing warnings of impending crises and the austere measures that will follow if these warnings are not heeded. If a debt crisis does occur, the debt managers want those responsible for creating the crisis to pay a substantial price for financial misbehavior. To contain moral hazard, governments should not bail out either those who have borrowed unwisely or those who have unwisely loaned to overly risky borrowers. This proposal represents a change from the usual procedure of rolling over the debt, rather than letting the loans default and countries or corporations go into bankruptcy.[91]

Since there are no agreed-upon standards of what constitutes debt excess, the debt managers often seek to get recalcitrant borrowers to emulate the good examples of those who perform well, without spelling out exactly why those examples have been chosen. For example, the Maastricht Treaty is not specific about what methodology should be used to calculate basic reference values; it simply cites Norway, Korea, and Finland as the three best national examples of what it wants other nations to achieve, while citing Italy, Belgium, and Greece as examples of poor public debt management. Arbitrary standards are better than no standards at all, they argue; and when a general standard is not thought possible, then the official targets established by individual governments themselves are often used as guidelines for creditable debt management. Overall, the debt managers take a practical rather than a doctrinaire approach.

Where public and private debt crises have been limited, sporadic, of short duration, and largely confined to the periphery of the global system rather than occurring at the core, the debt management approach has been quite effective. In other words, where the crisis is in fact temporary and exceptional, managing those crises is a reasonable approach to the problem. It is also an effective approach to getting nations, corporations, and households to change direction—from increasing indebtedness to decreasing indebtedness—provided they have the will and sufficient time to do so. In normal times, "muddling through" is generally an approach to addressing debt crises that do not threaten to derail the global economy. But in a global system where public debt has already risen above 70 percent of GDP and is still rising, and where net public pension liabilities characteristically exceed 100 percent of GDP, simply *managing* already high and rising debt may not be adequate to the challenge. Moreover, when corporate debt/GDP ratios reach 40 percent of GDP or higher, when asset and equity bubbles develop, or when household debt/disposable income ratios are approaching 100 percent and still rising, simply trying to manage the situation may not be sufficient to avoid a crisis or to prevent contagion. When *both* public and private debt levels have entered the danger zone, it may be time for a much more radical approach.

The problem with the debt management approach when both public and private debt levels have been rising for decades, and when attempts to reverse these upward trends have met with only temporary and moderate success, is twofold: (1) Debt management may not be an adequate approach to the challenges of a sustained debt buildup that has infected the international community for many years. In these circumstances debt growth may have become self-generating. In other words, a vicious cycle may have been created, requiring a major shock to reverse course. (2) Debt management may not be adequate to address a major crisis, such as a global market crash or a prolonged recession which has, itself, been partly caused by trying merely to manage an ever-rising debt trend rather than reversing it. In these situations, stronger medicine is called for.

Crisis Management: When Things Turn Really Bad

In normal times, the *management* of debt, not the level of debt, is the primary focus of public and corporate officials. In debt crisis situations, it is the *crisis* itself which takes precedence. With rising debt levels, borrowers find themselves more and more exposed to changes in interest rates and exchange rates and also find their debts more difficult to measure as a result of innovations in financial markets. Increasingly complex new debt instruments—especially derivatives—which can result in debt exposure of several multiples of recorded debts, as we saw in the Long Range Capital Management case, now become commonplace. Debt, merely unruly in normal times, can create manias and panics in crisis periods when the unsoundness of previous lending is exposed. The longer the period of previous debt buildup, the greater the crisis is likely to be. Sharp and rapid revisions in investor perceptions are common in crisis situations, and contagion effects are multiplied. Excessive optimism often turns into excessive pessimism. What could be managed in good times now must be reformed, often radically.

It is an old Keynesian principle that sustained economic expansion requires continuously increasing contributions to the flow of income, according to Wynne Godley, emeritus professor of applied economics and fellow of King's College, Cambridge, and his colleague George McCarthy, an assistant professor of economics at Bard College.[92] During the growth of the welfare state, that stream of outside or exogenous funding was provided to the U.S. economy by federal expenditures based on deficit spending. As the welfare state was modified or cut back during the Reagan-Bush years, the required financial stimulus to the economy was provided by private expenditures based on household borrowing. This private credit boom, along with rising asset prices, pushed the current expansion to unexpected lengths.

Godley and McCarthy based their findings primarily on data through 1996. Since then, borrowing trends in the United States support their main thesis even more graphically, as Table 6.2 shows. Since 1993, the federal government has cut back its net borrowing, from $256 billion annually in 1993 to a *minus* $137 billion in the third quarter of 1998. Surprisingly, when the government finally decided to balance its accounts, total borrowing did not decline; it rose dramatically. Household debt more than doubled in those years of declining federal borrowing, and corporate debt exploded from $52 billion in 1993 to $405 billion in 1998. Growing household and corporate debt more than made up the difference in declining federal borrowing. The total debt increase in 1998 is even more striking, since U.S. household financial assets, minus mutual funds and corporate equities, have been falling since 1996; and the year-to-year percentage change in U.S. corporate after-tax profits has been declining since 1995.[93] Truly, rising *private* debt has been the economic stimulus for the U.S. economy in the 1990s, just as rising *public* debt was the catalyst in the 1980s. By early 1999, the American economy may have entered the period that Hyman Minsky describes as "financial fragility," as outlined above.

The S&P 500 price/earnings index reached 32 in late January 1999, the highest level in at least forty years and more than double the average value since 1959.[94] According to the President's Council of Economic Advisors, there has been "a substantial fall in the perceived riskiness of U.S. financial assets."[95] Many believe that shares are overvalued in America. Because consumers have used their newfound paper wealth to go on a consumption binge and corporations have used *their* newfound wealth to go on an investment binge (double the average of previous expansions), the U.S. economy is vulnerable to a collapse. What might trigger the collapse? The *Economist* thinks a reversal in the near-vertical climb of Internet share prices might provide the catalyst. "Just as tulips only became truly manic when ordinary people started trading bulbs in Dutch taverns," write the editors, "so the trebling of Internet values since September [1998] has been accompanied by a surge of trading among people unskilled in the art of valuation and unburnt by past losses. All this is likely to reverse with brutal rapidity."[96] There is now a serious possibility that the U.S. economy could go abruptly into reverse, although virtually no one is predicting that this will happen.[97] Household savings have disappeared, household debt as a percentage of disposable income is the highest it has ever been, and corporate debt as a percentage of GDP is also the highest it has been in recent decades. Moreover, total taxes as a percentage of income are the highest ever, thus making further tax increases very unlikely. Household capacity to fund this level of indebtedness has not increased much. Real compensation per hour in the United States has not increased since 1992, and the median net worth of American families where the head of the family is between the ages of thirty-five and sixty-five has actually fallen since 1989.[98] Much of the increase in household net wealth is based on the rising values of equity funds, especially mutual funds, which are largely dependent on a strong stock market. Since most households hold stock in some form, the rapid rise in the stock market has made them feel good. This paper wealth could evaporate very rapidly in a sustained market decline, but the unprecedentedly high levels of debt would remain. This is not a situation that anybody would want to be in.

Table 6.2

Total Net Borrowing by U.S. Domestic, Nonfinancial Sectors:
Households, Corporations, and the Federal Government, 1993–1998
(in billions of dollars)

Year	Total[a]	Households	Corporations	Federal government
1993	588	208	52	256
1994	527	311	143	156
1995	700	344	237	144
1996	727	370	171	145
1997	770	356	265	23
1998[b]	931	473	405	−137

Source: Federal Reserve Bulletin, January 1999, p. A37.
[a]Total includes all sectors, not just the three listed here.
[b]Third quarter data.

Alan Greenspan has publicly criticized the White House's rosy estimates for budget surpluses in the coming years. Greenspan has also compared the internet stock market mania of January 1999 to buying a lottery
ticket, and has compared investing in stocks at those valuations to gambling.[99] I am not inclined to read these statements as idle chatter. The
American stock market rose faster and further than all the other markets
in the G–7 in the 1990s by a wide margin. If these markets have now
reached bubble proportions, as I believe they have, then American equities may fall the fastest and the furthest when the bubbles burst. If that
happens, either government expenditures must rise or taxes must be cut
to achieve the necessary and continuing stimulus the system needs to
prosper. Since neither tax increases nor massive spending cuts are likely,
a recession is likely if the market bubble bursts. This is in keeping with
the Fisher-Minsky-Kindleberger model that financial crises are an essential part of the upper turning point of the business cycle. The cycle
turns downward because of an excessive accumulation of debt during
the previous boom years. According to this thesis, the economy becomes
ever more fragile until something shocks the system and triggers a sell-
off of assets. A panic results which culminates in a market crash and recession follows.[100]

Perhaps the most likely shock to precipitate a debt crisis of major magnitude would be a stock market crash similar to Japan's 1990 crash. When
Japan's equity bubble burst, its market lost 50 percent of its peak value in
two years and had fallen more than 60 percent by the end of 1998. The U.S.

equity bubble, which began about the same time as the Japanese bubble did and has risen much higher and over a much longer period, could theoretically burst at any time for a variety of reasons. Unprecedented household and corporate debt levels, an unsustainable and rapidly growing current account deficit, zero household savings, a weakening dollar, and fragile financial markets worldwide—all make the United States increasingly vulnerable to adverse shocks. The Asian crisis of 1997–1998 revealed fundamental weaknesses in the debt structure of those countries, requiring profound reforms. Should a similar debt crisis emerge in the United States—or in other G–7 countries, for that matter—it is not unreasonable to expect that profound changes will be required there as well.

A very high and growing U.S. trade deficit acted as a safety valve in the past—importation of cheap goods helped to keep inflation low, while imports of capital helped to keep interest rates low. In such times, "irrational exuberance" is certainly a risk. If risk were to turn to reality, and the market crashed and stayed in the doldrums for several years—as it has done in Japan and as it has always done in the United States over the long term—what might be the best policy for addressing this debt crisis? What would be the best course of action should a crash cause income to fall? What if imports—which have tended to keep prices low—also fall, causing inflation to rise again? What if foreign capital—which has tended to compensate for our low savings—begins to flee, and interest rates therefore begin to rise again? Should American officials try to manage the debt crisis under these conditions? Or should government officials and the public generally take a much more radical approach? If a market decline turns into an economic decline—and if both last for several years—how should we pick up the pieces from the debt bomb explosion?

A precipitous drop in the stock market—even as much as 60 percent—does not *necessarily* require any counteraction from federal authorities. Falling and rising markets are simply part of the capitalist system and a necessary part of repricing risk. Even a market that goes down for several years, as it always has in the past in real terms, should not, by itself, be cause for alarm. Alan Greenspan, in December 1996, when the DJIA reached 6,437, uttered the most memorable phrase of his long career: "irrational exuberance." Two years later, when the market reached 9,600, almost 50 percent higher, it must be even more irrational, by Greenspan's reckoning. Although Greenspan no longer issues characterizations of the stock market—Vice Chair Alice Rivlin now has that role—it is reliably reported that both Greenspan and U.S. Secretary of the Treasury Robert Rubin are worried about the consequences of a market this high.[101] Were the market to fall, even dramatically (thus restoring some rationality by reducing the ratio of its capitalization to GDP, which was three times its long-term historical average in early 1999), and adjusting downward the price/earnings ratios (which reached twice the historical average by early 1999), such a dive could arguably be a good thing in the long run.[102] A falling market might also encourage people to transfer some of their wealth from equities to savings or government bonds, which could be a good thing in the long run as well. For example, in 1980, American households had about 29 percent of their financial assets in corporate bonds, mutual funds, and pension fund reserves; in 1997 that figure had risen to 56 percent.[103] That is a very high figure in a falling market. Moreover, mutual funds, which have grown from $135 billion in 1980 to $4,490 billion in 1997, are very likely overrated as a way to save for retirement if the market is falling, especially since these funds are not insured and generally are heavier in stocks than bonds.

There have been several relatively small debt crises that have caught the world's attention, but the crisis has not yet spread to a majority of the world's major nations. Except in Japan, major world markets have not crashed; depressions are not yet upon us. There is still time, therefore, to deal with the growing risk of a major debt crisis. Below are some new or at least relatively little-known approaches that would effectively address the current crisis.

First, a stock market drop of limited duration should be welcomed, not feared. Bubbles are an inherent part of the capitalist system, according to the Minsky-Kindleberger thesis, and they always burst sooner or later. Rationally, we should hope they burst sooner rather than later. Those who will be hurt the most when the market crashes are those who have risked the most and have made the greatest profits as the bubble grew. Few tears need be shed for them. More importantly, a sustained market drop may be the only sure way to end, or at least modify significantly, the fiscal illusion and excessive optimism that infects all bubble societies, once the bubble has reached a certain level. A sustained market drop—especially were it to last for several years and extend worldwide—would likely encourage people to think more in terms of historical cycles, and less about illusionary "new paradigms."

A deep and prolonged market crash would also likely change peoples thinking in other ways. Surely such an event would encourage people to save more and to do so in more secure ways. Household saving rates in Japan rose after the market crashed there, even though the rate of saving in Japan was already more than twice as high as it was in the United States.[104] Debt/equity ratios in manufacturing corporations in Japan also fell after the Japanese market crashed.[105] Perhaps American corporations would also reduce their debt, rather than simply rolling over their debt, as they have done in the past. After their market bubble burst in Japan, credit tightened, and the Japanese became more cautious in their patterns of consumption. Pressure was put on the banks to get their house in order. The Japanese are clearly not out of the woods yet, and their equity bubble before their crash was smaller by far than the American bubble is currently. Surely this should give Americans some pause. Rather than chastising the Japanese for not being more like Americans in their spending habits, Americans ought to be focusing on how effectively the Japanese handled the bursting of their equity bubble and what Americans can learn from that experience.

Second, to really defuse the global debt bomb would require a profound change in the way the world views credit and debt. Since ever-growing debt gradually enfeebles our sensitivities to the normal risks of debt and makes us think that we are richer than we really are, people need to experience something that will reestablish the concept of natural limits. All events have their due measure; all have boundary limits, seen or unseen. Over the years, excessive debt can detach the normal connections between cause and effect. As Pope said, "shallow draughts intoxicate the brain;" constant overdrafts smothered by yet another dose of credit can numb the mind. Debt—once, like vice, a "monster of frightful mien"—becomes just a pussycat at the Jellicle Ball.

Here is where Minsky's and Kindleberger's insights are most useful. Combining economics with history, these economists show how debt crises develop and, more importantly, how they solve themselves—minor disturbances through a lender of last resort and major ones, by burning themselves out, since no organization extant is capable of solving a major fiscal problem in a G–7 nation. The defusing of the global debt bomb is more a historical than an economic or a political process. As we have tried to demonstrate in the previous chapters, it begins by recognizing "the fragility of the monetary system and its propensity to disaster"; it attaches great importance to the role of rapidly increasing debt, which eventually results in a boom.[106] The boom—energized in the United States by *public* debt in the 1980s and *private* debt in the 1990s—inevitably generates euphoria and the urge to speculate, eventually creating a bubble. At the top of the market (perhaps close to where we are now), there is volatility and hesitation. Then something unforeseen happens. There is a rush to liquidity, and the bubble pops. Markets crash despite the best efforts of economists; governments falter despite the best intentions of politicians.

Each debt bubble carries the seeds of its own destruction. There is no equilibrium; there are only cycles. Those who ride highest on the previous debt crest often suffer the most when that debt wave crashes. Few claim to understand how this process really works; no one claims to be able to predict it. Experience is our only guide, but experience is incommensurable and speaks with many voices. And so we "muddle through," waiting our turn for our own experience to tell us where life's financial boundaries are. No one can predict, of course, when or how such a message may be transmitted. But we can rest assured that the indomitable and inexorable cycles of history will certainly produce some event sufficiently powerful to redress the excesses and delusions of our generation, just as they have in generations past.

Notes

Chapter 1. An Introduction to the Debt Culture

1. Mortimer B. Zuckerman, "The Second American Century," *Foreign Affairs*, May/ June 1998, pp. 27–28.

2. Rudi Dornbusch, "Growth Forever," *Wall Street Journal*, July 30, 1998, p. A20.

3. James Grant, "The Coming Bust," *Wall Street Journal*, August 28, 1998, p. A20.

4. Bernard Wysocki Jr., "No Problem?" *Wall Street Journal*, September 18, 1999, p. R22.

5. Vito Tanzi and Domenico Fanizza, "Fiscal Deficit and Public Debt in Industrial Countries, 1970–1994," pp. 238–39.

6. Table, *Economist*, April 25, 1995, p. 123.

7. Keith M. Carlson, "On the Macroeconomics of Private Debt," pp. 53–66.

8. The household debt/savings ratios are published monthly in the *Federal Reserve Bulletin*; for corporate debt/equity ratios, see E.P. Davis, *Debt, Financial Fragility, and Systemic Risk*, p. 34.

9. IMF, *World Economic Outlook*, May 1995, ch. 5.

10. For this development in the United States, see David M. Tucker, *The Decline of Thrift in America*; and IMF, "Savings in a Growing World Economy," *World Economic Outlook*, May 1995, ch. 5.

11. IMF, *World Economic Outlook*, May 1998, p. 214.

12. Ibid., Interim Assessment, January 1993, ch. 2.

13. *Economist*, October 24, 1998, p. 116.

14. IMF, *World Economic Outlook*, May 1998, p. 69.

15. Many scholars and experienced market participants are beginning to predict a substantial decline in stock prices over the next several years. See, for example, John H. Campbell and Robert J. Shiller, "Valuation Ratios and Long-Run Stock Market Outlook," p. 11. For the views of a major market participant, see George Soros, *The Crisis of Global Capitalism*. The *Economist* has long argued that U.S. shares in general are overvalued.

16. "Profits of Doom," *Economist*, January 2, 1999, p. 66.

17. Alan Murray, "U.S. Oasis Is Hot Topic in Snowy Swiss Alps," *Wall Street Journal*, February 1, 1999, p. A1.

18. "America's Bubble Economy," *Economist*, April 18, 1998, pp. 15–16; "The Central Banker as God," *Economist*, November 14, 1998, pp. 23–25.

19. U.S. Bureau of the Census, *Statistical Abstract of the United States: 1998*, p. 513.

20. Ibid., p. 515.

21. Tanzi and Fanizza, "Fiscal Deficit and Public Debt," pp. 238–39.

22. Davis, *Debt, Financial Fragility, and Systemic Risk*, p. 35.

23. IMF, *World Economic Outlook*, May 1992, p. 50.

24. Ibid., October 1998, p. 94.

25. Davis, *Debt, Financial Fragility, and Systemic Risk*, p. 75.

26. Adam Smith, in *The Theory of Moral Sentiments*, quoted in Charles Kindleberger, *Manias, Panics, and Crashes*, p. 2.

27. U.S. OMB, *Budget of the United States Government, Fiscal Year 1999*, p. 10.

28. Adjusted for inflation, defense outlays were one-third less in the United States in 1997 than they were in 1990. The number of active-duty military has also been cut by about one-third. But future defense expenditures are scheduled to rise modestly.

29. See the Federal Reserve Board, "Monetary Policy Report to the Congress, February 24, 1998," *Federal Reserve Bulletin*, March 1998, pp. 155, 163.

30. The pressures of demographics and rising health-care costs will become severe in just a few years, according to the CBO, *Long-Term Budgetary Pressures and Policy Options*. The dates of the crisis vary according to which study one consults, but the FY 1999 budget of the United States puts the onset of fiscal problems at 2010 for Medicare and 2012 for Social Security.

31. See, for example, CBO, *Long-Term Budgetary Pressures and Policy Options*; Alan J. Auerbach, "Quantifying the Current U.S. Fiscal Imbalance," pp. 387–98; and Guillermo Calvo and Mervyn King, *The Debt Burden and Its Consequences for Monetary Policy*. Perhaps the foremost long-term advocate of paying down the public debt in the United States is Alan Greenspan. President Bill Clinton formally subscribed to this position in his FY 2000 budget presentation in February 1999.

32. Empirically, the impact of deficits on interest rates is mixed, as are the data on the impact on balance of payments. The appropriate rate of savings is also much contested, but growing public debt does appear to increase current consumption relative to saving and tends to shift lifetime consumption from future to current generations. For an extended discussion of these issues, see Daniel Shaviro, *Do Deficits Matter?* esp. ch. 4. For a review of the literature, see IMF, *World Economic Outlook*, May 1996, ch. 3.

33. IMF, *World Economic Outlook*, May 1998, p. 72.

34. See the review of Peter Hartcher's *The Ministry*, in *Economist*, April 18, 1998, p. 9.

35. See "America Bubbles Over," *Economist*, April 18, 1998, pp. 15, 67; Greg Ip and Aaron Tucchetti, "For Thousands of Stocks, Bear Market Is Here," *Wall Street Journal*, July 30, 1998, p. C1; Louis Uchitelle, "The Joint Is Still Jumping, but the Floor Is Shaking," *New York Times*, January 3, 1999, p. BU-4; "Why Internet Shares Will Fall," *Economist*, January 30, 1999, pp. 17–18; "The World Economy," *Economist*, February 20, 1999, pp. 19–22; John H. Campbell and Robert J. Shiller, "Valuation Ratios and Long-Run Stock Market Outlook."

36. "America Bubbles Over," *Economist*, April 18, 1998, p. 67.

37. "Shareholdings," *Economist*, September 19, 1998, p. 125.

38. George Soros, *The Crisis of Global Capitalism*, ch. 7.

39. Paul Krugman, "America the Boastful," pp. 32–45.

40. Federal Reserve Board, "Monetary Policy Report to the Congress," pp. 155–73.

41. IMF, *World Economic Outlook*, October 1998, p. 19.

42. Wynne Godley and George McCarthy, "Fiscal Policy Will Matter," pp. 52–58.

43. IMF, *World Economic Outlook*, May 1996, pp. 44–62.

44. See especially, ch. 2.

45. IMF, *World Economic Outlook*, October 1998, p. 94.

46. U.S. Bureau of the Census, *Statistical Abstract: 1998*, p. 566.

47. As quoted in Kindleberger, *Manias, Panics, and Crashes*, p. 66.

48. As quoted in ibid., p. 160.

49. For a highly useful distillation of Minsky's model, see Charles J. Whalen, "Money-Manager Capitalism and the End of Shared Prosperity," 517–23; see also Kindleberger, *Manias, Panics, and Crashes*.

50. Whalen, "Money-Manager Capitalism," p. 521.

51. As quoted in Herbert Sloan, *Principle and Interest*, p. 202.

52. As quoted in ibid., p. 104.

53. This pattern is the opposite of what generally causes exceptionally good years in the market. See Martin S. Fridson, *It Was a Very Good Year*, pp. 221–27.

54. There is an extraordinary consistency in this cycle of stock market bubbles in the hundred-year history of the Dow Jones Industrial Average (DJIA), once nominal prices are converted to real prices. See figure 1.2.

55. IMF, "Financial Crises: Characteristics and Indicators of Vulnerability," *World Economic Outlook*, May 1998, pp. 74–97.

56. Ibid., p. 81.

57. Ibid., p. 96.

58. Share prices and money supply data are from the data sheets of the *Economist*, May 2, 1998, p. 97.

59. Charles Kindleberger, interviewed by *Challenge*, p. 21.

60. Compare the two charts in "Financial Indicators," *Economist*, September 19, 1998, p. 125, and January 30, 1999, p. 105.

61. Most notably Mortimer B. Zuckerman, "a Second American Century," 18–31. For the mainstream view see Victor Zarnowitz, "Theory and History Behind Business Cycles: Are the 1990s the Onset of a Golden Age?" *Journal of Economic Perspectives*, 13 (Spring 1999), pp. 69–90.

62. Campbell and Shiller, "Valuation Ratios," p. 24, forecast a substantial decline in stock prices in the United States over the next ten years.

63. For an excellent analysis of global stock markets over the long term see Philippe Jorson and William N. Goetzmann, "Global Stock Markets in the Twentieth Century," *Journal of Finance*, LIV (June 1999), pp. 953–980.

64. Anne O. Krueger, "Whither the World Bank and the IMF?"

65. Ibid., p. 2014.

66. See "A Lender of Last Resort" (editorial), *Wall Street Journal*, October 29, 1998, A22; the *Journal* has been critical of the IMF for some time.

67. Charles Kindleberger, *The World Economy and National Finance in Historical Perspective*, p. 37.

68. A similar minor debt crisis occurred in the United States and the United Kingdom during the recession of the early 1990s. See IMF, *World Economic Outlook*, May 1992, Annex I.

69. See James Grant, *The Trouble with Prosperity*.

70. For an excellent analysis of this problem, see Paul Krugman, "The Return of Depression Economics," pp. 56–74.

Chapter 2. The Global Debt Picture

1. C. Eugene Steuerle and Masahiro Kawai, eds., *The New World Fiscal Order*. This excellent volume focuses on the interrelationships between fiscal policy and demography, our aging population, prior governmental commitments, and savings and investment.

2. Public debt held by the public was $3.8 trillion in 1998. The *burden* of public debt

in the United States was, of course, much less in the United States than, for example, in Italy and Belgium, measured as a ratio of public debt to GDP. Total credit market debt (which includes all forms of debt) for the United States was $22 trillion in 1998, or 251 percent of GDP. See, for example, the appendix in any 1998 issue of the monthly *Federal Reserve Bulletin*.

3. Edward M. Graham and Paul R. Krugman, *Foreign Direct Investment in the United States*, p. 24.

4. The OECD, headquartered in Paris, gathers data regularly on about twenty-six countries, including data on debt.

5. See *Economic Report of the President, 1994*, ch. 1; and *Economic Report of the President, 1997*, ch. 7. For a world perspective, see OECD, *Economic Outlook*, June issues; and IMF, *World Economic Outlook*, May and October issues. For a provocative and insightful analysis of global problems generally, see William Greider, *One World, Ready or Not*.

6. For an excellent analysis of these fiscal crises, see Martin Feldstein, ed., *The Risk of Economic Crisis*.

7. U.S. Bureau of the Census, *Statistical Abstract of the United States: 1997*, p. 506. For the most recent data, see the current issue of the *Federal Reserve Bulletin*.

8. David Asher, "Japan Can't Rescue Asia," *Wall Street Journal*, November 23, 1998, p. A22. For private debt, see especially the excellent work of E.P. Davis in *Debt, Financial Fragility, and Systemic Risk*. For public debt trends, see Steuerle and Kawai, *The New World Fiscal Order*.

9. Davis, *Debt, Financial Fragility, and Systemic Risk*, pp. 197 ff.

10. U.S. Bureau of the Census, *Historical Statistics of the United States, Colonial Times to 1970*, Bicentennial Edition, part 2, ch. 10. For more recent years, see 1996 *U.S. Statistical Abstract*, Flow of Funds Account, sect. 16.

11. The most recent author to take this view for the United States is Daniel Shaviro in his excellent analysis, *Do Deficits Matter?* p. 308. The IMF has taken the same position for all the advanced countries in its *World Economic Outlook, May 1996*, ch. 3. Also useful is Francis X. Cavanaugh, *The Truth About the National Debt*. For a recent contrary view, see James Medoff and Andrew Harless, in *The Indebted Society*, who argue for increasing taxes on the rich rather than reducing the amount of public debt.

12. Published monthly in the *Federal Reserve Bulletin* under "Flow of Funds."

13. OECD, *Economic Outlook*, June 1998, Appendix; and IMF, *World Economic Outlook*, May 1998, pp. 19, 29.

14. IMF, *World Economic Outlook*, Interim Assessment, January 1993, pp. 31–37.

15. "Consumer Debt," *CQ Researcher* (pamphlet), November 15, 1996.

16. Ibid., p. 1012.

17. IMF, *World Economic Outlook*, May 1996, ch. 4, "Fiscal Policy Issues in Developing Countries," p. 63.

18. World Bank, *World Debt Tables, 1993–1994*; and Harold Laser, "The Debt Won't Be Paid," p. 3.

19. Ibid., p. 65.

20. At this writing, Canada shows the most promise among the G–7 nations of solving its public deficit problem, at least temporarily. The IMF forecast a surplus for Canada beginning in 1997 (excluding social security transactions), and a surplus for the United States beginning in 1998. Both forecasts were accurate, with additional surpluses predicted until 2003. The last G–7 country to have a surplus in its general government balance was Japan in 1992; before that, it was the United Kingdom in 1989.

21. The IMF believes that public budget deficits in almost all industrial countries have become too large for sustainability, especially when invisible debt is taken into

account. *World Economic Outlook*, May 1996, p. 61. Shaviro, in *Do Deficits Matter?* p. 150, says the problem of policy sustainability is quite acute. Cavanaugh, in *The Truth About the National Debt*, p. 62, says the federal budget will never be balanced unless interest is excluded but calls for the immediate balance in the program budget (spending minus interest costs). A contrary view is put forward by James Medoff and Andrew Harless in *The Indebted Society*. They call for a larger federal deficit and increased taxes on the wealthy. Robert Eisner, *The Misunderstood Economy*, ch. 5, also says federal deficits are well within prudent limits; but see Shaviro's critique, *Do Deficits Matter?* pp. 113–19. Regarding the sustainability of private debt levels, E.P. Davis, *Debt, Financial Fragility, and Systematic Risk*, is the primary authority, albeit somewhat dated. His overall view is that a degree of vigilance remains appropriate (p. 277).

22. U.S. OMB, *Budget of the United States Government: Analytical Perspectives, Fiscal Year 1997*, p. 198.

23. Cavanaugh, *The Truth About the National Debt*, ch. 7.

24. The best account of this fiasco is Lawrence J. White, *The S&L Debacle*.

25. Cavanaugh, *The Truth About the National Debt*, p. 92.

26. "The World Economic Survey," *Economist*, October 7, 1995, p. 23.

27. IMF, *World Economic Outlook*, May 1998, p. 200.

28. Ibid., 1996, ch. 3.

29. Ibid., p. 29. For the technical aspects behind the 60 percent figure, see Guglielmo Maria Caporale, "Fiscal Solvency in Europe," p. 69.

30. Shaviro, *Do Deficits Matter?* p. 305.

31. Ibid., ch. 5; and Peter Peterson, *Will America Grow Up Before It Grows Old?* ch. 6.

32. Garry J. Schinasi and Monica Hargraves, "'Boom and Bust' in Asset Markets in the 1980s."

33. IMF, *World Economic Outlook*, October 1993, p. 60.

34. OECD, *Economic Outlook*, June 1994, p. A62.

35. IMF, *World Economic Outlook*, May 1995, p. 24.

36. For an excellent analysis, see Lewis Evans et al., "Economic Reform in New Zealand, 1984–95," pp. 1856–84.

37. "Kiwis Turn Sour," *Economist*, October 19, 1996, p. 19.

38. "Two Economies in Ireland," *Economist*, May 17, 1997, p. 22.

39. Vito Tanzi and Domenico Fanizza, "Fiscal Deficit and Public Debt in Industrial Countries, 1970–1994," pp. 229–31.

40. Quoted in ibid., p. 148.

41. For the United States, see Martin Feldstein, ed., *The Risk of Economic Crisis*; and Martin H. Wolfson, *Financial Crises*. For Canada, see Richard G. Harris, ed., *Deficits and Debt in the Canadian Economy*. For the rest of the G–7, see Davis, *Debt, Financial Fragility, and Systemic Risk*; and recent issues of IMF, *World Economic Outlook*, and OECD, *Economic Outlook*.

42. For a typical example, see C. Alan Garner, "Can Measures of the Consumer Debt Burden Reliably Predict an Economic Slowdown?" p. 63.

43. Steven Weber, "The End of the Business Cycle?" p. 65.

44. For an extended discussion, see Michael Bordo, ed., *Financial Crises*, vol. 1.

45. Shaviro, *Do Deficits Matter?* p. 309.

46. Greider, *One World*, pp. 11–26.

47. For the shift to consumerism in the 1920s, see President's Research Committee on *Recent Social Trends in the United States*, ch. 17. This outstanding volume of more than 1,500 pages has no listed editor but includes essays by more than a score of experts. For a longer view, see David M. Tucker, *The Decline of Thrift in America*.

48. Herbert Stein, *The Fiscal Revolution in America*, p. 458.

49. Ron Chernow, *The House of Morgan*, esp. ch. 34. This attitude was perhaps most concentrated in the savings and loan sector, and was well described by Martin Mayer in *The Greatest-Ever Bank Robbery*.

50. James Grant, *The Trouble with Prosperity*, p. 245.

51. Chernow, in *The House of Morgan*, coined this phrase and dated the beginning of the attitude he describes to 1948 (see p. 483).

52. Tucker, *The Decline of Thrift*, p. 137.

53. As quoted by Tucker, ibid.

54. Andrew Hacker, *Money*, p. 86.

55. Peter G. Peterson, "Entitlement Reform," pp. 39, 44.

56. Stein, *The Fiscal Revolution in America*, p. 580.

57. John H. Makin and Norman J. Ornstein, *Debt and Taxes*, p. 282.

58. Lester R. Brown et al., *State of the World, 1991*, p. 8.

Chapter 3. The Nature of Debt

1. James Grant, *Money of the Mind*, p. 5.

2. See, for example, Proverbs 21:20, Matthew 25:1–12, 1 Timothy 6:10.

3. Herbert E. Sloan, *Principle and Interest*, p. 3.

4. Ibid., ch. 1.

5. Quoted in ibid., p. 329, note 78.

6. Andrew Carnegie, *The Empire of Business*, 3.

7. Frederick Martin Townsend, *Things I Remember*, pp. 238–43.

8. See President's Research Committee on Social Trends, *Recent Social Trends in the United States*, p. 857. Also useful is Moses Rischin, ed., *The American Gospel of Success*.

9. Robert Lynd, quoted in President's Research Committee, *Recent Social Trends*, p. 867.

10. R.H. Tawney, *The Acquisitive Society*, esp. pp. 28–32.

11. David M. Tucker, *The Decline of Thrift in America*; and James Medoff and Andrew Harless, *The Indebted Society*.

12. U.S. Bureau of the Census, *Historical Statistics of the United States*, p. 989.

13. Ron Chernow, *The House of Morgan*, esp. pp. 12, 36.

14. No one then or since has captured this spirit better than Thorstein Veblen in *The Theory of the Leisure Class: An Economic Study of Institutions* (1899).

15. See Richard H. Fink and Jack C. High, eds., *A Nation in Debt*, especially James Buchanan's "The Moral Dimension of Debt Financing," pp. 102–7.

16. From "Of Public Debt," by Adam Smith reprinted in Fink and High, pp. 1–34. Quote is on p. 19.

17. Herbert Stein, *The Fiscal Revolution in America*, p. 458.

18. For an excellent and readable discussion on this point, see Arthur Benavie, *Deficit Hysteria*, ch. 1.

19. For an extended analysis on this point, see William Greider, *One World, Ready or Not*, ch. 13.

20. "Analysis of Economic and Financial Conditions," internal newsletter, published by Hoisington Investment Management Co., Austin, TX, February 1997. This newsletter analyzes data from the Federal Reserve Board, Bureau of Economic Analysis, third quarter, 1996.

21. U.S. OMB, *Budget of the United States Government: Analytical Perspectives*, *Fiscal Year 1997*, p. 198.

22. "What Did It Get Us?" *Wall Street Journal*, January 20, 1999, p. A22.

23. "Lender Without Limit," *Economist*, October 10, 1998, p. 85.

24. IMF, *World Economic Outlook*, October 1998, p. 92.

25. Benavie, in *Deficit Hysteria*, pp. 1–12, asserts that morality has no role whatsoever in public budgeting.

26. For a lengthy discussion, see Mario Blejer and Adrienne Cheasty, "The Measurement of Fiscal Deficits," p. 1644. For a good overview of the complexities of private debt, see Keith Carlson, "On the Macroeconomics of Private Debt," p. 53. For a good though dated study that integrates both public and private debt, see Committee on Economic Policy, "Debt: Public and Private."

27. Most notably Robert Eisner, *The Misunderstood Economy*, esp. ch. 5.

28. IMF, *World Economic Outlook*, October 1993, p. 57. Net public debt for the United States 1992 was 54 percent of GDP; net total debt was 140 percent of GDP. For the United Kingdom, those figures were 29 percent and 160 percent, and for Japan, 4 percent and 220 percent. Japan has the most heavily indebted private sector, followed by Switzerland, Sweden, Germany, Britain, Holland, and the United States. See Statistics Sheet, *Economist*, October 28, 1995, p. 123.

29. Robert Eisner, "Which Budget Deficit?" p. 138.

30. A particularly balanced and sophisticated recent study on this point is IMF, "Fiscal Challenges Facing Industrial Countries," *World Economic Outlook*, May 1996, ch. 3.

31. (Boston: Little, Brown & Co., 1992), p. 178.

32. Buchanan's most interesting book, from a theoretical perspective, is arguably *Democracy in Deficit*, written with Richard Wagner.

33. For an excellent analysis of Buchanan's and others' theories of deficit spending, see Sung Deuk Hahm, Mark L. Kamlet, and David C. Mowery, "Influences on Deficit Spending," p. 183.

34. See Eisner, "Is the Deficit a Friendly Giant After All?" pp. 140–48.

35. Virtually all the decline in savings in the major industrial nations since the 1970s took place in the public sector. See IMF, "Saving in a Growing World Economy," *World Economic Outlook*, May 1995, pp. 67–89.

36. Ibid., p. 88.

37. IMF, *World Economic Outlook*, October 1993, p. 61.

38. Peter G. Peterson, "Entitlement Reform," p. 39.

39. Ibid., *Facing Up*, pp. 321–85.

40. A falling birth rate and rising unemployment—which puts Germany's social security system at grave risk—is a greater concern in Germany than debt. See Ifo Institute for Economic Research and Sakura Institute of Research, *A Comparative Analysis of Japanese and German Economic Success*, ch. 8.

41. Stein, *The Fiscal Revolution in America*, p. 580.

42. OECD, *Economic Surveys: Italy, Paris*, January, 1995, p. 41.

43. Ibid., *Economic Outlook*, December 1997, p. A63.

44. Barry Bosworth, Gary Burtless, and John Sabelhous, "The Decline in Saving: Evidence from Household Surveys," *Brookings Papers on Economic Activity*, 1991, vol. 1, pp. 183–199. For a longer view, see Tucker, *The Decline of Thrift in America*.

45. IMF, *World Economic Outlook*, May 1995, p. 88.

46. U.S. Bureau of the Census, *State Government Finances: 1992*, p. 34.

47. See James Hines, *Constitutional Restrictions Against State Debt*.

48. For an extensive analysis of the whole entitlement system, see Peterson, *Facing Up*. The three to five times figure comes from Peterson, "Entitlement Reform," p. 44.

49. Vito Tanzi and Domenico Fanizza, "Fiscal Deficit and Public Debt in Industrial Countries, 1970–1994," pp. 228–31.

50. IMF, *World Economic Outlook*, May 1996, p. 41.

51. Quoted in Walter Eltis, "Financial Crises and Credit Cycles," p. 48.

52. Hahm, Kamlet, and Mowery, "Influences on Deficit Spending."

53. An excellent analysis of this problem is Martin Feldstein, ed., *The Risk of Economic Crisis.*

54. For an excellent discussion of derivatives, see "A Survey of Corporate Risk Management," *Economist*, February 10, 1996, Survey, pp. 1–22. On the dangers of derivatives, see Philippe Jorion, *Big Bets Gone Bad*, ch. 16.

55. Chernow, *House of Morgan*, part 3; James Grant, *The Trouble with Prosperity*, esp. ch. 5.

56. Quoted in Paul Zachary, "Global Growth Attains a New, Higher Level That Could Be Lasting," *Wall Street Journal*, March 13, 1997, p. A1.

57. Louis Uchitelle, "The Joint Is Still Jumping, but the Floor Is Shaking," *New York Times*, January 3, 1999, p. BU-4.

58. Blejer and Cheasty, "The Measurement of Fiscal Deficits," p. 1644.

59. For a good discussion of the usual errors of deficit and debt definitions, see Eisner, *The Misunderstood Economy*, ch. 5.

60. For an overview of these derivatives, see "A Survey of Corporate Risk Management," fn. 53.

61. Robert Eisner et al., "Is the Deficit a Friendly Giant After All?" p. 93.

62. John J. Seater, "Ricardian Equivalence," pp. 142–90.

63. According to a special IMF issue on fiscal policy, "the preponderance of research" clearly suggests that, while there is some tendency for private savers to compensate for reduced public-sector saving, "the offset is far from complete." IMF, *World Economic Outlook*, May 1996, p. 50.

64. Chernow, *House of Morgan*, p. xvii. See esp. ch. 35.

65. Charles Kindleberger, *Manias, Panics, and Crashes.* See also James Grant, *Money of the Mind*; and Robert Sobel, *Panic on Wall Street.*

66. IMF, *World Economic Outlook*, October 1996, p. 204.

67. *Economic Report of the President, 1997*, p. 251.

68. See, for example, Benjamin Friedman's "U.S. Fiscal Policy in the 1980s," p. 149. See also Paul Volker, "Facing Up to the Twin Deficits," p. 154.

69. See Paul Kennedy, *The Rise and Fall of the Great Powers*; and Paul Kennedy, *Preparing for the Twenty-First Century*, esp. ch. 13.

70. Benjamin M. Friedman, *Day of Reckoning*, p. 158.

71. IMF, *World Economic Outlook*, October 1996, p. 1.

72. For an analysis of this 60 percent, see Guglielmo Caporale, "Fiscal Solvency in Europe," p. 69.

73. IMF, *World Economic Outlook*, May 1996, p. 50.

74. Tim Congdon, *The Debt Threat*, p. 206.

75. IMF, *World Economic Outlook*, May 1995, p. 86.

76. Ibid., p. 86. This is Blanchard's model, for those familiar with this methodology. See O.J. Blanchard, "Suggestions for a New Set of Fiscal Indicators."

77. Statistics Sheet, *Economist*, October 28, 1995, p. 123.

78. OECD, *Economic Outlook*, December 1997, p. A29.

79. See also Peter G. Peterson, "Entitlement Reform," p. 39.

80. Lester Thurow, *The Future of Capitalism*, p. 97.

81. Peter G. Peterson, *Facing Up*, p. 106.

82. Thurow, *The Future of Capitalism*, p. 98.

83. Herbert Stein, *The Fiscal Revolution in America*, esp. the final chapter.

84. U.S. Bureau of the Census, *Statistical Abstract of the United States: 1995*, p. 399.

85. Federal Reserve Board, *Federal Reserve Bulletin*, July 1994, p. 571.

86. Ibid.

87. U.S. Bureau of the Census, *State Government Finances: 1992.*

88. Ibid., p. 34.

89. James Poterba, "Budget Institutions and Fiscal Policy in the U.S. States," pp. 395, 399.

90. Simply stated, the Ricardian equivalence theorem denies that an increase in the federal deficit leads to an increase in the GDP, a rise in interest rates, or a crowding out of private investment, because private citizens, realizing that future taxes will be increased to cover the deficit, take measures to protect themselves from this eventuality.

91. See, for example, Eisner, *The Misunderstood Economy.*

92. For an extensive analysis of these correlations in thirty-two countries, see Georgios Karras, "Macroeconomic Effects of Budget Deficits," p. 190.

93. (New York: Basic Books, 1999).

94. Ibid., p. xiii.

95. Statistical Sheet, *Economist*, July 8, 1995, p. 115.

96. IMF, *World Economic Outlook*, October 1993, p. 56.

97. Quoted in Richard H. Fink and Jack C. High, eds., *A Nation in Debt*, p. 16.

98. See Sloan, *Principle and Interest*, pp. 50–51.

99. U.S. OMB, *Budget . . . Fiscal Year 1999*, p. 31.

100. Peterson, *Facing Up*, p. 78.

101. See Stein, *The Fiscal Revolution in America*; James Buchanan et al., *Deficits*, esp. part 1; and Donald Stabile and Jeffrey Cantor, *The Public Debt of the United States.*

102. Buchanan began to challenge the "new or orthodoxy," for deficit spending in 1958 when he published *Public Principles of Public Debt* (Homewood, IL: Richard D. Irwin, 1958).

103. Harrie A.A. Verbon and F.A.A.M. Van Winden, eds., *The Political Economy of Government Debt*, ch. 1.

104. See esp. Walter Bagehot's introduction to *Lombard Street*, where he explains how familiarity blinds us to the nature of this system.

105. For an excellent overview of the issues in public debt crises, see Martin Feldstein, ed., *The Risk of Economic Crisis.* The most recent extended analysis is in IMF, *World Economic Outlook*, May 1996, in the special section on fiscal policy.

106. For a landmark study, see Blanchard, "Suggestions for a New Set of Fiscal Indicators."

107. "Housing Costs," *Economist*, May 28, 1999, p. 101.

108. Congdon, *The Debt Threat*, p. 2.

109. IMF, *World Economic Outlook*, May 1994, p. 44.

110. Peterson, *Facing Up*, p. 290.

111. (New York, Random House, 1993), esp. ch. 9.

112. Steuerle and Kawai, *The New World Fiscal Order*, esp. ch. 7; Paul Posner and Barbara Bovbjerg, "Deficit Reduction Around the World"; John H. Makin and Norman J. Ornstein, *Debt and Taxes*, part 5; and IMF, *World Economic Outlook*, May 1996, ch. 3; but see IMF *World Economic Outlook*, October 1998, pp. 26–28, for a more optimistic outlook.

113. Posner and Bovbjerg, "Deficit Reduction Around the World," p. 137.

114. Congdon, *The Debt Threat*, Appendix.

115. Robert J. Samuelson, *The Good Life and Its Discontents*, p. 39.

116. Jeffrey Madrick, *The End of Affluence*, p. 141. See also Donald Bartlett and James Steele, *America: What Went Wrong?* ch. 9.

117. Makin and Ornstein, *Debt and Taxes*, p. 276.

118. IMF, *World Economic Outlook*, May 1996, pp. 61–62; Steuerle and Kawai, *The New World Fiscal Order*, introduction; Richard Cebula, John Killingsworth, and Willie

J. Belton Jr., "Federal Government Budget Deficits and the Crowding Out of Investment in the United States," p. 168.

119. The best study on this subject is Frank Levy and Richard Murnane, "U.S. Earnings Levels and Earnings Inequality," pp. 1333–81.

120. IMF, "Lessons from Fiscal Consolidation Experiences," *World Economic Outlook*, May 1996, pp. 61–62; Posner and Bovbjerg, "Deficit Reduction Around the World," p. 135; "The Burdensome National Debt," *Economist*, February 10, 1996, pp. 68–69; and Stephen Moore, ed., *Restoring the Dream*. For a contrary view, see Wallace Peterson, *Silent Depression*.

121. Fritjof Capra in *The Turning Point* argues interestingly that debt is one intricate piece in a web of relationships, through which the whole system constantly renews itself in cycles.

Chapter 4. Private Debt

1. John Kenneth Galbraith, *A Short History of Financial Euphoria*, p. 12.

2. Charles Kindleberger, *The World Economy and National Finance in Historical Perspective*, p. 97.

3. Thomas J. Stanley and William D. Danko, *The Millionaire Next Door*, p. 2.

4. Andrew Hacker, *Money*, p. 86.

5. Ibid., p. 43.

6. Walter Bagehot, *Lombard Street*, p. 78.

7. Ibid., p. 162.

8. "Bubble Babble," *Economist*, December 5, 1998, p. 87.

9. Ibid., p. 90.

10. For an extended discussion of this problem, see David Thelen, "The Practice of American History," esp. part 2, "History and Students."

11. Richard F. Kohn, "History and the Culture Wars," p. 1063.

12. Steven Weber, "The End of the Business Cycle?" pp. 65–83; and Francis Fukuyama, "The End of History?" pp. 3–18.

13. Quoted by Jacob M. Schlesinger, an economics reporter for the *Wall Street Journal*, in *Wall Street Journal Almanac: 1999*, p. 117.

14. IMF, *World Economic Outlook October 1998*, p. 1.

15. Statistics Sheet, *Economist*, December 19, 1998, p. 149.

16. Ibid., December 5, 1998, p. 121.

17. Quoted by Schlesinger, *Wall Street Journal Almanac: 1999*, p. 117. Greenspan spoke on this issue at length: "Statement by Alan Greenspan, Chairman, Board of Governors of the Federal Reserve System Before the Committee on the Budget, U.S. Senate, September 23, 1998," p. 936.

18. Alan Greenspan's famous statement is carefully analyzed in "The Central Banker as God," *Economist*, November 14, 1998, pp. 23–25.

19. See IMF, *World Economic Outlook*, October 1998, chs. 1–4; George Soros, *The Crisis of Global Capitalism*; "America's Bubble Economy," *Economist*, April 18, 1998, p. 15; Daniel Yergin and Joseph Stanislaw, *The Commanding Heights*, esp. ch. 5; Susan George, *The Debt Boomerang*, on Third World debt; and Thomas J. Stanley and William D. Danko, *The Millionaire Next Door*, on personal debt.

20. OECD, *Economic Outlook*, December 1997, p. A29.

21. "Statement by Alan Greenspan, Chairman, Board of Governors of the Federal Reserve System, before the Committee on Banking and Financial Services, U.S. House of Representatives, January 30, 1998," pp. 186–90.

22. Ibid., p. 187.

23. IMF, *World Economic Outlook*, October 1998, pp. 102–6. For an extended analysis, see "Special Issue on the Asian Crisis," *Cambridge Journal of Economics.*

24. Ibid., p. 92.

25. The best account of the Korean debt crisis is William H. Overholt, "Korea: To the Market Via Socialism."

26. IMF, *World Economic Outlook, Interim Assessment*, January 1993, p. 35.

27. Ibid.

28. These data are most readily accessed in U.S. Bureau of the Census, *Statistical Abstract of the United States*, annually, in the Banking Section under "Flow of Funds." For greater detail, see the monthly *Federal Reserve Bulletin.*

29. For recent years, see "Summary of Credit Market Debt Outstanding," *Federal Reserve Bulletin*, November 1998, p. A40. For earlier years, see U.S. Bureau of the Census, *Historical Statistics of the United States, Colonial Times to 1970*, part 2, p. 973.

30. E.P. Davis, *Debt, Financial Fragility, and Systemic Risk*, pp. 35, 77.

31. For a similar but more recent analysis, see "Consumer Debt," *CQ Researcher*, November 15, 1996, pp. 1009–32.

32. Keith Carlson, "On the Macroeconomics of Private Debt," pp. 53, 58.

33. Davis, *Debt, Financial Fragility, and Systemic Risk*, p. 39.

34. IMF, *World Economic Outlook*, Interim Assessment, p. 36.

35. "Deeper in Debt," *Wall Street Journal Almanac: 1999*, p. 301.

36. See Benjamin Friedman, "New Directions in the Relation Between Public and Private Debt," pp. 397–403.

37. *Economic Report of the President, 1994*, p. 62.

38. Davis, *Debt, Financial Fragility, and Systemic Risk*, pp. 32–39.

39. Carlson, "On the Macroeconomics of Private Debt," p. 55.

40. *Economic Report of the President, 1994*, p. 61.

41. Fact Sheet, *Economist*, September 17, 1994, p. 117.

42. See Garry Schinasi and Monica Hargraves, "'Boom and Bust' in Asset Markets in the 1980s." For U.S. corporations, see especially U.S. Senate, Committee on Banking, Housing, and Urban Affairs, *Corporate Debt.*

43. Ibid.

44. U.S. Bureau of the Census, *Statistical Abstract of the United States: 1994*, p. 547.

45. Davis, *Debt, Financial Fragility, and Systemic Risk*, p. 59.

46. U.S. Bureau of the Census, *Statistical Abstract of the United States: 1997*, p. 557.

47. Davis, *Debt, Financial Fragility, and Systemic Risk*, p. 71.

48. Ibid., p. 72.

49. IMF, *World Economic Outlook*, October 1994, p. 153.

50. Ibid.

51. Davis, *Debt, Financial Fragility, and Systemic Risk*, pp. 34–35.

52. See Davis, *Debt, Financial Fragility, and Systemic Risk*, ch. 2. But Britain's continued long-term relative decline is troubling, as is its growing inequality, both regionally and in terms of income distribution.

53. IMF, *World Economic Outlook*, October 1998, p. 21.

54. A. Gary Shilling, *Deflation*, p. 194.

55. Peter G. Peterson, *Facing Up*, p. 342.

56. *Economic Report of the President, 1997*, p. 178.

57. Shilling, *Deflation*, p. 206.

58. Davis, *Debt, Financial Fragility, and Systemic Risk*, ch. 3.

59. *Economic Report of the President, 1998*, p. 66.

60. "Analysis of Economic and Financial Conditions" (internal newsletter), Hoisington Investment Management Co., Austin, TX, February 1997.

61. "Bankruptcy Filings," *Wall Street Journal Almanac: 1999*, p. 303.
62. Ibid.
63. *Economic Report of the President*, 1998, p. 74.
64. "Consumer Debt," p. 1014.
65. Peter S. Yoo, "Charging Up a Mountain of Debt," p. 3.
66. Ibid.
67. "Consumer Confidence Index," *Wall Street Journal Almanac: 1999*, p. 135.
68. Peter Gottschalk, "Inequality, Income Growth, and Mobility," p. 27.
69. U.S. Bureau of the Census, *Statistical Abstract of the United States: 1998*, p. 524.
70. Ibid., p. 523.
71. "Taking Credit," *Economist*, November 2, 1996, p. 75.
72. OECD, *Economic Outlook*, June 1993, p. 140.
73. U.S. Bureau of the Census, *Statistical Abstract: 1998*, p. 522.
74. Ibid., p. 521.
75. See Schinasi and Hargraves, "Boom or Bust," p. 1.
76. Ibid., p. 9.
77. See testimony of John P. LaWare, Federal Reserve Board of Governors, *Federal Reserve Bulletin*, July 1994, p. 581; and U.S Bureau of the Census, *Statistical Abstract: 1997*, p. 727.
78. U.S. Bureau of the Census, *Statistical Abstract: 1998*, p. 522.
79. Ibid., p. 728.
80. Davis, *Debt, Financial Fragility, and Systemic Risk*, 88.
81. James Grant captures this spirit well in *Money of the Mind*, esp. ch. 11. Also useful is David M. Tucker, *The Decline of Thrift in America*.

Chapter 5. Public Debt

1. Vito Tanzi and Domenico Fanizza. "Fiscal Deficit and Public Debt in Industrial Countries, 1970–1994," pp. 238–39; and IMF, *World Economic Outlook*, May 1997, p. 22.
2. For an overall view of the public debt problem see: CBO, *Long-Term Budgetary Pressures and Policy Options*, pp. xi–xxiv; Robert T. Golembiewski and Jack Rabin, eds. *Public Budgeting and Finance*; Robert Eisner, *The Misunderstood Economy*, pp. 89–119; Preston J. Miller and William Roberds, "How Little We Know About Deficit Policy Effects," pp. 2–10. The best single-volume study on deficit spending in the United States is Daniel Shaviro, *Do Deficits Matter?* The most readable book debunking the excessive concern for deficits by conservatives is Arthur Benavie, *Deficit Hysteria*. An excellent and authoritative view of deficits and debt in the modern industrial world is International Monetary Fund, "Fiscal Challenges Facing Industrial Countries," *World Economic Outlook*, May 1996, pp. 44–62.
3. IMF, *World Economic Outlook*, October 1997, p. 22.
4. See IMF, "Fiscal Challenges Facing Industrial Countries," pp. 44–62; Shaviro, *Do Deficits Matter?* p. 2; Francis X. Cavanaugh, *The Truth about the National Debt*, p. 2. Cavanaugh emphasizes undisciplined government spending more than the growing debt that results therefrom. For an agnostic view, see Miller and Roberds, "How Little We Know About Deficit Policy Effects," pp. 2–11. For the administration's view, see *Economic Report of the President, 1999*.
5. An excellent and current analysis of the aging problem is presented by Peter G. Peterson, "Gray Dawn," pp. 42–55.
6. See IMF, *World Economic Outlook*, May 1995, p. 68. Savings rates have fallen in *every* major industrial country except Japan.

7. Ibid.

8. "Fiscal Virtuosos," *Economist*, October 25, 1997, p. 36. Italy, the United States, and the United Kingdom are projected to reduce their public indebtedness in this period as well, but *only* if prosperity continues, if promised but not yet enacted cuts are in fact accomplished, and if further tax cuts are not initiated—a quite unlikely scenario.

9. IMF, *World Economic Outlook*, October 1998, p. 28.

10. Peterson, "Gray Dawn," p. 46.

11. See Joseph J. Cordes, "How Yesterday's Decisions Affect Today's Budget and Fiscal Options," p. 113. For the United States, see especially Cavanaugh, *The Truth About the National Debt*, ch. 10; and Shaviro, *Do Deficits Matter?* p. 2.

12. IMF, *World Economic Outlook*, May 1996, p. 55.

13. IMF assumptions for near-term deficit projections are spelled out in its *World Economic Outlook*, October 1998, pp. 26–27.

14. U.S. OMB, *Budget of the United States Government: Analytical Perspectives, Fiscal Year 1999*, p. 12.

15. This is not a fanciful idea and is supported by the CBO itself in *Long-Term Budgetary Pressures and Policy Options*, p. xvi.

16. Paul Posner and Barbara Bovbjerg, "Deficit Reduction Around the World," p. 137.

17. IMF, *World Economic Outlook*, May 1996, p. 46.

18. Ibid., p. 45.

19. Ibid., p. 46.

20. "What Economists Don't Know about Growth: Interview with Moses Abramovitz," *Challenge*, January–February 1991, pp. 81–91; Jeffrey Madrick, *The End of Affluence*; Frank Levy and Richard J. Murnane, "U.S. Earnings Levels and Earnings Inequality," pp. 1333–81.

21. See IMF, "Meeting the Challenges of Globalization in the Advanced Economies," *World Economic Outlook*, May 1997, pp. 45–71.

22. *Economic Report of the President, 1999*, p. 31.

23. For an excellent overview, see Peter Gottschalk, "Inequality, Income Growth, and Mobility."

24. James Buchanan and Richard Wagner, in *Democracy in Deficit*, say that this tendency is endemic to democracy and that the public is incapable of changing course.

25. Herbert Stein, *The Fiscal Revolution in America*, part 2.

26. See Shaviro, *Do Deficits Matter?* ch. 4.

27. C. Eugene Steuerle and Masahiro Kawai, "The New World Fiscal Order," p. 7.

28. John H. Makin and Norman J. Ornstein, *Debt and Taxes*, ch. 13.

29. Cordes, "How Yesterday's Decisions Affect Today's Budget and Fiscal Options," p. 112.

30. Toshihiro Ihori, "Prior Commitments, Sustainability, and Intergenerational Redistribution in Japan," pp. 117–34.

31. IMF, *World Economic Outlook*, May 1996, p. 47.

32. U.S. OMB, *Budget . . . Fiscal Year 1999*, p. 254.

33. Benavie, *Deficit Hysteria*, p. 9.

34. Ibid., ch. 9.

35. For a sustained examination, see John J. Seater, "Ricardian Equivalence," pp. 142–90.

36. See, as typical editorials, "Invincible Ignorance," *Wall Street Journal*, July 2, 1997, p. A14; and "The GOP's Party," *Wall Street Journal*, January 16, 1998, p. A14.

37. "Debt Heads," *Wall Street Journal*, August 6, 1998, p. A14.

38. For a recent example, see Owen Ullmann, "Forget Saving, America. Your Job Is to Spend," p. 54.

39. Peter Yoo, "Is Increasing Wealth a Substitute for Savings?" pp. 1–2; U.S. Bureau of the Census, *Statistical Abstract of the United States: 1998*, p. 482.

40. J.P. Morgan, *World Financial Markets*, p. 54.

41. Seater, "Ricardian Equivalence," pp. 142–90.

42. Shaviro, *Do Deficits Matter?*, especially ch. 4.

43. Alan S. Blinder, "Is the National Debt Really—I Mean, *Really*—a Burden?" p. 217.

44. Quoted in Gordon Wood, "Virtue and Politics in the Convention," p. 171.

45. For an overview of Keynes's views on public debt from a variety of perspectives, see Richard H. Fink and Jack C. High, eds., *A Nation in Debt*, ch. 2.

46. For an intense, theoretical, and highly sophisticated analysis of the Ricardian equivalence issue, see Seater, "Ricardian Equivalence," pp. 142–90. For an excellent overview and critique, see Shaviro's *Do Deficits Matter?* For a clear and relatively brief statement by Robert J. Barro himself, see "The Ricardian Model of Budget Deficits," pp. 133–49. I am indebted to all three.

47. Shaviro, *Do Deficits Matter?* p. 71.

48. Ibid., p. 78.

49. IMF, *Economic Outlook*, May 1996, p. 50.

50. Ibid., May 1997, p. 27.

51. Miller and Roberds, "How Little We Know," pp. 2–11.

52. For an extended analysis, see Shaviro, *Do Deficits Matter?* ch. 6.

53. IMF, *World Economic Outlook*, May 1996, p. 50.

54. For a full analysis, see Peter G. Peterson, *Facing Up*.

55. See Cavanaugh, *The Truth About the National Debt*, ch. 5.

56. Ibid., p. 77.

57. Ibid., p. 85.

58. U.S. OMB, *Budget of the United States Government: Analytical Perspectives, Fiscal Year 1998*, p. 21.

59. See Blinder, "Is the National Debt Really—I Mean, *Really*—a Burden?" p. 210. Shaviro, *Do Deficits Matter?* p. 151, calls this phenomenon "tax lag."

60. Blinder, "Is the National Debt Really—I Mean, *Really*—a Burden?" p. 211.

61. For the classical view of the burden question, see especially Lakis C. Kaounides and Geoffrey E. Wood, *Debt and Deficits*, vol. 1. For a current classical view, see James Buchanan, "Concerning Future Generations"; and Lee M. Cohen, ed., *Justice Across Generations*. For the originator of "generational accounting," see Laurence J. Kotlikoff, *Generational Accounting*.

62. IMF, *World Economic Outlook*, May 1996, p. 52.

63. Kotlidsoff, *Generalized Accounting*, pp. 172–184.

64. Ibid., p. 53.

65. Ibid., p. 52.

66. Ibid., p. 53.

67. For an extended analysis, see Shaviro, *Do Deficits Matter?* ch. 5. On the rise of budgetary cynicism, see Makin and Ornstein, *Debt and Taxes*, ch. 13. For an account of the modest efforts to do something about this problem, see Posner and Bovbjerg, "Deficit Reduction Around the World," pp. 135–62.

68. *Economic Report of the President, 1997*, p. 414; and U.S. OMB, *Budget . . . Fiscal Year 1999*, p. 254.

69. U.S. OMB, *Budget . . . Fiscal Year 1998*, p. 227.

70. Benjamin M. Friedman, "U.S. Fiscal Policy in the 1980s," p. 156; and Shaviro, *Do Deficits Matter?* pp. 192–98.

71. Shaviro, *Do Deficits Matter?* p. 193.

72. Friedman, "U.S. Fiscal Policy in the 1980s," pp. 149–72; Blinder, "Is the National Debt Really—I Mean, *Really*—a Burden?" pp. 209–26. Friedman wrote that the United States went on a consumption binge; Blinder declared that we "threw a party";

and James Rock and Timothy Smeeding added the part about the wealthy being especially invited. See Rock, *Debt and the Twin Deficits Debate*, p. 221.

73. See Paul Kennedy, *Preparing for the Twenty-First Century*, p. 334.

74. IMF, *World Economic Outlook*, October 1997, p. 184.

75. This idea is at least as old as the work of David Hume, who believed that using debt to finance governments allowed politicians to "make a great figure" without raising taxes or creating public hostility. Deluding the public in this way causes "fiscal illusion." Lakis C. Kaounides and Geoffrey E. Wood, *Public Debt and Classical Political Economy*, vol. 1, p. xvii. Adam Smith was even more pointed. He thought governments often raised taxes even in wartime to conceal the real financial burden of that war. As quoted in Shaviro, *Do Deficits Matter?* p. 29.

76. Steuerle and Kawai, "The New World Fiscal Order," p. 14. Stein, in his classic *The Fiscal Revolution in America*, p. 458, says that Americans have not seriously wanted a balanced budget—if it means real sacrifices—since the late 1930s.

77. Quoted in Shaviro, *Do Deficits Matter?* pp. 29–30.

78. James M. Buchanan and Richard E. Wagner, *Democracy in Deficit*, pp. 58–59.

79. See Shaviro, *Do Deficits Matter?* pp. 93–103; and Sung Deuk Hahm, Mark L. Kamlet, and David C. Mowery, "Influences on Deficit Spending in Industrialized Democracies," pp. 183–97.

80. Blinder, "Is the National Debt Really—I Mean, *Really*—a Burden?" p. 221.

81. Cole S. Brembeck, *Congress, Human Nature, and the Federal Debt*.

82. Lance T. LeLoup, Carolyn N. Long, and James N. Giordano, "President Clinton's Fiscal 1998 Budget," pp. 3–32.

83. Makin and Ornstein, *Debt and Taxes*, p. 282.

84. U.S. OMB, *Budget . . . Fiscal Year 1999*, pp. 251–53.

85. Shaviro, *Do Deficits Matter?* p. 16.

86. Ibid., pp. 243–47.

87. James Hines, *Constitutional Restrictions Against State Debt*; and James M. Poterba, "Budget Institutions and Fiscal Policy in the U.S. States," pp. 395–400.

88. See "This Year's Surplus-Spending Binge Will Compound Next Year's Headaches," p. 2797.

89. See IMF, *World Economic Outlook*, October 1998, p. 28.

90. Jacob M. Schlesinger and Greg Hitt, "Clinton Budget Balances Spending Rise Aimed at Democrats with Items for GOP," pp. A2, A8.

91. It is hard to overestimate the importance of Herbert Stein's insights on this point, so persuasively argued in *The Fiscal Revolution in America*. We simply no longer have any widely shared rules on why we should balance the budget; hence, each political party and every political interest group tries to maximize the benefits flowing to its constituents, with little concern for the whole or for the long run.

92. "Hey, Big Spenders," *Economist*, March 28, 1998, pp. 26–27.

93. LeLoup, Long, and Giordano, "President Clinton's Fiscal 1998 Budget," pp. 3–32.

94. Editorial, *Wall Street Journal*, October 9, 1997, p. A18.

95. Editorial, *New York Times*, July 30, 1997, p. A16.

96. Quoted in "A Balanced Budget Deal Won, a Defining Issue Lost," pp. 1831–36.

97. U.S. OMB, *Budget . . . Fiscal Year 1999*, p. 367.

98. IMF, *World Economic Outlook*, October 1997, p. 167.

99. Quoted in *Wall Street Journal*, November 3, 1997, p. 1.

100. "Fiscal Virtuosos," *Economist*, October 25, 1997, p. 36.

101. IMF, *World Economic Outlook*, October 1997, p. 22; see also D'Arch Jenish, *Money to Burn*; and Richard G. Harris, ed., *Deficits and Debt in the Canadian Economy*.

102. Christopher J. Chipello, Michael T. Malloy, and John Urquhart, "Day of Reckon-

ing," *Wall Street Journal*, August 27, 1992, p. 1; Alastair Fernie, "Canada's Debt Crisis," pp. 613–17; and Paul Martin, "The Canadian Experience in Reducing Budget Deficits and Debt," p. 11.

103. IMF, *World Economic Outlook*, October 1998, p. 28.

104. Ibid.

105. IMF, "Japan's Economic Crisis and Policy Options," *World Economic Outlook*, October 1998, pp. 107–22; and "Hurtling Towards Paralysis," *Economist*, March 21, 1998, pp. 21–28.

106. IMF, *World Economic Outlook*, October 1997, p. 22.

107. For the United States, see especially three works of Kevin Phillips: *The Politics of Rich and Poor*; *Boiling Point*; and *Arrogant Capital*. For a world perspective, see Lester Thurow, *The Future of Capitalism*, ch. 15.

108. This is the goal of New Zealand, the most heralded debt reformer, which has reduced its net public debt from 52 percent of GDP to 35 percent in the past decade and plans to reduce it to 20 percent of GDP in the near future. See Lewis Evans et al., "Economic Reform in New Zealand, 1984–95," pp. 1856–1902.

109. U.S. OMB, *Budget . . . Fiscal Year 1999*, p. 3.

110. See CBO, *Long-Term Budgetary Pressures and Policy Options*. This report was updated for the near term in U.S.OMB, *Budget . . . Fiscal Year 1999*, pp. 51–140.

111. CBO, *Long-Term Budgetary Pressures and Policy Options*, p. xv.

112. Ibid., p. xvii.

113. "Italy Survey," *Economist*, November 8, 1997, p. 25.

114. IMF, *World Economic Outlook*, May 1996, p. 55.

115. *Goldberg v. Kelly*, 397 U.S. 254.

116. Peterson, *Facing Up*, p. 106; condensed in Peter G. Peterson "Entitlement Reform," p. 44.

117. Examples include the implosion of the Japanese real estate market, followed by its stock market crash and banking crisis, and, more recently, the enormous losses in Southeast Asia. See Martin H. Wolfson, *Financial Crises*; and, for a longer view, Charles P. Kindleberger, *Manias, Panics, and Crashes*.

Chapter 6. Disarming the Debt Bomb

1. IMF, *World Economic Outlook*, October 1998, p. 208.

2. Arthur M. Schlesinger, Jr., *The Cycles of American History*; Martin Feldstein, *The Risk of Economic Crisis*; Martin H. Wolfson, *Financial Crises*; and Harold R. Kerbo, *Social Stratification and Inequality*.

3. For a brief discussion, see Wolfson, *Financial Crises*, part 1. For a more detailed analysis, see Hyman Minsky, "Longer Waves in Financial Relations," pp. 83–92. An excellent sourcebook is Michael Bordo, ed., *Financial Crises*, 2 vols.

4. Charles J. Whalen, "Money-Manager Capitalism and the End of Shared Prosperity," pp. 517–23. This article analyses Minsky's writings.

5. Feldstein, *The Risk of Economic Crisis*, p. 17; and Wolfson, *Financial Crises*, ch. 14.

6. Steven Weber, "The End of the Business Cycle?" pp. 65–83.

7. Pascal Zachary, "The Right Mix, Global Growth Attains a New, Higher Level That Could Be Lasting," cited in *Wall Street Journal*, March 13, 1997, p. A1.

8. IMF, *World Economic Outlook*, May 1997, p. 2.

9. Quoted in Pedro-Pablo Kuczynski, "Debt Crisis," pp. 582–84.

10. Quoted in Charles Kindleberger, "Financial Crises," 1:46–47; Walter Eltis, "Financial Crises and Credit Cycles," pp. 47–51.

11. Feldstein, *The Risk of Economic Crisis*, p. 1.

12. Paul Krugman, "The International Aspects of Financial Crises," p. 85.

13. Ibid., p. 87.

14. Bordo, *Financial Crises*, pp. xiii–xiv.

15. Gary A. Dymski, "Deciphering Minsky's Wall Street Paradigm."

16. Ibid., pp. 506–7.

17. Whalen, "Money-Manager Capitalism and the End of Shared Prosperity," pp. 517–24.

18. Charles P. Kindleberger, *Manias, Panics, and Crashes*, ch. 6.

19. Ibid., Appendix B, "A Stylized Outline of Financial Crises, 1720–1987," pp. 249–57.

20. IMF, *World Economic Outlook*, May 1998, p. 88.

21. Ibid., pp. 88–89.

22. Benjamin M. Friedman, "New Directions in the Relation Between Public and Private Debt," pp. 397–403.

23. These figures include foreign credit market debt held in the United States, as well as credit market debt owed by financial sectors of the economy. See *Federal Reserve Bulletin*, August 1998, p. A40; U.S. Bureau of the Census, *Statistical Abstract of the United States: 1997*, p. 510; and *Economic Report of the President, 1998*, p. 280.

24. IMF, *World Economic Outlook*, May 1998, p. 229.

25. Ibid., May 1996, p. 44.

26. Ibid., October 1998, p. 191.

27. Data are for 1970 to 1994. See Vito Tanzi and Domenico Fanizza, "Fiscal Deficit and Public Debt in Industrial Countries, 1970–1994," pp. 223–52.

28. Virtually all experts recognize the growing public concern over rising public debt, but they are divided on how much the public is willing to do about it, especially in the United States, and to what extent it is a "burden." For a good, brief account of those who feel public debt levels are now a burden for the G–7, see IMF, "Focus on Fiscal Policy," *World Economic Outlook*, May 1996, pp. 44–63. For a good account arguing that the burden in the United States is not public debt but public spending, see Francis X. Cavanaugh, *The Truth About the National Debt.*

29. For the United States, see especially Herbert Stein, *The Fiscal Revolution in America*; John H. Makin and Norman J. Ornstein, *Debt and Taxes*; and OMB, *Budget of the United States Government*, published annually. For the international perspective, see IMF, "Focus on Fiscal Policy," *World Economic Outlook*, May 1996; C. Eugene Steuerle and Masahiro Kawai, eds., *The New World Fiscal Order*; Harrie A. A. Verbon and F.A.A.M. Van Winden, eds., *The Political Economy of Government Debt*; and for a more technical account John Seater, "Ricardian Equivalence," pp. 142–90.

30. For an excellent discussion of the major economic theories (and their limitations) that attempt to explain the explosion of public indebtedness, see Sung Deuk Hahm, Mark S. Kamlet, and David C. Mowery, "Influences on Deficit Spending in Industrialized Democracies," pp. 183–97.

31. IMF, *World Economic Outlook*, May 1996, pp. 45–46.

32. OECD, *Economic Outlook*, December 1997, p. A38.

33. Richard A. Musgrave, "A Brief History of Fiscal Doctrine," p. 46.

34. Colin Thain and Maurice Wright, *The Treasury and Whitehall.*

35. IMF, *World Economic Outlook*, October 1998, p. 1.

36. This point is discussed at length by Robert J. Samuelson, *The Good Life and Its Discontents.*

37. See Wolfson, *Financial Crises*, esp. ch. 14.

38. Tanzi and Fanizza, "Fiscal Deficit and Public Debt in Industrial Countries, 1970–

1994," esp. 241–50; and IMF, *World Economic Outlook*, May 1995, pp. 67–89.

39. IMF, *World Economic Outlook*, May 1996, p. 47.

40. Makin and Ornstein, *Debt and Taxes*, ch. 13. For a longer view of public ambivalence toward deficits, see Stein, *The Fiscal Revolution in America*, part 2.

41. Makin and Ornstein, *Debt and Taxes*, p. 282.

42. See Francis X. Cavanaugh, *The Truth About the National Debt*, p. 79. By the mid-1990s, that figure had fallen back to about 50 percent.

43. David Wessel, "Spending Assumptions Shaped to Fit Within Caps," *Wall Street Journal*, February 2, 1999, p. A8.

44. Paul Posner and Barbara Bovbjerg, "Deficit Reduction Around the World," p. 138.

45. See IMF, "Lessons from Fiscal Consolidation Experiences," *World Economic Outlook*, May 1996, pp. 61–62; Lewis Evans et al., "Economic Reforms in New Zealand, 1984–85: The Pursuit of Efficiency," *Journal of Economic Literature* 34 (December 1996): 1856–94; and "A Kiwi Conundrum," *Economist*, May 2, 1998, pp. 70–71.

46. Stein, *The Fiscal Revolution in America*, p. 454.

47. Ibid., pp. 580, 600.

48. Lance T. LeLoup, Carolyn N. Long, and James N. Giordano, "President Clinton's Fiscal 1998 Budget," pp. 3–32.

49. Alan J. Auerbach, "Quantifying the Current U.S. Fiscal Imbalance," pp. 387–98.

50. Ibid., p. 392.

51. Posner and Bovbjerg, "Deficit Reduction Around the World," pp. 135–68; IMF, *World Economic Outlook*, May 1995, p. 30.

52. Italy has done little to reduce its budget deficit, which is not expected to fall much in the near term. Canada's prospects are somewhat better, although a majority of Canadians may actually benefit from a continuation of deficit spending, thus lessening the chances for a major policy change. On this point, see Isabella Horry and Michael Walker, *Government Spending Facts*. For current public debt levels, see IMF, *World Economic Outlook*, October 1998, p. 28.

53. Paul Martin, "The Canadian Experience in Reducing Budget Deficits and Debt," pp. 11–25.

54. For a good general discussion of private debt since the 1950s, see Keith M. Carlson, "On the Macroeconomics of Private Debt," pp. 53–66. For current "Credit Market Debt Outstanding," see monthly issues of the *Federal Reserve Bulletin* under "Domestic Financial Statistics."

55. For the growth of corporate debt in recent years, see U.S. Senate, Committee on Banking, Housing, and Urban Affairs, *Corporate Debt*.

56. Ibid., p. 2.

57. Ibid.

58. Davis, *Debt, Financial Fragility, and Systemic Risk*, p. 72.

59. See U.S. Senate, *Corporate Debt*, p. 10; Davis, *Debt, Financial Fragility, and Systemic Risk*, ch. 2; Margaret M. Blair, *The Deal Decade*, ch. 1; Tim Congdon, *The Debt Threat*, part 3; Feldstein, ed., *The Risk of Economic Crisis*; and Wolfson, *Financial Crises*.

60. U.S. Bureau of the Census, *Statistical Abstract of the United States: 1998*, p. 512.

61. Leon Levy, president of the Institute for Advanced Study in Princeton, believes this may be the case. Quoted in Jeffrey Madrick, "Wall Street Blues," *New York Review of Books*, October 8, 1998, pp. 8–10.

62. George Zuckerman, "U.S. Corporations Load on Debt at Rapid Clip," *Wall Street Journal*, December 31, 1998, pp. C1, C15.

63. Ibid.

64. *Economic Report of the President: 1999*, p. 219.

65. James Medoff and Andrew Harless, *The Indebted Society*, esp. part 2.

66. "New Home Prices," *Wall Street Journal Almanac: 1999*, p. 328.

67. U.S. Bureau of the Census, *Statistical Abstract of the United States: 1998*, p. 524.

68. Laurie Hays, "Banks' Marketing Blitz Yields Rash of Defaults," *Wall Street Journal*, September 25, 1996, pp. B1, B7.

69. Ibid.

70. Robert Sobel, *The Great Bull Market*, esp. ch. 7. John Kenneth Galbraith, in his classic *The Great Crash, 1929*, pp. 78–79, also emphasizes that the well-established financial services, including financial information in newspapers like the *New York Times*, were the most conservative participants in that era.

71. James Grant, *Money of the Mind*, ch. 11.

72. As quoted in David M. Tucker, *The Decline of Thrift in America*, p. 137.

73. Andrew Hacker, *Money*, p. 86.

74. See Galbraith, *The Great Crash*, ch. 10; and Robert Sobel, *Panic on Wall Street*, ch. 11.

75. See Carlson, "On the Macroeconomics of Private Debt," p. 59.

76. U.S. Bureau of the Census, *Statistical Abstract of the United States: 1995*, p. 517.

77. See Edward Altman, *Corporate Financial Distress and Bankruptcy*, p. 3.

78. "Bankruptcy Filings," *Wall Street Journal Almanac: 1999*, p. 303.

79. For a good recent example, see Laurie Hays, "Banks' Marketing Blitz Yields Rash of Defaults," *Wall Street Journal*, September 25, 1996, pp. B1, B7. A less recent but more extended example of journalistic alarm is James Dale Davidson and Lord William Rees-Mogg, *The Great Reckoning*.

80. See Feldstein, ed., *The Risk of Economic Crisis*; and Wolfson, *Financial Crises*.

81. *Economic Report of the President, 1999*, p. 69.

82. See E.P. Davis, *Debt, Financial Fragility, and Systemic Risk*, p. 34.

83. Ibid., p. 275.

84. *Economic Report of the President, 1999*, p. 450.

85. IMF, *World Economic Outlook*, October 1998, pp. 21, 69; and *Economist*, February 6, 1999, p. 109.

86. "Statement by Alan Greenspan, . . . before the Committee on Banking and Financial Services, . . . October 1, 1998," pp. 1046–50.

87. "Statement by William J. McDonough, President, Federal Reserve Bank of New York, before the Committee on Banking and Financial Services, U.S. House of Representatives, October 1, 1998," pp. 1050–54.

88. George Soros, *The Crisis of Global Capitalism*, p. xi.

89. Ibid., p. 170.

90. IMF, *World Economic Outlook*, October 1998, ch. 1.

91. Ibid., pp. 10–12; U.S. OMB, *Budget of the United States Government: Analytical Perspectives, Fiscal Year, 1999*, ch. 4; Makin and Ornstein, *Debt and Taxes*, ch. 13.

92. Wynne Godley and George McCarthy, "Fiscal Policy Will Matter," pp. 52–54.

93. Table, *Federal Reserve Bulletin*, January 1999, pp. A37, A41.

94. *Wall Street Journal*, January 25, 1999, p. C3; *Economic Report of the President, 1999*, pp. 58–59.

95. *Economic Report of the President, 1999*, p. 57.

96. "Why Internet Shares Will Fall," *Economist*, January 30, 1999, pp. 17–18.

97. Like most analysts, the President's Council of Economic Advisors is predicting "sustained job creation and continued noninflationary growth," *Economic Report of the President, 1999*, p. 98.

98. *Economic Report of the President, 1998*, p. 338; *The Wall Street Journal Almanac: 1999*, p. 316; and U.S. Bureau of the Census, *Statistical Abstract . . . 1998*, p. 482. The most recent figure for family net worth is for 1995.

99. As quoted in *Wall Street Journal*, January 29, 1999, p. A2, C-15.

100. Michael Bordo, ed., *Financial Crises*, pp. xiii–xiv.

101. David Wessel, "Stock Market Weighs Heavily Upon the Fed," *Wall Street Journal*, January 18, 1999, p. 1.

102. On January 25, 1999, the DJIA price/earnings ratio was 24/1; the S&P 500 ratio was 32.17/1, based on the diluted per-share earnings for the previous four quarters. The historical average for price/earnings ratios is around 15/1.

103. U.S. Bureau of the Census, *Statistical Abstract . . . 1998*, p. 514.

104. OECD, *Economic Outlook*, December 1997, p. A38.

105. IMF, *World Economic Outlook*, October 1998, p. 94.

106. Kindleberger, *Manias, Panics, and Crashes*, p. 17; see also ch. 2.

Bibliography

Altman, Edward. *Corporate Financial Distress and Bankruptcy*, 2d ed. New York: John Wiley & Sons, 1993.

Auerbach, Alan J. "Quantifying the Current U.S. Fiscal Imbalance." *National Tax Journal* 50, no. 3 (1997): 387–98.

———, and Martin Feldstein, eds. *Handbook of Public Economics*, 2 vols. Amsterdam: North Holland Press, 1985.

Bagehot, Walter. *Lombard Street: A Description of the Money Market*. Westport, CT: Hyperion Press, 1962.

"A Balanced Budget Deal Won, a Defining Issue Lost." *Congressional Quarterly Weekly Report* (August 2, 1997): 1831–36.

Barro, Robert J. "The Ricardian Model of Budget Deficits." In *Debt and the Twin Deficits Debate*, ed. James M. Rock, pp. 133–48. Mountain View, CA: Mayfield, 1991.

Bartlett, Donald, and James Steele. *America: What Went Wrong?* Kansas City: Andrews and McMeel, 1992.

Benavie, Arthur. *Deficit Hysteria: A Commonsense Look at America's Rush to Balance the Budget*. Westport, CT: Praeger, 1998.

Blair, Margaret M. *The Deal Decade*. Washington, DC: Brookings Institution, 1993.

Blanchard, O.J. "Suggestions for a New Set of Fiscal Indicators." *OECD Working Paper No. 79*, 1990.

Blejer, Mario, and Adrienne Cheasty. "The Measurement of Fiscal Deficits: Analytical and Methodological Issues." *Journal of Economic Literature* 29 (December 1991): 1644–78.

Blinder, Alan S. "Is the National Debt Really—I Mean, *Really*—a Burden?" In *Debt and the Twin Deficits Debate*, ed. James M. Rock, pp. 209–26. Mountain View, CA: Mayfield, 1991.

Bordo, Michael, ed. *Financial Crises*, 2 vols. Brookfield, VT: Edward Elgar, 1992.

Bosworth, Barry; Gary Burtless; and John Sabelhous. "The Decline in Saving: Evidence from Household Surveys." *Brookings Papers on Economic Activity*, vol. 1 (1991):183–256.

Brembeck, Cole S. *Congress, Human Nature, and the Federal Debt: Essays on the Political Psychology of Deficit Spending*. New York: Praeger, 1991.

Brown, Lester R., et al. *State of the World 1991*. New York: W.W. Norton, 1991.

Browning, Martin, and Annamaria Lusari. "Household Saving: Micro Theories and Micro Facts." *Journal of Economic Literature* 34 (December 1996): 1797–1855.

Buchanan, James. "Concerning Future Generations." In *Public Debt and Future Generations*, ed. James M. Ferguson. Chapel Hill: University of North Carolina Press, 1964.

————. "The Moral Dimension of Debt Financing." In *A Nation in Debt: Economists Debate the Federal Budget Deficit*, eds. Richard H. Fink and Jack C. High, pp. 102–7. Frederick, MD: University Publications of America, 1987.

————, and Richard E. Wagner. *Democracy in Deficit: The Political Legacy of Lord Keynes.* New York: Academic Press, 1977.

————, Charles K. Rowley, and Robert T. Tollison. *Deficits.* New York: Basil Blackwell, 1987.

"Budget Deficits and Debt: Issues and Options." A Symposium Sponsored by the Federal Reserve Bank of Kansas City, Jackson Hole, Wyoming, August–September 1995. Kansas City: Author, 1995.

Calvo, Guillermo, and Mervyn King. *The Debt Burden and Its Consequences for Monetary Policy.* London: Macmillan Press, 1998.

Campbell, John H., and Robert J. Shiller. "Valuation Ratios and Long-Run Stock Market Outlook." *Journal of Portfolio Management* 25 (Winter 1998): 11–24.

Caporale, Guglielmo. "Fiscal Solvency in Europe: Budget Deficits and Government Debt Under European Monetary Union." *National Institute Economic Review*, no. 140 (May 1992): 69–77.

Capra, Fritjof. *The Turning Point.* New York: Bantam, 1982.

Carlson, Keith M. "On the Macroeconomics of Private Debt." *Economic Review* (January–February 1993): 53–66.

Carnegie, Andrew. *The Empire of Business.* New York: Doubleday, Page, 1902.

Cavanaugh, Francis X. *The Truth About the National Debt: Five Myths and One Reality.* Boston: Harvard Business School Press, 1996.

Cebula, Richard; John Killingsworth; and Willie J. Belton Jr. "Federal Government Budget Deficits and the Crowding Out of Investment in the United States." *Public Finance* 49 (1994): 168–78.

Chernow, Ron. *The House of Morgan: An American Banking Dynasty and the Rise of Modern Finance.* New York: Touchstone Books, 1990.

Cohen, Lee M., ed. *Justice Across Generations: What Does It Mean?* Washington, DC: Public Policy Institute of the American Association of Retired Persons, 1993.

Committee on Economic Policy. "Debt: Public and Private." Pamphlet. Washington, DC: Chamber of Commerce of the United States, 1957.

Congdon, Tim. *The Debt Threat.* Oxford, UK: Basil Blackwell, 1988.

Congressional Budget Office. *Long-Term Budgetary Pressures and Policy Options.* Report to Senate and House Committees on the Budget. Washington, DC: Government Printing Office, March 1997.

"Consumer Debt." *CQ Researcher* (November 15, 1996): 1009–32.

Cordes, Joseph J. "How Yesterday's Decisions Affect Today's Budget and Fiscal Options." In *The New World Fiscal Order: Implications for Industrialized Nations*, eds. C. Eugene Steuerle and Masahiro Kawai, pp. 95–116. Washington, DC: Urban Institute Press, 1966.

W. Michael Cox and Richard Alm, *Myths of Rich and Poor, Why We're Better Off Than We Think* (New York: Basic Books, 1999).

Davidson, James Dale, and Lord William Rees-Mogg. *The Great Reckoning: Protect Yourself in the Coming Depression.* New York: Simon & Schuster, 1993.

Davis, E.P. *Debt, Financial Fragility, and Systemic Risk.* Oxford: Clarendon Press, 1992.

Dymski, Gary A. "Deciphering Minsky's Wall Street Paradigm." *Journal of Economic Issues* 31 (June 1997): 501–7.

Economic Report of the President, 1994. Washington, DC: Government Printing Office, 1994.

————, 1997. Washington, DC: Government Printing Office, 1997.

————, 1998. Washington, DC: Government Printing Office, 1998.

————, 1999. Washington, DC: Government Printing Office, 1999.

Eisner, Robert. *The Misunderstood Economy: What Counts and How to Count It.* Boston: Harvard Business School Press, 1994.

————. "Sense and Nonsense About Budget Deficits." *Harvard Business Review* 71 (May–June 1993): 99–111.

————. "Which Budget Deficit? Some Issues of Measurement and their Implications." *American Economic Review* 24 (May 1984): 138–43.

————, et al. "Is the Deficit a Friendly Giant After All?" *Harvard Business Review* 71 (July–August 1993): 140–48.

Eltis, Walter. "Financial Crises and Credit Cycles." In *The New Palgrave Dictionary of Money and Finances*, vol. 1, eds. Peter Newman, Murray Milgate, and John Eatwell, vol. 1, pp. 47–51. New York: Stockton Press, 1992.

Evans, Lewis, et al. "Economic Reform in New Zealand, 1984–95: The Pursuit of Efficiency." *Journal of Economic Literature* 34 (December 1996): 1856–1902.

Feldstein, Martin. "The Missing Piece in Policy Analysis: Social Security Reform." *American Economic Review* 36 (May 1996): 1–43.

————, ed. *The Risk of Economic Crisis.* Chicago: University of Chicago Press, 1991.

Fernie, Alastair. "Canada's Debt Crisis." In *Vital Speeches of the Day*, pp. 613–17. Mount Pleasant, SC: City News, 1993.

Figgie, Harry E. *Bankruptcy 1995: The Coming Collapse of America and How to Stop It.* Boston: Little, Brown, 1992.

Fink, Richard H., and Jack C. High, eds. *A Nation in Debt: Economists Debate the Federal Budget Deficit.* Frederick, MD: University Publications of America, 1987.

Fridson, Martin S. *It Was a Very Good Year: Extraordinary Moments in Stock Market History.* New York: John Wiley & Sons, 1998.

Friedman, Benjamin M. *Day of Reckoning.* New York: Random House, 1998.

————. "New Directions in the Relation Between Public and Private Debt." *Science* (April 24, 1987): 397–403.

————. "U.S. Fiscal Policy in the 1980s: Consequences of Large Budget Deficits at Full Employment." In *Debt and the Twin Deficits Debate*, ed. James M. Rock, pp. 149–72. Mountain View, CA: Mayfield, 1991.

Fukuyama, Francis. "The End of History?" *The National Interest* (Summer 1989): 3–18.

Galbraith, John Kenneth. *The Great Crash, 1929.* Boston: Houghton Mifflin, 1961.

————. *A Short History of Financial Euphoria.* Knoxville, TN: Whittle Direct Books, 1990.

Garner, C. Alan. "Can Measures of the Consumer Debt Burden Reliably Predict an Economic Slowdown?" *Economic Review* 81 (Fourth Quarter 1996): 63–76.

George, Susan. *The Debt Boomerang.* London: Pluto Press, 1992.

Godley, Wynne, and George McCarthy. "Fiscal Policy Will Matter." *Challenge* (January–February 1998): 52–58.

Golembiewski, Robert T., and Jack Rabin, eds. *Public Budgeting and Finance*, 4th ed. New York: Marcel Dekker, 1997.

Gottschalk, Peter. "Inequality, Income Growth, and Mobility: The Basic Facts." *Journal of Economic Perspectives* 11 (Spring 1997): 21–40.

Graham, Edward M., and Paul R. Krugman. *Foreign Direct Investment in the United States*, 2d ed. Washington, DC: Institute for International Economics, 1991.

Grant, James. *Money of the Mind: Borrowing and Lending in America from the Civil War to Michael Milken.* New York: Farrar, Straus, Giroux, 1992.

————. *The Trouble with Prosperity: The Loss of Fear, the Rise of Speculation, and the Risk to American Savings.* New York: Random House, 1996.

Greenspan, Alan. "Statement by Alan Greenspan, Chairman, Board of Governors of the Federal Reserve System, Before the Committee on Banking and Financial Services, U.S. House of Representatives, January 30, 1998." *Federal Reserve Bulletin* (March 1998): 186–90.

———. "Statement by Alan Greenspan, Chairman, Board of Governors of the Federal Reserve System, Before the Committee on Banking and Financial Services, U.S. House of Representatives, October 1, 1998." *Federal Reserve Bulletin* (December 1998): 1046–50.

———. "Statement by Alan Greenspan, Chairman, Board of Governors of the Federal Reserve System, Before the Committee on the Budget, U.S. Senate, September 23, 1998." *Federal Reserve Bulletin* (November 1998): 936–38.

Greider, William. *One World, Ready or Not: The Manic Logic of Global Capitalism.* New York: Simon and Schuster, 1997.

Hacker, Andrew. *Money: Who Has How Much and Why.* New York: Scribner, 1997.

Hahm, Sung Deuk; Mark L. Kamlet; and David C. Mowery. "Influences on Deficit Spending in Industrialized Democracies." *Public Policy* 31 (Summer 1995): 183–97.

Harris, Richard G., ed. *Deficits and Debt in the Canadian Economy.* Kingston, ON: John Deutsch Institute for the Study of Economic Policy, 1993.

Hines, James. *Constitutional Restrictions Against State Debt.* Madison: University of Wisconsin Press, 1963.

Horry, Isabella, and Michael Walker. *Government Spending Facts, 2.* Vancouver, BC: Fraser Institute, 1994.

Ifo Institute for Economic Research and Sakura Institute of Research. *A Comparative Analysis of Japanese and German Economic Success.* Bonn: Springer, 1997.

Ihori, Toshihiro. "Prior Commitments, Sustainability, and Intergenerational Redistribution in Japan." In *Debt and the Twin Deficits Debate,* ed. James M. Rock, pp. 117–29. Mountain View, CA: Mayfield, 1991.

International Monetary Fund. *World Economic Outlook.* Cited by date.

Jenish, D'Arch. *Money to Burn.* Toronto: Stoddart, 1996.

Jorion, Philippe. *Big Bets Gone Bad: The Largest Municipal Failure in U.S. History.* San Diego: Academic Press, 1995.

Kaounides, Lakis C., and Geoffrey E. Wood, eds. *Debt and Deficits,* 2 vols. London: Elgar Reference Collection, 1992.

———. *Public Debt and Classical Political Economy.* 2 vols. London: Elgar Reference Collection, 1992.

Karras, Georgios. "Macroeconomic Effects of Budget Deficits: Further International Evidence." *Journal of Economics, Money, and Finance* 27 (April 1994): 190–205.

Kennedy, Paul. *Preparing for the Twenty-First Century.* New York: Random House, 1993.

———. *The Rise and Fall of the Great Powers.* New York: Random House, 1987.

Kerbo, Harold J. *Social Stratification and Inequality: Class Conflict in Historical and Comparative Perspective,* 3d ed. New York: McGraw-Hill, 1996.

Kindleberger, Charles. Interviewed by *Challenge.* "Manias and How to Prevent Them." *Challenge* (November–December 1997): 21.

———. *Manias, Panics, and Crashes: A History of Financial Crises,* 2d ed. New York: Basic Books, 1978. [Reprinted in 1989.]

———. *The World Economy and National Finance in Historical Perspective.* Ann Arbor: University of Michigan Press, 1995.

———. eds. Peter Newman, Murray Milgate, and John Eatwell, "Financial Crises." In *The New Palgrave Dictionary of Money and Finance,* pp. 46–47. New York: Stockton Press, 1992.

Kohn, Richard F. "History and the Culture Wars: The Case of the *Enola Gay* Exhibition." *Journal of American History* 82 (December 1995): 1036–63.

Kotlikoff, Laurence J. *Generational Accounting: Knowing Who Pays, and When, for What We Spend.* New York: Free Press, 1992.

Krueger, Anne O. "Whither the World Bank and the IMF?" *Journal of Economic Literature* 36 (December 1998): 1983–2020.

Krugman, Paul. "America the Boastful." *Foreign Affairs* 77 (May–June 1998): 32–45.

———. "The International Aspects of Financial Crises." In *The Risk of Economic Crisis*, ed. Martin Feldstein, pp. 85–109. Chicago: University of Chicago Press, 1991.

———. "The Return of Depression Economics." *Foreign Affairs* 78 (January–February 1999): 56–74.

Kuczynski, Pedro-Pablo. "Debt Crisis." In *The New Palgrave Dictionary of Money and Finance*, eds. Peter Newman, Murray Milgate, and John Eatwell, eds., pp. 582–84. New York: Stockton Press, 1992.

Laser, Harold. "The Debt Won't Be Paid." *New York Review of Books* (June 28, 1984): 3–5.

LeLoup, Lance T.; Carolyn N. Long; and James N. Giordano. "President Clinton's Fiscal 1998 Budget: Political and Constitutional Paths to Balance." *Public Budgeting and Finance* 18 (Spring 1998): 3–32.

Levy, Frank, and Richard J. Murnane. "U.S. Earnings Levels and Earnings Inequality: A Review of Recent Trends and Proposed Explanations." *Journal of Economic Literature* 30 (September 1992): 1333–81.

Madrick, Jeffrey. *The End of Affluence: The Causes and Consequences of America's Economic Dilemma.* New York: Random House, 1995.

Makin, John H., and Norman J. Ornstein. *Debt and Taxes: How America Got into Its Budget Mess and What to Do About It.* New York: Times Books, 1994.

Martin, Paul. "The Canadian Experience in Reducing Budget Deficits and Debt." *Economic Review* (First Quarter 1996): 11–25.

Mayer, Martin. *The Greatest-Ever Bank Robbery: The Collapse of the Savings and Loan Industry.* New York: Macmillan, 1992.

McDonough, William J. "Statement by William J. McDonough, President, Federal Reserve Bank of New York, Before the Committee on Banking and Financial Services, U.S. House of Representatives, October 1, 1998." *Federal Reserve Bulletin* (December 1998): 1050–54.

Medoff, James, and Andrew Harless. *The Indebted Society: Anatomy of an Ongoing Disaster.* Boston: Little, Brown, 1996.

Miller, Preston J., and William Roberds. "How Little We Know About Deficit Policy Effects." *Quarterly Review* (Winter 1992): 2–11.

Minsky, Hyman. "Longer Waves in Financial Relations: Financial Factors in the More Severe Depressions II." *Journal of Economic Issues* 19 (March 1985): 83–92.

Moore, Stephen, ed. *Restoring the Dream: The Bold New Plan by House Republicans.* New York: Times Books, 1995.

Morgan, J.P. *World Financial Markets* (Fourth Quarter 1998): 54.

Musgrave, Richard A. "A Brief History of Fiscal Doctrine." In *Handbook of Public Economics*, vol. 2, eds. Alan J. Auerbach and Martin Feldstein, eds., pp. 1–59. Amsterdam: North Holland Press, 1985.

Newman, Peter; Murray Milgate; and John Eatwell, eds. *The New Palgrave Dictionary of Money and Finance*, 3 vols. New York: Stockton Press, 1992.

Organization for Economic Cooperation and Development. *Economic Outlook.* Cited by date in the notes.

———. *Economic Surveys: Italy.* Paris: OECD, 1994–95.

Overholt, William H. "Korea: To the Market Via Socialism," July 21, 1998, pp. 1–26, typescript research report, available from BankBoston in Singapore, at Website <woverholt@bkb.com>.

Peterson, Peter G. "Entitlement Reform: The Way to Eliminate the Deficit." *New York Review of Books* (April 7, 1994): 39, 44.

———. *Facing Up: How to Rescue the Economy from Crushing Debt and Restore the American Dream.* New York: Simon & Schuster, 1993.

———. "Gray Dawn: The Global Aging Crisis." *Foreign Affairs* 78 (January–February 1999): 42–55.

———. *Will America Grow Up Before It Grows Old?* New York: Random House, 1996.

Peterson, Wallace. *Silent Depression: The Fate of the American Dream.* New York: W.W. Norton, 1994.

Phillips, Kevin. *Arrogant Capital.* Boston: Little, Brown, 1994.

———. *Boiling Point.* New York: Random House, 1993.

———. *The Politics of Rich and Poor.* New York: Random House, 1990.

Posner, Paul, and Barbara Bovbjerg. "Deficit Reduction Around the World." In *The New World Fiscal Order: Implications for Industrialized Nations,* eds. C. Eugene Steuerle and Masahiro Kawai, pp. 135–68. Washington, DC: Urban Institute Press, 1996.

Poterba, James M. "Budget Institutions and Fiscal Policy in the U.S. States." *AEA Papers and Proceedings* 86 (May 1996): pp. 395–400.

President's Research Committee on Social Trends. *Recent Social Trends in the United States.* New York: McGraw-Hill, 1933.

Rischin, Moses, ed. *The American Gospel of Success: Individualism and Beyond.* Chicago: Quadrangle Books, 1965.

Rock, James M., ed. *Debt and the Twin Deficits Debate.* Mountain View, CA: Mayfield, Bristlecone Books, 1991.

Rosenau, Pauline Marie. *Post-Modernism and the Social Sciences: Insights, Inroads, and Intrusions.* Princeton, NJ: Princeton University Press, 1992.

Samuelson, Robert J. *The Good Life and Its Discontents: The American Dream in the Age of Entitlement, 1945–1995.* New York: Random House, Times Books, 1995.

Schinasi, Garry J., and Monica Hargraves. "'Boom and Bust' in Asset Markets in the 1980s: Causes and Consequences." In *Studies for the World Economic Outlook,* eds. Washington, D.C.: IMF, 1993.

Schlesinger, Arthur M., Jr. *The Cycles of American History.* Boston: Houghton Mifflin, 1986.

Schlesinger, Jacob M. "The U.S. Economy." In *Wall Street Journal Almanac: 1999,* pp. 116–23. New York: Ballantine Books, 1998.

———, and Greg Hitt. "Clinton Budget Balances Spending Rise Aimed at Democrats with Items for GOP." *Wall Street Journal* (February 2, 1999): A2, A8.

Seater, John J. "Ricardian Equivalence." *Journal of Economic Literature* 31 (March 1993): 142–90.

Shaviro, Daniel. *Do Deficits Matter?* Chicago: University of Chicago Press, 1997.

Shilling, A. Gary. *Deflation: Why It's Coming, Whether It's Good or Bad, and How It Will Affect Your Investments, Business, and Personal Affairs.* Short Hills, NJ: Lakehills, 1998.

Sloan, Herbert E. *Principle and Interest: Thomas Jefferson and the Problem of Debt.* New York: Oxford University Press, 1995.

Sobel, Robert. *The Great Bull Market: Wall Street in the 1920s.* New York: W.W. Norton, 1968.

———. *Panic on Wall Street: A History of America's Financial Disasters.* New York: Collier Books, 1968.

Soros, George. *The Crisis of Global Capitalism: Open Society Endangered.* New York: Public Affairs, 1998.

Stabile, Donald, and Jeffrey Cantor. *The Public Debt of the United States: An Historical Perspective, 1775–1990.* New York: Praeger, 1991.

Stanley, Thomas J., and William D. Danko. *The Millionaire Next Door: The Surprising Secrets of America's Wealthy.* Atlanta: Longstreet Press, 1996.

Stein, Herbert. *The Fiscal Revolution in America: Policy in Pursuit of Reality,* 2d ed. rev. Washington, DC: AEI [American Enterprise Institute] Press, 1996.

Steuerle, C. Eugene, and Masahiro Kawai. "The New World Fiscal Order: Introduction." In *The New World Fiscal Order: Implications for Industrialized Nations,* eds. C. Steuerle and Masahiro Kawai, pp. 1–18. Washington, DC: Urban Institute Press, 1996.

———, eds. *The New World Fiscal Order: Implications for Industrialized Nations.* Washington, DC: Urban Institute Press, 1996.

Tanzi, Vito, and Domenico Fanizza. "Fiscal Deficit and Public Debt in Industrial Countries, 1970–1994." In *The New World Fiscal Order: Implications for Industrialized Nations,* eds. C. Eugene Steuerle and Masahiro Kawai, pp. 223–52. Washington, DC: Urban Institute Press, 1996.

Tawney, R.H. *The Acquisitive Society.* New York: Harcourt, Brace & World, 1920.

Thain, Colin, and Maurice Wright. *The Treasury and Whitehall: The Planning and Control of Public Expenditures, 1976–1993.* Oxford: Clarendon Press, 1995.

Thelen, David. "The Practice of American History." *Journal of American History,* 81 (December 1994): 933–60.

"This Year's Surplus-Spending Binge Will Compound Next Year's Headaches." *Congressional Quarterly Weekly Report* (October 17, 1998): 2797.

Thurow, Lester. *The Future of Capitalism: How Today's Economic Forces Shape Tomorrow's World.* New York: William Morrow, 1996.

Townsend, Frederick Martin. *Things I Remember.* London: E. Nash, 1913.

Tucker, David M. *The Decline of Thrift in America: Our Cultural Shift from Saving to Spending.* New York: Praeger, 1991.

Uchitelle, Louis. "The Joint Is Still Jumping, but the Floor Is Shaking." *New York Times* (January 3, 1999): BU4.

Ullmann, Owen. "Forget Saving, America. Your Job Is to Spend." *Business Week* (December 28, 1998): 54.

U.S. Bureau of the Census. *Historical Statistics of the United States, Colonial Times to 1970,* Bicentennial Edition, Part 2. Washington, DC: U.S. Department of Commerce, 1975.

———. *State Government Finances: 1992.* Washington, DC: Government Printing Office, 1993.

———. *Statistical Abstract of the United States: 1995.* Washington, DC: Government Printing Office, 1995.

———. *Statistical Abstract of the United States: 1997.* Washington, DC: Government Printing Office, 1997.

———. *Statistical Abstract of the United States: 1998.* Washington, DC: Government Printing Office, 1998.

U.S. Office of Management and Budget. *Budget of the United States Government: Analytical Perspectives, Fiscal Year 1997.* Washington, DC: Government Printing Office, 1997.

———. *Budget of the United States Government: Analytical Perspectives, Fiscal Year 1998.* Washington, DC: OMB, 1998.

———. *Budget of the United States Government: Analytical Perspectives, Fiscal Year 1999.* Washington, DC: OMB, 1998.

U.S. Senate, Committee on Banking, Housing, and Urban Affairs, 102d Cong., 1st Sess. *Corporate Debt: A Perspective on Leverage*. Washington, DC: Government Printing Office, 1991.

Veblen, Thorstein. *The Theory of the Leisure Class: An Economic Study of Institutions* (1899). In *The Portable Veblen*, ed. Max Lerner, pp. 53–214. New York: Viking Press, 1948.

Verbon, Harrie A.A., and F.A.A.M. Van Winden, eds., *The Political Economy of Government Debt*. Amsterdam: North Holland Press, 1993.

Volker, Paul. "Facing Up to the Twin Deficits." In *A Nation in Debt: Economists Debate the Federal Budget Deficit*, eds. Richard H. Fink and Jack C. High, pp. 154–61. Frederick, MD: University Publications of America, 1987.

Wall Street Journal Almanac: 1999. New York: Ballentine Books, 1998.

Weber, Steven. "The End of the Business Cycle?" *Foreign Affairs* 76 (July–August 1997): 65–83.

Whalen, Charles J. "Money-Manager Capitalism and the End of Shared Prosperity." *Journal of Economic Issues* 31 (June 1997): 517–23.

White, Lawrence J. *The S&L Debacle: Public Policy Lessons for Bank and Thrift Regulation*. New York: Oxford University Press, 1991.

Wolfson, Martin H. *Financial Crises: Understanding the Postwar U.S. Experience*, 2d ed. Armonk, NY: M.E. Sharpe, 1994.

Wood, Gordon. "Virtue and Politics in the Convention." In *Major Problems in American Constitutional History*, vol. 1: *The Colonial Era Through Reconstruction*, ed. Kermit Hall, pp. 169–77. Lexington, MA: D.C. Heath, 1992.

World Bank. *Averting the Old Age Crisis*. New York: Oxford University Press, 1994.

———. *World Debt Tables, 1993–1994*. Washington, DC: World Bank, 1994.

Yergin, Daniel, and Joseph Stanislaw. *The Commanding Heights: The Battle Between Government and the Marketplace That Is Remaking the Modern World*. New York: Simon & Schuster, 1998.

Yoo, Peter S. "Charging Up a Mountain of Debt: Accounting for the Growth of Credit Card Debt." *Review of the Federal Reserve Bank of St. Louis* (March–April 1997): pp. 3–13.

———. "Is Increasing Wealth a Substitute for Savings?" *National Economic Trends* (February 1998): 1–2.

Zachary, Paul. "Global Growth Attains a New, Higher Level That Could Be Lasting." *Wall Street Journal* (March 13, 1997): A1.

Zuckerman, Mortimer B. "A Second American Century." *Foreign Affairs* 77 (May–June 1998): 18–31.

Index

About the Author

James L. Clayton is a professor of history at the University of Utah. His research has focused on U.S. economic history, fiscal policy, defense and welfare spending, and debt. Professor Clayton's major publications include: editor, *The Economic Impact of the Cold War* (New York: Harcourt, Brace & World, 1970); *A Farewell to the Welfare State* (Salt Lake City: University of Utah Press, 1976); *Does Defense Beggar Welfare?* (New York: National Strategy Information Center, 1979); and *On the Brink: Defense, Deficits, and Welfare Spending* (New York: Ramapo Press, 1984). He has also published articles in *Western Political Quarterly*, *Pacific Historical Review*, and other scholarly journals, as well as articles for *The Nation*, *Playboy Magazine*, and *Vital Speeches*. Professor Clayton, a former provost of the University of Utah, has won several teaching and research awards.